应用型人才培养规划教材·经济管理系列

国际商务礼仪

（双语版）

张　真　刘玲玉◎主编

雷　倩◎参编

清華大学出版社

北京

内 容 简 介

　　国际商务礼仪是在国际商务活动中体现各国相互尊重的行为准则。本书从十个方面系统介绍了国际商务礼仪的基本规范及实用知识，帮助学生了解我国与西方国家礼仪文化的差异，传授从日常商务活动到求职面试等多方面的国际商务礼仪和社会准则，以利于学生在全球经济一体化的今天，面对社会挑战，突围而出，在拥有专业知识的同时，拥有良好、优雅的专业形象和卓越的商务礼仪。

　　本书主要适于用作高等院校商务英语、国际贸易、涉外旅游等相关专业的本科生教材，同时对职场商务人士提升礼仪素养也有一定的指导意义。

图书在版编目（CIP）数据

　　国际商务礼仪：双语版/张真，刘玲玉主编. — 北京：清华大学出版社，2015（2023.7重印）
　　应用型人才培养规划教材·经济管理系列
　　ISBN 978-7-302-39866-0

　　I. ①国… II. ①张… ②刘… III. ①国际商务－礼仪－双语教学－高等学校－教材 IV. ①F718

　　中国版本图书馆CIP数据核字（2015）第080714号

责任编辑：陈仕云
封面设计：刘　超
版式设计：郑　坤
责任校对：马军令
责任印制：沈　露

出版发行：清华大学出版社
　　　　　网　　　址：http://www.tup.com.cn，http://www.wqbook.com
　　　　　地　　　址：北京清华大学学研大厦A座　　　　　　邮　　编：100084
　　　　　社 总 机：010-83470000　　　　　　　　　　　　邮　　购：010-62786544
　　　　　投稿与读者服务：010-62776969，c-service@tup.tsinghua.edu.cn
　　　　　质量反馈：010-62772015，zhiliang@tup.tsinghua.edu.cn
印 装 者：三河市君旺印务有限公司
经　　销：全国新华书店
开　　本：185mm×230mm　　印　　张：17.75　　字　　数：360千字
版　　次：2015年12月第1版　　印　　次：2023 年 7 月第 9 次印刷
印　　数：13501～15000
定　　价：49.80元

产品编号：042397-03

前 言
Preface

随着世界经济一体化步伐的加快，我国与世界各国的经济贸易往来方兴未艾，具有商务礼仪知识和良好外语能力的复合型人才成为社会急需人才，因此培养具备商务英语运用能力的应用型人才就成为高校教学科研迫在眉睫的任务。

本书正是为满足希望跻身商界的学生以及各行各业的商务人士对国际商务礼仪知识的渴求，对英语交流能力的需要而编写的。本书的特色主要体现在以下几个方面。

一、体例新颖。各章节在导入环节设置自我测试（test yourself）模块，激发读者的阅读兴趣，进而启发读者带着问题深入思考。

二、双语编写。这种编写模式既方便读者理解国际商务礼仪知识，又有助于了解相应的英语表达方式。

三、涵盖全面。本书内容全面而实用，主要包括国际商务礼仪概念、仪容仪表、电话礼仪、接待礼仪、餐饮礼仪、求职与面试礼仪、商务信函礼仪、谈判礼仪、旅行礼仪以及各国商务文化礼仪和禁忌等。

四、练习多样。实践环节包括案例分析在内的各种练习，既有助于巩固读者对各篇章的理解，又强化了对国际商务礼仪知识的掌握。

五、拓展阅读。利用网络资源补充大量最新的阅读材料，读后活动设计多元化，引导读者由课内延伸到课外，拓宽了礼仪知识的输入渠道，同时增强了教材的趣味性。

本书可作为高等院校经贸类专业、商务英语专业在校学生使用的教材，也可以作为其他有志于从事国际商务或企业在职商务人士的参考读本。

本书是集体智慧的结晶，武汉轻工大学张真老师负责第1、3、4、5、7章的编写，该校刘玲玉老师负责第2、6、8、9、10章的编写及练习答案的制作，雷倩负责前期资料搜集、课件制作和全书校对工作。在编著过程中，我们参考了国内外相关专著、书刊以及大量网上资料，在此对有关专家、学者表示深深的谢意！本书的出版更离不开责任编辑的辛勤劳动，在此一并表示由衷的感谢！

由于时间紧迫，加之编者水平有限，书中错误和不妥之处在所难免，恳请专家、学者及广大读者不吝赐教。

编 者

目 录
Contents

Chapter One
The Importance of Business Etiquette
商务礼仪的重要性

📖 Objectives（学习目标）

After you have studied this chapter, you should be able to:

❑ Realize the necessity of learning business etiquette

❑ Analyze the concept of etiquette theoretically and recognize the characteristics of etiquette

❑ Cultivate the cross-cultural awareness in business communication

🐾 Lead-in（导读）

Good manners are cost-effective because they not only increase the quality of life in the workplace, contribute to optimum employee morale, and embellish the company image, but also play a major role in generating profit. Succeeding in business today requires not only mastery of one's job but also mastery of the common courtesies of give and take and of consideration for others. Put them to work today, and you will find that they will work for you in your whole career.

良好的礼仪不但能愉悦工作氛围，提升员工士气，美化公司形象，而且能有效地创造商业效益，可谓本轻利厚。如今，商业成功不仅仅取决于掌握专业工作技能，而且还要求遵循为对方考虑、适当让步等商务礼仪。将礼仪应用于商务活动，有助于未来的职业发展。

🔍 Test yourself（自我测试）

Some of the questions that arise regarding etiquette are greeting visitors, making introductions, table manners, choice of clothing, the etiquette of business letters, business entertaining, proper forms of address, smoking, conversation business relationships between men and women in the office, gift giving, planning seminars, meetings, and many, many more. In the following chosen situations, make your own judgment and hence commence with learning about business etiquette.

1. When you have a business meeting in the UK, you should

A. get down to business straight away   Yes ☐ No ☐

B. spend time eating and drinking and getting to know each other   Yes ☐ No ☐

2. The most ill-mannered things to do at a business meal is

A. order a lot of food   Yes ☐ No ☐

B. use a mobile phone   Yes ☐ No ☐

3. You have a meeting with a client but are expecting a call. You should

A. turn your mobile phone off   Yes ☐ No ☐

B. tell your client you are expecting a phone call   Yes ☐ No ☐

4. When you receive someone else's business card you should

A. immediately pass them your business card   Yes ☐ No ☐

B. look at the card and acknowledge it   Yes ☐ No ☐

5. When expressing thanks to a business client who has given you a gift, you should

A. send an e-mail because it is faster and more efficient   Yes ☐ No ☐

B. send a handwritten note   Yes ☐ No ☐

6. When you're being introduced to someone, you should

A. stand up   Yes ☐ No ☐

B. sit because it helps establish your presence   Yes ☐ No ☐

7. To show your politeness, you should

A. only say "thank you" once or twice during a conversation. Otherwise, you may make yourself seem somewhat helpless and needy   Yes ☐ No ☐

B. say as many thanks as possible   Yes ☐ No ☐

8. In a business setting, you should

A. follow the social gender rules, always pull a female client's chair out for her   Yes ☐ No ☐

B. never pull out someone's chair for them regardless of gender   Yes ☐ No ☐

9. When dining during professional occasions, you can

A. never ask for a to-go box because you are there for business, not for the leftovers

     Yes ☐ No ☐

B. ask for a to-go box to avoid the waste of money   Yes ☐ No ☐

10. As a female host, you should

A. always pay for a bill regardless of gender   Yes ☐ No ☐

B. fight a bill over if a male guest insists on paying   Yes ☐ No ☐

Part I   The Concept of Business Etiquette
商务礼仪的概念

In China, good manners are very important. Manners develop a person's personality. Well-mannered people are always welcome to everyone. Manners are something used every day to make a good impression on others and to feel good about someone. No matter where you are—at home, work, or with friends—practicing good manners is important.

But, it is surprising that many people get confused about good manners or etiquette. Because sometimes when we try to impress others in a polite way, we do not achieve the desired results. Consequently, we should first have a study of etiquette to find out the reasons.

在中国，拥有良好的举止显得尤为重要。礼仪培养人的性格。有教养的人通常会受欢迎。每天保持礼貌的言行举止会给大家留下良好的印象。良好的举止是衡量一个人修养的评判标准之一。无论在家、在工作场所，还是和朋友在一起，礼貌得体的举止都是很重要的。

但令人不解的是，很多人却对良好的举止或礼仪产生了困惑。这是因为，有时当我们试图用礼貌的方式与别人交往时，却常常得不到预期的效果。因此，有必要首先研究一下什么是礼仪，以便找出出现这种现象的原因。

1. The Concept of Business Etiquette 商务礼仪的概念

As is known to all, etiquette is one of the most misunderstood words in the English language. Most people, when asked what etiquette means to them, reply, "Manners", "Politeness", "Thank-you notes", "Rules".

American etiquette expert Emily Post defined etiquette as: "Whenever two people come together and their behavior affects one another, you have etiquette. Etiquette is not some rigid code of manners; it's simply how persons' lives touch one another." Actually, etiquette is about building relationships, plain and simple.

Etiquette is a set of practices and forms which are followed in a wide variety of situations. Each society has its own distinct etiquette, and various cultures within a society also have their own rules and social norms. Because the social norms of different cultures are so different, so people should study etiquette before traveling or entering a new social circle to ensure that they do not cause offense or embarrass themselves. Nobody actually wants to cause offense, but as business becomes ever more international, it is increasingly easy to get it wrong. Sometimes the person lacking the etiquette simply does not realize the action taken is offensive.

众所周知，"礼仪"是最不好理解的词汇之一。当询问一些人有关这个词的含义时，他们的理解就是"有礼貌""温文尔雅"，或者是"多说谢谢""遵规守纪"等。

美国礼仪专家艾米丽·波斯特对此的定义是"无论任何时候，只要两个人在一起，并且他们的行为相互影响着对方，就产生了礼仪。礼仪并不像电脑程序一样，都是些死板的礼节编码，而是使人们的生活联系在一起的纽带"。礼仪是建立人与人之间关系的方法，朴实而简单。

礼仪是在各种环境下通过练习逐渐塑造形成的。每种形态的社会都有其独特的礼仪规范，而且不同的文化背景也有其不同的规则和社会规范。由于不同文化背景下的社会规范不同，因此人们在出行或进入一个新的社交圈前应学习礼仪，以避免犯错或陷入尴尬的境地。实际上，没有人愿意犯错，但随着国际化和一体化的加强，人们犯错的机会也越来越多，更何况缺乏礼仪观念的人，根本就意识不到自己的行为是错的。

2.The Effects of Business Etiquette 商务礼仪的作用

(1) It coordinates employee relations

Professionals are aware of the many advantages of proper business etiquette. In professional situations, extending proper courtesies can help you to make a good impression on colleagues. In addition, it will make the office environment much more pleasant and will make for better-quality work when employees treat each other well. Proper etiquette will also make it more likely that a team of workers will come together to complete a project, which further means that deadlines will be met and employees will feel less burned out.

很多商务人士意识到一些收获得益于得体的商务礼仪。在很多场合，正确运用礼仪能给别人留下良好的印象。例如，礼仪使同事们相处融洽，有助于营造愉悦的工作氛围，提高工作质量。恰当的礼仪还有利于工作团队的彼此协调，按时完成项目任务。

(2) It creates a good image of employees and companies

Business etiquette is a kind of civilization accumulation of human being. It is also kind of standard behavior observed by employees. Of course, it can regulate employee's behavior while employees represent the companies they work for. The best intrinsic quality of each employee comes from the continuous penetration by proper etiquette. As it is well known good manners make a positive impression. Etiquette, therefore, keeps employees' goodwill as well as maintains the company's image and reputation.

商务礼仪既是人类文明的积累，也是员工遵守的行为准则。它可以指导员工的行为举止，而员工代表他们所在的公司，因此商务礼仪还同时影响公司形象。员工内在的优秀品格源于持续不断的礼仪熏陶。众所周知，良好的仪态必将树立正面的形象。可见，礼仪不仅可以使员工的友善得以保持，而且还可以使公司的形象及声誉得以维护。

(3) It helps international business negotiation more effectively

International business negotiation focuses more and more techniques and tactics. But this does not mean that the success of negotiation will depend only on techniques and tactics. Sometimes human emotion also plays a significant role. Etiquette is the code of conduct and guidelines of communication in business activities. A small mistake in etiquette might lead to embarrassment or even break up the negotiation. Etiquette in business negotiation is essentially about building relationship between/among negotiation parties. That is why "etiquette" is considered to be a part of negotiation. Most negotiators have two main goals: creating strong deals and building good relationships. In today's business climate, it is critical that negotiators achieve both goals. And etiquette plays an important role in helping achieve the goals.

国际商务谈判越来越注重策略与战术，但这并不意味着谈判的成功完全取决于策略及战术。有时谈判者的情感也在谈判中发挥相当大的作用。礼仪是人们在商务活动交往与沟通中的行为准则和指南。在谈判中，只要出现一个小小的礼仪错误就可能使谈判者陷入窘迫，或导致谈判失败。礼仪在商务谈判中的重要性体现在帮助双方或多方之间建立良好的关系。这就是礼仪甚至被看成是商务谈判的一部分的原因。大多数谈判者在谈判时都设立了两个主要目标：一是多达成交易；二是与对方建立良好的关系。对于谈判者而言，尤其在当今的商务环境下，更要同时实现这两个目标，而礼仪正在这其中发挥着重要作用。

So, learning international business etiquette is beneficial to associate with others. It gives us clues as to how we should act and what we should do in any given situation, so that we can be as successful as possible in our interactions with the people around us. Far from stifling your personality in a strait jacket, etiquette—by giving you the confidence to handle a wide variety of situations with ease and aplomb—actually lets you focus on being your own, relaxed self, and the real you.

因此，学习国际商务礼仪有利于人们与他人的交往。它是指导人们在任意场合应该如何做和做什么的依据，也是帮助人们建立良好人际关系的基础。礼仪不是束缚人的枷锁，相反它会给予人们在任何场合轻松坦然应对的信心，并使之在与他人的交往中关注自己、放松自己，找到真正的自己。

Part II   The Principles of Business Etiquette
商务礼仪的原则

International business etiquette is not easy to establish or maintain. Although we communicate by using faster media, such as facsimiles, e-mail, and wireless phones, we do not necessarily communicate more intelligently. In order to avoid the occurrence of this kind of circumstance, we should have a clear study of the principles of international business etiquette so that we can have a deep and through understanding about the etiquette.

国际商务礼仪很难养成或保持。尽管如今，我们通过使用一些更便捷的通信媒体来进行沟通，例如，传真、电子邮件、无线电话，但我们未必能够智慧地与他人交谈。为了避免这种情况发生，我们首先来学习国际商务礼仪原则，以便能够更深层次、更透彻地理解礼仪。

1.Etiquette and Manner 礼仪与礼节

Etiquette is the power that fuels our relationships, by helping us know how to act and how to expect others to act in any kind of situation. Etiquette accomplishes this through a powerful combination of manners and principles.

礼仪使我们知道，在何种情况下应如何表现，如何正确地待人接物。礼仪是礼节和原则的有力结合，正是这种结合使礼仪推动了人与人之间关系的发展。

In many situations, manners can help us determine the right thing to do, but there are always exceptions, and so we have to judge when a manner applies and when we should do something differently rather than by the book. Manners tell us two types of things:

(1)What to do in all kinds of situations—What fork to use; whether to hold a door for someone else; How to introduce yourself to another person?

(2)What we can expect other people to do?

在很多情况下，礼节都能正确地指导行为举止，但也会有例外，所以我们需要判断是否采纳某个礼节，决定何时使用礼节而非从书本上生搬硬套。

礼节告诉我们以下两件事：

（1）在各种场合中我们应该怎样做——如何使用叉子；是否为别人开门；如何向别人介绍自己？

（2）希望得到别人怎样的回应？

If you extend your hand to shake hands, you fully expect the other person to reciprocate. When he does, everything is fine. If he does not extend his hand, however, you immediately start to wonder if you have body odor or bad breath, or if you did something to insult him. In essence, manners are guidelines to help us as we interact with the people around us, by sketching out the appropriate actions, appearance, and words that will help us build successful relationships.

如果你主动与别人握手，你肯定希望对方能把手伸出来配合你。如果他与你握手了，一切正常。但是，如果他没有把手伸出来，你立刻就会想到自己是不是有体味或是口臭，还是自己做了某件事侮辱了他。从本质上来说，礼节是我们与周围人相互交流的指南，因此我们要通过合适的行为举止、外表和言辞来建立良好的人际关系。

2. The Three Principles That Govern All Etiquette 礼仪的三个原则

Principles are the guiding concepts on which all manners are based. Among other things, they tell us:

- ❑ Why a certain manner is called for?
- ❑ What to do when there is no prescribed manner or a manner does not work?
- ❑ How to resolve relationship situations?

For example, while attending a business dinner, an elderly client begins to excuse herself from the table. Since business etiquette is meant to be non-gender specific, the appropriate "manner" states that you, as a male, should not stand as she gets ready to leave the table. But you also know the client is old-school—and so you decide that, despite the latest guideline or "rule", you will stand. As you do, she smiles and says, "Thank you." By understanding the unique circumstances of the situation, and showing respect for your dinner companion by standing in spite of what the "rule" says, you have made her appreciate you much more. In turn, you have helped yourself and your company builds a better relationship with her.

Virtually, all the manners you will find in etiquette books—and, indeed, all the choices that you will ever make about your actions, appearance, and words—are governed by three principles: consideration, respect, and honesty.

In order to understand these principles and how they are used in etiquette, it is necessary to define each of them:

礼仪的三个原则是所有礼仪形成的指导思想，即所有礼仪都是在这个基础上建立起来的。这三个原则具体如下：

- ❑ 为什么需要特定的礼仪？
- ❑ 在某些场合，没有特定的礼仪或已有的礼仪派不上用场该怎么办？
- ❑ 应如何解决人际关系中发生的某些状况？

例如，在一个商务晚宴上，一位年老女客户正准备离开桌子（在商务礼仪中是没有性别区分的），作为男性的你不应该在她离开桌子时起立，但是因为你知道这位客户是你的老校友，所以你决定不顾礼仪课上的指导或是规定，站了起来。当你站起来时，她微笑着并对你说"谢谢"！通过对特殊环境的理解，以及出于对与你共同进餐的人的尊重而起立，虽然这并不是按照"规矩"做，但你获得了她对你的深深谢意，并且有利于你和你的公司与她建立起更好的关系。

事实上，所有礼节都可以在礼仪书中找到，而且所有关于行为举止、外表和语言的选择都是基于体谅、尊重和真诚这三个原则。

为了使你了解这些原则，并清楚如何使用它们，有必要给它们下个定义。

（1）Consideration 体谅

Consideration means looking at the current situation and assessing how it affects everyone who is involved. This is Why etiquette—defined simply as being sincerely considerate, respectful, and honest—is invaluable. Etiquette allows the real you to thrive, by giving you the skills and confidence to build the best relationships possible, which in turn will give you the opportunity to be as successful as you want to be. With the help of etiquette, the sky is the limit.

体谅，即观察周围的环境，评估一下它对参与其中的每个人的影响。礼仪是无价的——真诚地体谅他人、尊重他人，并诚实地对待他人。礼仪可以让你真正有所发展，它赋予你建立良好的人际关系的能力和信心，同时也给了你实现成功的机会。有了礼仪的帮助，成功将变得触手可及。

（2）Respect 尊重

Respects means looking at how your possible actions will affect others in the future. To respect the others is the essential etiquette in interpersonal communication. Respect is often displayed in the trifles, such as listening to the others attentively, not interrupting the other's conversation, remembering the names of new acquaintances, replying promptly to the letters, phone calls and messages.

尊重，即观察你可能有的举动，在未来将会如何影响周围的人。人际沟通中的基本礼仪是尊重他人。要尊重生活中的每一件事，即使是琐事。例如，聚精会神地倾听对方，不要打断别人的谈话，牢记新结识的人的名字，及时回复信件、电话和邮件。

（3）Honesty 真诚

Honesty means acting sincerely and being truthful, not deceitful. Contrary to what some people may think, a concerted effort to make a good impression through the use of etiquette does not mean putting on airs, playing games, betraying yourself, or compromising your integrity. Phoniness and pretentiousness are one thing; observing guidelines of behavior that have evolved over time to serve the common good is quite another. Therefore, it is not enough to be considerate, respectful, and honest; you must also be sincere in the use of these principles. If you are not, people will see through your vender. "Jim seems like a nice guy, but there's something about him that strikes me as phony." That is not the impression you want to make.

The more considerate, respectful, and honest business people sincerely are to one another, the better their relationships will be with coworkers, employees, customers, and suppliers. Etiquette greases the wheels of social interaction.

Being in command of proper etiquette really means knowing how to use your own common sense in applying one or more of the above principles to determine the best course of action in any situation. The man standing up at the dinner table knew that in this case, being respectful of his companion was more important than following the "rule"—so he rose.

真诚，即表现得诚恳并且要诚实不要欺骗。与某些人的想法正相反，通过礼仪努力给别人留下一个好的印象，并不意味着装腔作势、玩弄手段、伪装自己。骗术和自命不凡是一回事，遵守行为准则并将其不断发展为平常生活和服务完全又是另外一回事。因此，对于体贴、尊重与诚实还是有很多要做的：你要抱着真诚的态度使用这些原则。否则，人们将会看透你的伪装。"吉姆看起来是个好人，但是他的有些事让我感觉他像个骗子。"这不是你想留给别人的印象。

越是考虑周到、尊重他人并且诚实的商务人员，对待合作者、员工、客户和供货商就会越真诚。礼仪是人际交往的润滑油。

在礼仪的指挥下，你要知道如何在你的日常言行中加入上述原则中的一条或多条，从而在任何情况下表现出最好的行为。在餐桌前起立的那个男士深知在这种情况下，尊重他的同伴比遵循"规矩"更加重要，所以他起立了。

Succeeding in business today requires not only mastery of one's job but also mastery of the common courtesies of give and take and of consideration for others. Not only does this make the office a pleasanter place to be, it helps you leave a favorable impression behind, whatever you do, whether you are making a first impression during a job interview or representing your company to others, your manners are often counted as highly as your knowledge of your subject matter or your brilliance in the conference room. Put them to work today, and you will find that they will work for you in all your professional days to come.

当今商界的成功不仅仅要求个人的工作能力，还要求个人具有谦让和对他人体贴考虑的精神。这会使办公室成为一个令人心仪的处所。无论你做什么，都会给他人留下美好的印象。不论你求职面试，还是代表你的公司，你的行为举止会和你的才识一样被人看重。在实际工作中运用这些准则，会在未来的职业生活中助你一臂之力。

Situational practice for etiquettes 礼仪口语实景

Make up or search for more situational conversations that may occur when talking about etiquette and put them into practice.

A:Excuse me, Mary, what does the word E-t-i-q-u-e-t-t-e in the notice mean?

B:Oh, etiquette. It's a French word which means manners.

A:So I have been asked to attend the etiquette training. Mary, how is the word pronounced?

B:E-ti-ket. Q-u make the sound of k, instead of that of q, e-ti-ket.

A:I come here to work, not to attend the parties. Why should I learn the etiquette?

B:Etiquette is very important to business. Whether an employee treats his clients politely influences the business a lot.

A:To make it clear, what does etiquette refer to here?

B:Etiquette is a set of rules that allow us to interact with others in a civilized manner.

A:To interact with others in a civilized manner?

B:Precisely, it means treating other people with courtesy and respect and making them feel comfortable with you.

A:En, treating other people with courtesy and respect and making them feel comfortable with you. It isn't hard to me. I'm always polite and courteous to others.

B:But the topic of the training is focused on the western etiquette which is different from Chinese etiquette as cultural differences exist.

A:So etiquette is not the same in different countries. I'd like to hear about that.

 Terminology related 相关礼仪术语

Business etiquette

Business etiquettes are not only the way to maintain and develop interpersonal relationships but also symbol of human civilization and social progress. Good manners are not only indispensable in society, but they have a very practical value in the business world.Business etiquettes are the behaviors followed in the world of business and corporate culture. They consist of certain universally applicable and acceptable rules. Business etiquettes are the way you handle yourself in a business and social environment. The basics of social manners include dressing etiquette, meeting etiquette, conversation etiquette, gift-giving etiquette, dining etiquette and so on. In general, social manners are the social guidelines to follow in society when dealing with others.

商务礼仪不仅是维护和发展人际关系的方式，而且是人类文明和社会进步的象征。举止礼貌得体不但在社会生活中不可或缺，而且在商界也很实用。商务礼仪是商界和企业文化遵循的行为准则，它包含被广泛适用和被接受的规则。商务礼仪指导人们在生意中和社会环境中如何为人处世。基本的商务礼仪包括服装礼仪、会议礼仪、会话礼仪、赠礼礼仪、餐饮礼仪等。总之，商务礼仪是在商业场合与他人相处应遵循的社会准则。

Useful expressions for etiquettes 礼仪用语集锦

Study and interpret the following idioms or quotations centered on etiquette.

❑ Courtesy costs nothing.
　　礼仪本轻利厚。

❑ A smart coat is a good letter of introduction.
　　得体的装束是一封最佳的介绍信。

❑ Do as the Romans do.
　　礼仪随俗。

❑ Apparel makes the man.
　　人靠衣装。

❑ A good face is a letter of recommendation.
　　良好的面貌是最佳推荐信。

❑ The hardest thing children face today is learning good manners without seeing any.
　　今天年青一代难以学习良好礼仪是因为榜样难寻。

❑ By treating another person with appropriately high levels of politeness, you interact with the other person more as a role than as a human being.
　　用得体的、高水准的礼仪对待他人，是把对方当作一个人物而非一般人对待。

❑ Politeness and consideration for others is like investing pennies and getting dollars back.　　　　　　　　　　　　　　　　　　　　—Thomas Sowell
　　对他人礼仪周全等同于小投资、大回报。　　　　　　　——托马斯·索维尔

❑ Wherever you go, no matter what the weather, always bring your own sunshine.
　　　　　　　　　　　　　　　　　　　　　　—Anthony J. D. Angelo
　　无论身在何处，无论环境如何，永远要阳光在身，乐观积极。
　　　　　　　　　　　　　　　　　　　　　　——安东尼·安吉乐

❑ You shouldn't say it is not good. You should say you do not like it; and then, you know, you're perfectly safe.　　　　　　　　　　　　　　—James Whistler

在表述时，不要说这不好，而应该说你只是不喜欢它。这样的表述不会惹出麻烦。

——詹姆斯·惠斯勒

❑ When you blame others, you give up your power to change.　—Douglas N. Adams
当你指责他人的时候，你放弃了用自己的力量去改变。

——道格拉斯·亚当斯

Exercises（课后练习）

I. Questions and answers: answer the following questions according to the information you have got in the previous reading.

1.What is your understanding of the quotation "*Etiquette is simply how persons' lives touch one another*"?

2.Why do we define etiquette as a powerful combination of manners and principles?

3.What is the function of the three principles that govern all etiquette?

4.How can you avoid betraying yourself or compromising your integrity when using etiquette?

5.What can you learn from the case of "the man standing up at the dinner table" in the text?

II.Expressions: match the terms in column A with the Chinese equivalents in column B.

A	B
distinguished guest	友好访问
host country	时间管理
transnational corporation	贵宾
time management	跨国公司
goodwill visit	东道国

III. Translation: translate the following statements into Chinese to ensure your understanding of etiquette.

1.Etiquette refers to a kind of standardized behavior in interpersonal contacts. It goes through a certain common procedures to show respects to the people we are talking to from the beginning to the end.

2.Etiquette is in the level higher than that of politeness with wider and deeper meaning. It is the integrity of system and process.

3.Etiquette can be said to be the external manifestations of a person's inner cultivation and quality.

4.Etiquette can be defined as the code of people's interaction.

5.Etiquette can be described as an art in interpersonal activities or a communicative means or method.

6.Etiquette is a formal beauty which reflects people's soul.

7.Business etiquette can be defined as behavior norms that should be abided by business people in their activities.

8.Compared with other subjects, business etiquette has its own unique characteristics which can be reflected in five aspects: normative, qualificative, operable, inheritable and changeable.

9.One of the functions of business etiquette is that it helps to improve people's self-cultivation.

10.Another function of business etiquette is that it contributes to the promotion of business communication and improving people's interpersonal relationship.

IV. Cloze: choose the suitable statements from the box and complete the passage.

> A. Valuing time
> B. Honoring space issues
> C. Understanding the handshake
> D. Exchanging business cards
> E. Observing the hierarchy

_____1_____. It is not always a simple matter to know who is the highest-ranking member when you are dealing with a group. To avoid embarrassment, err on the side of age and masculine gender, only if you are unable to discover the protocol with research. If you are interacting with the Japanese, it is important to understand that they make decisions by consensus, starting with the younger members of the group. By contrast, Latin people have a clear hierarchy that defers to age.

_____2_____. With a few exceptions, business people around the world use the handshake for meeting and greeting. However, the American style handshake with a firm grip, two quick pumps, eye contact and a smile is not universal. Variations in handshakes are based on cultural differences, not on personality or values. The Japanese give a light handshake. Germans offer a firm shake with one pump, and the French grip is light with a quick pump. Middle Eastern people will continue shaking your hand throughout the greeting. Don't be surprised if you are occasionally met with a kiss, a hug, or a bow somewhere along the way.

_____3_____. The key to giving out business cards in any culture is to show respect for the other person. Present your card so that the other person does not have to turn it over to read your information. Use both hands to present your card to visitors from Japan, China, Singapore, or Hong Kong. When you receive someone else's business card, always look at it and acknowledge it. In most cases, wait until you have been introduced to give someone your card.

_____4_____. Not everyone in the world is as time conscious as Americans. Don't take it personally if someone from a more relaxed culture keeps you waiting or spends more of that commodity than you normally would in meetings or over meals. Stick to the rules of punctuality, but be understanding when your contact from another country seems unconcerned.

_____5_____. Americans have a particular value for their own physical space and are uncomfortable when other people get in their realm. If the international visitor seems to want to be close, accept it. Backing away can send the wrong message. So can touching. You shouldn't risk violating someone else's space by touching them in any way other than with a handshake.

V.Case study: get into the groups, discuss and find out:

1.Any specific examples to prove the importance of learning about etiquette.

2.The differences between Chinese and Western etiquette.

3.The characteristics of business etiquette.

Extension（拓展阅读）

I Want You to Do a Better Job—Building Relationship

"I want you to do a better job—building relationships" is what your boss could tell you in a job performance review. If she did, how would you go about fulfilling such a request? Chances are, you wouldn't have a clue where to begin. If, however, you shift your focus from improving your "relationships" in general to evaluating how well you handle the specific factors that influence all relationships, this goal will start to look much more attainable（可到达的）. This is easier than you might think, because there are really only three things that affect a relationship: your actions, your appearance, and your words.

❑ Actions

The thing we do can have various impacts. Imagine: you sit down at a restaurant table with a client. After a few minutes, your mobile phone starts ringing. You answer it and start talking. Clearly, we are all aware that this action would create a negative atmosphere at your business lunch. What is a better action, one that will improve your relationship with your client? Simple: either turn off your phone before meeting your client or let your client knows that you're expecting a call, and then excuse yourself to the lobby or restroom area when your phone vibrates （震动）.

❑　Appearance

The importance of clothes and grooming is obvious. Dress like a slob, and the people you are with will think of you as a slob. Body odor （气味） and bad breath—those are no-brainers. What about body language? That falls under appearance as well: twitching （ 颤 动 ） your foot during a meeting says you are either nervous or apprehensive （焦虑）, or you can't wait for the meeting to end. Improve your appearance by keeping your foot still—and staying calm, alert, and twitch-free in general—and you will build better relationships with the people you do business with.

❑　Words

Coarse （粗鲁的） language is clearly out of bounds. But say you're in a meeting and you blurt out （脱口而出）, "Oh my God, Sally, what a great idea!" Later, you discover that some of the people present were offended that you took the Lord's name in vain. Suddenly, instead of thinking about Sally's great idea, those participants are focused on you and their negative perception of you.

When everything is going well as far as your actions, appearance, and words are concerned, your focus—and the focus of the people you are with—will be on the content of your discussion. Slip up （弄错） with any one of these factors, however, and the focus will suddenly shift to the failure ("I can't believe he just did that"). By being aware of your actions, appearance, and words, and working to improve your performance in all three areas, you can directly enhance the quality of your relationships.

After-reading tasks（读后任务）

When you finish reading the text above, get into the groups and discuss with your group members about the following tasks and fulfill them.

Task 1

Give a speech to talk about your own experiences in building relationship, first in your group, then before class.

Task 2

As mentioned in the text, there are really only three things that affect a relationship: your

actions, your appearance, and your words. Do you think you have paid attention to these factors in your career life? Share your successful examples or failure in these aspects with group members.

Task 3

This unit is a general introduction to business etiquette. Find out your understanding of business etiquette and plans of how to learn about business etiquettes by talking with your group members. Each group should elect a representative to speak for your group.

Self-study（自学反馈）

If possible, summarize what you have learned in this unit with the help of the following table.

Focus of this unit:
Guidelines for etiquette: 1. 2. 3. ...
Summary:
Application: 1. 2. 3. ...
Feedback:

Chapter Two
Business Image Etiquette
商务礼仪形象

Objectives（学习目标）

After you have studied this chapter, you should be able to:

- ❑ Know the corresponding etiquettes in setting a successful and professional image
- ❑ Handle some problem situations concerning physical appearance and dressing
- ❑ Cultivate the cross-cultural awareness when communicating with people from different cultural background

Lead-in（导读）

First impression last. Dressing the body for public concern and expectations is much like marketing a commodity. As with any other product, the visible elements of one's person (speech, dress, body language, and manners) must reflect the individual's inner talents and aspirations and give others an idea of the kind of person with whom they are associating. The way we dress has an impact on the people we meet professionally or socially. It affects their treatment of us.

第一印象影响持久。如何穿衣着装才能受到公众关注，被寄予期望，这类似于商品营销。和其他商品一样，一个人的外在因素，如言谈、着装、身体语言和礼仪，会反映其内在素质，对方会由此判断出你属于哪一类人。无论在商务场合还是社交场合，着装都会影响对方对你的印象，同时也决定了对方的态度。

Test yourself（自我测试）

To start with, take a test to see to obtain the knowledge of how to set up a professional image in the business world. You can use Yes or No to make responses to the following statements.

1. A successful dresser is someone who changes from being formal to being relaxed, from wearing solid basic colors to lighter colors and more colorful accessories (women's blouses, men's shirts and ties) to fit the occasion.　　　　　　　Yes ☐ No ☐
2. If others perceive us as lacking in polish or finesse or sophistication in our dress or manner, we convey the message that we have not developed into well-rounder and mature

professional persons.   Yes ☐ No ☐

3.Women as well as men are free to wear casual slack outfits as times change.   Yes ☐ No ☐

4.Both men and women must look well groomed and select the clothes that best suit them and are compatible with the business environment.   Yes ☐ No ☐

5.Professional women do not have to be like uniformed clones of men, e.g. by dressing in suits that resemble men's attire.   Yes ☐ No ☐

6.Shorts or jeans are an absolute no to professional women.   Yes ☐ No ☐

7.Avoid too much makeup in the office.   Yes ☐ No ☐

8.Cocktail and party wear dress has no place in the office. It leaves the impression that you are at heart a party girl rather than a professional business person.   Yes ☐ No ☐

9.Avoid too long hair. It sheds, gets into the typewriter and clings to computers, papers, and desks.   Yes ☐ No ☐

10.Beware of scuffed heels and unpolished shoes or runs in stockings. All these leave an impression of carelessness.   Yes ☐ No ☐

Part I   Grooming
仪容形象修饰

Appearance usually refers to the person's appearance, physiognomy, but it mainly means person's countenance. In the process of interpersonal communication, our appearance claims other's first attention. After a elaborate care, the appearance embodies the beauties and etiquette of appearance. The appearance is usually influenced by two factors. One is congenital factor of each individual, formed by nature; the other is adscititious decorate and care. As the French renowned enlightened thinker Montesquieu put it, "A person only has one way to be beautiful, but he can be lovely by using hundred thousands ways." Person's appearance is innate and cannot be changed, but we can also acquire a completely new outlook by taking careful and special care. For this effect, you need to know some common knowledge of beauty, and master some basic grooming techniques.

仪容通常是指人的外观、外貌，重点是指人的容貌。在人际交往过程中，首先引起对方注意的就是仪容，仪容通过精心修饰体现了仪容美，也展示了仪容礼仪。仪容通常受两方面因素影响：一为个人的先天条件，自然形成；二为后天的修饰和保养。正如法国启蒙思想家孟德斯鸠所说："一个人只有一种方式是美丽的，但他可以通过十万种方式使自己变得可爱。"个人容貌是天生的、相对定型的，但通过细心保养、精心修饰就可以焕然一新。要想达到这种效果，就需要懂得一些美容常识，掌握一些基本的修饰技巧。

1.Beauty of Nature 自然美

（1）Hair 头发

Proper hair care will lead to healthier and better looking hair. Bad hair care tactics or not taking care of your hair can lead to breakage, frizzy, split ends, dull hair, and early hair loss.

Wash your hair often enough to keep it from looking greasy. Avoid both the super-blow-dried look and the gelled-to-the-skull look.

正确地护理头发将会使你的头发更健康、更好看。反之，则会导致头发破损、卷曲、开叉、无光泽，甚至早期脱发。

要经常清洗头发，让头发保持干净清爽，既不要看起来很干，也不要看起来很油。

A woman will attract attention with her hair when she has a flattering cut or healthy, shiny hair that simply begs to be admired. What about length? There's no longer a true rule, but on the job, hair should be kept out of the eyes: tuck it behind your ears, pull it back in a ponytail, or pull it out of your eyes with a barrette. Unusual ornaments are risky unless you're a senior vice president who has earned the right to be a little au courant.

一个讨人喜欢的发型，或者有一头健康有光泽的头发，这样的女士很容易吸引人们的目光。至于头发的长度多长为好？这个并没有严格的规定。但是，在办公室内，头发以不能遮住眼睛为宜，可以把头发梳到耳朵后面，扎成一个马尾辫；或用发卡别住头发，使其不遮挡眼睛。"与众不同"的打扮是危险的，除非你是高级副总裁，有权引起大家关注。

It is not advisable for men to keep long hair. Men's hair should not cover their ears or forehead. Keep a small brush in the office for whisking flakes off your shoulders. One morning a week at least, gentlemen should check to see if their nose hairs need to be clipped or your ears tweezed, otherwise, do it yourself at home, not in a office restroom.

男士则不建议留长发。男士的头发以不遮住耳朵或额头为宜。在办公室里准备一把小刷子，专门用来清理肩膀上的头皮屑。一个星期至少有一天检查自己的鼻毛是不是需要修剪，看看耳毛是不是需要拔掉。另外，这些事情在家里做就好，千万别在办公室里处理。

（2）Nails 指甲

Nails should always be kept clean and trimmed. Dirt can mysteriously appear under your fingernails when you least expect it. So keep a nail clipper with a cleaning tool in your desk drawer.

The best length for women's nails in most business environments is just over the tip of the finger. Men's nails should be trimmed straight across with about one-sixteenth of an inch of white showing. Clear nail polish is the best choice if you're uncertain.

指甲必须保持干净，要勤修剪。指甲很容易进灰尘，因此要在桌子抽屉里准备一把指甲剪，以便随时修剪。

对于商务女性来说，指甲的最佳长度是长出指尖一点点。对于商务男性来说，则应把指甲剪齐，露出 1/16 英寸就可以了。在办公室里，不建议使用彩色指甲油，如果你不确定，最好选用透明指甲油。

（3）Tooth 牙齿

To make your smile more attractive and keep your breath fresh, you should brush your teeth in the morning, at night and after each meal. Bring your toothbrush to work so that you can brush after lunch. Brushing the back of the tongue helps control odor, and a breath mint or two during the day should keep you from offending.

为了使你的笑容更加迷人，并保持口气清新，你必须早晚以及饭后刷牙。上班时带上牙刷以便午餐后刷牙。清理舌头后面的部分可以防止口臭。每天嚼一两片口香糖也是不错的选择。

（4）Body 身体

In order to stay clean and odor-free, a daily shower is needed. It is the best defense against body odor. And a deodorant or antiperspirant is the second best.

想要让自己保持干净、无气味，必须每天洗澡，这是防止体味最有效的办法。除臭剂和止汗药是第二选择。

2.Beauty of Cosmetics 修饰美

（1）Make-up principles 化妆原则

As a rule, use a light touch, makeup should enhance, not dominate. Extreme eye makeup, very unusual lip color, a lot of lip liner that is obvious contrast to the lipsticks, these are poor choices in most workplace.

一般情况下，建议化淡妆作简单的点缀，而不应浓妆艳抹。与口红不搭配的很浓的眼妆、颜色独特的唇彩、与口红颜色对比鲜明的厚重的唇线，在绝大多数工作场合中都是很不明智的选择。

（2）Tricks of make-up 化妆的技巧

❑ Before makeup, clean and moisturize your face daily are essential to maintain glistening skin. Different moisturizer fit various types of skin. For oily and combination skin, an oil-free formulation and regulating extra oil formulation. For dry skin, a rich hydrating cream suits the best. As for normal skin, use a light moisturizing lotion.

❑ Do not forget the most important part of your face—the eyes. Use light eye cream so that the eye concealer later put on covers smoothly.

❑ When the skin looks dull, you can scales off the dead skin cells by an exfoliant.

❑ Put on paper facial masks to moisturize the face once or twice a week.

❑ Remove excessive small hair around your eyebrows. A pair of clear, sharp eyebrows is a core of the entire face.

化妆前，做好日常的清洁与保湿对保持闪耀发光的肌肤非常重要。不同的保湿水适合不同肤质。对于油性和混合性的肌肤，适用无油配方和调节多余油脂的配方。对于干性皮肤，滋养的保湿霜最合适。对于正常的皮肤，可以使用轻柔的保湿乳液。千万不要忘了脸部最重要的部位——眼睛。使用清爽的滋润眼霜可以使之后上的眼妆服帖。当皮肤看起来暗沉时，你可以使用磨砂膏去除脸上死皮。每星期做一次或两次面膜以滋润面部。除去眉毛周围过多的小毛发。一双清晰、锐利的眉毛是整个面部的核心。

（3）Make-up tools 化妆工具

These things you'll need: foundation, mascara, eye shadow brushes, blush brush, face powder, blush, waterproof mascaras, lipstick, lip gloss, and eye shadow.

你需要的化妆工具有：粉底、睫毛膏、眼影刷、腮红刷、粉饼、腮红、防水睫毛膏、口红、唇彩、眼影。

（4）Make-up procedure 化妆步骤

An energetic and charming face is a critical factor to give a favorable impression. However, many businesswomen will feel difficult and time-consuming in doing a satisfying nude makeup in a haste morning. Follow these eight simple steps will do a perfect makeup for yourself.

一个充满活力并散发迷人光彩的面孔是给对方留下美好印象的关键因素。然而很多商务女性认为在匆忙的早上化一个令人满意的裸妆是一件困难并耗费时间的事情。按照以下八个步骤，你可以给自己化一个完美的妆容。

Step one

The foundation of the whole face is the main importance for the success of a makeup. Put on UV sunscreen to shade the ultraviolet ray to protect your skin. Follow by a colored base which can improve your skin color and enhance makeup hold. Choose foundation that matches your skin tone exactly. Apply it in dots over the central part of your face, and then blend it out with a makeup sponge until it covers your entire face. Use a loose or pressed powder to keep foundation and concealer on longer. Use pressed powder to touch up when you're away from home.

步骤一：整个面部的基础，是化妆成功的重要因素。使用防晒霜遮挡紫外线，保护你的皮肤。接下来，使用有颜色的隔离霜，以提亮皮肤，并提高整体妆容观感。选择一款与你皮肤基调完全匹配的粉底液。在脸部中央打点，然后使用海绵涂匀直到遮盖全部脸部肌肤。使用散粉或粉饼定妆。当你离开家后，可以使用粉饼补妆。

Step two

Darken and shade your eyebrows using eyebrow powder instead of pencil, which can often look unnatural. Apply it with a hard, slanted brush. Choose the color that is the same as your eyebrows and hair. Start at the interior corner of the eyebrow, and trace its natural form in a soft movement. Finally, fill in sparse areas in the brow.

步骤二：用眉粉代替眉笔加深并描绘眉毛，因为用眉笔画显得不自然。使用硬的斜毛刷，选择和你的眉毛、头发一样颜色的眉粉，从眉毛内角开始，根据自然形状慢慢地往下刷。最后，补描眉毛稀疏的地方。

Step three

Apply a light eye shadow color from the eyelash line to the eyebrow bone. Choose color that makes you look energetic. Mind that not everyone matches purple and pink. Choose three colors of eye shadow: light, medium and dark. The closer to the eye, then use more dark shadow to apply. For longer-lasting look, use a long-wearing cream shadow, especially for oily skin.

步骤三：在睫毛线和眉骨之间涂上一层浅浅的眼影。选择让你看起来充满活力的颜色。记住不是所有人都适合紫色和粉色。建议选择三种颜色的眼影：浅色、中等色、深色。上眼影时以越接近眼睛颜色越深的方法来涂擦。为了使妆容持久，使用不易晕染的眼影，尤其是油性肌肤。

Step four

Apply eyeliner. Use eyeliner with a thin liner brush, or an eyeliner pencil, and line the lower lid below the lashes. Line only the outer two-thirds of the lower lid. Line up upper lid (just above the lash line and as close to the lashes as possible).

步骤四：画眼线。使用带有细细的眼线刷的眼线膏或眼线笔画眼睑下面的睫毛。从外眼角向内眼角由重到轻画到2/3处。上眼线全部画完（在睫毛根部上画，尽可能地接近睫毛）。

Step five

Choose waterproof mascara to prevent smudge. When applying mascara, sweep the lashes from the tip to the bottom, then from the bottom to tip. Wind the stick as you go to divide the lashes and avoid batches. In this way, it will look much better.

步骤五：选择防水睫毛膏防止晕妆。当使用睫毛膏时，应先从上往下刷，再从下往上刷。使用小棍棒将睫毛分成一根一根的，防止粘成一撮。这样看起来效果会更好。

Step six

Tap off excess powder blush from the brush, say "cheese" to give a smile and put on a natural shade of blush on the cheeks. Blend upward under the eye and then downward to lighten the color. A pink or orange color is also preferable.

步骤六：使用刷子上多余的腮红，一边说"cheese"展开笑脸，一边在脸颊上涂上最自然的腮红。向上在眼睛下方涂匀，然后向下缓和颜色。粉红色和橙色的腮红都可以。

Step seven

For the lips choose the lipstick or lip gloss that is close to the natural color of your lips.

步骤七：为双唇选择最接近你自然唇色的唇膏或唇彩。

Step eight

Line lips after applying lipstick. That way you won't end up with a dark circle of lip liner after your lipstick has worn off. Avoid combining very dark lip liner and pale lipstick.

步骤八：在涂完唇膏后画唇线。这样就不会在你涂完唇膏后，唇线就变成一个深色的圈。避免使深色的唇线配浅色的唇膏。

All in all, no matter in working environment or in private occasions, an eye-catching and pleasant face will give others a good impression. Remember "Practice makes perfect!"

总而言之，不管是在工作环境还是私人场所中，一张迷人愉快的脸会给对方留下良好的印象。同时记住"熟能生巧"。

Part II　Dress Code
着装规范

1.Dress Principles 着装原则

TPO dress prevailing principle is the world's most basic principles. T represents time, season; P is on behalf of place, situation, position; O is on behalf of the purpose, object.

TPO 着装原则是国际上通用的原则。T 代表时间、季节；P 代表地点、场合、职位；O 代表目的、对象。

（1）The principle of time 时间原则

Time refers to early, middle and later periods of a day, including the seasons change, and the different ages of life. The principle of time requires to consider the time factor, so the "when" dressing.

For example, one morning at home or outdoor activities, dress should be easy, free; you can choose sportswear, casual clothes. The dress of the working time should be based on the characteristics and nature of the work, dignified and generous principle. Clothing should also change with the season's change, not something new, to break the routine.

时间可以指每天早、中、晚三个时间段，也包括一年中四季的交替，还包括人生的不同年龄阶段。时间相符是指我们在选择服装时要考虑时间因素，做到"随时"穿衣。

例如，早晨在家中或进行户外活动时，着装应方便、随意，可选择运动服、休闲装等。工作时间的着装，则应根据工作性质及特点，以便于工作、庄重大方为原则。服饰还应当随着一年四季气候的变化随时更换，不宜标新立异，打破常规。

（2）The principle of place 地点原则

Clothing should be adapted to situation, environment. Different positions should be different dress; a particular environment should be accompanied by corresponding coordination of clothing in order to obtain visual and mental harmony beauty.

For example, professional dress is appropriate in formal work environment; wearing jeans, tennis skirt, sportwear in entertainment, shopping leisure, tourism; casual wear in the office and social occasions, hence, all the performance and environmental achieve harmony.

着装应与场合、环境相适应。不同身份不同的穿着。在一个特定的环境里，应穿着一致的、协调的服装，从而获得视觉和心理的和谐之美。

例如，在一个正规的工作环境中，应着职业套装。在娱乐、购物、休闲、旅游时，则穿牛仔裤、网球裙、运动装为宜。在办公室或一般商务活动场合，可以穿便装。所有的着装和环境是和谐统一的。

（3）The principle of object 对象原则

Choosing clothes requires to be in perfect harmony with the object and purpose, while attending various occasions. For example, state leader would choose to wear a dark suit when they meet leader, senior officials or diplomats of other countries. In addition, they prefer to wear plain, natural, casual clothing when having an inspection in the local area.

　　在出席各种场合时，服装的选择还需要注意与所要面对的对象、活动的目的协调一致。例如，国家领导人在接见他国领导人、高官或使节时会选择穿着深色的西装套装；到地方上视察工作与群众见面时适宜穿着简洁、自然的便装。

2.Guidelines for Dress 穿着指南

People begin to evaluate us before any words are ever spoken. "The way you dress affects the way you are perceived, and the way you are perceived, is the way you are treated." said by Buck Rodgers which is the former VP of marketing of IBM. After all, to wear appropriate is essential to all of us.

　　人们常在我们未开口前就开始打量我们。IBM 营销的前副总裁巴克·罗杰斯说过"你着装的方式影响着你被对方的认同，你被对方认同的程度，也就是对方如何看待你"。归根结底，合适的穿着对我们所有人来说都非常重要。

　　（1）Formal business attire 商务正装

Formal business attire suggests a formal, conservative dress style. Attention to detail, impeccable grooming, and a well-fitted suit are a must in formal business environment.

　　商务正装要求正式、保守。在正式的商务场合，务必做到注重细节、修饰完美、服装得体。

　　① Men's attire 男士服装

　　❑　Suit 西装

While you select a suit with care, think less of making a fashion statement than of finding something that fits well and feels comfortable, and that will stand the test of time. There's only one ironclad rule in choosing a fabric for a suit: No matter what the color, the surface should be matte—not shiny or iridescent. The choice in fabrics boils down to wool or cotton.

Dark colors have always been associated with authority, but tradition has also embraced suits in lighter shades of brown (tan and beige) and gray. Solids are always a safe choice, while pinstripes are a handsome alternative, with a very thin, light gray stripe preferred.

　　The pant leg should touch the front of the shoe and fall just above the heel in the back. Pants can either have cuffs or not. The suit jacket should be buttoned while standing and unbuttoned to sit. Do not button the bottom button of a three-piece or two-piece suit. Avoid suits with double-breasted jackets.

　　当选购西装时，对于是否时尚不要考虑太多，而要注意所选购的西装是否舒适，能不能经得起时间的考验。在选择西装的面料时有个铁定的准则：无论是什么颜色，材质不能是发亮或闪光的。西装面料最好是羊毛或棉的。

深色西装永远代表着庄重和权力，但传统的西装的颜色也包括浅褐色（棕色或米黄色）和灰色。纯色永远是安全的选择，细条纹面料的西装也是个不错的选择，特别是浅灰色纤细条纹的面料。

裤腿长度应触及鞋面，刚好在鞋后跟上方。裤脚有无翻边均可。西装扣子起立时应扣上，落座时则解开。穿着两件套或三件套西装时，不要扣最下面的扣子。避免穿双排扣西服。

❑ Dress shirt 衬衣

At work, more muted colors work better than loud colors. The only caveat is to make sure the jacket, shirt, and tie complement one another. White remains the dressiest choice. The buff or pale blue one is also ok. Pointed collars give a more professional image than button-down collars, yet both are acceptable. Avoid shirts with insignias on them. The shirt's sleeve should extend beyond the suit jacket sleeves by 1/2 inch.

工作中穿着颜色柔和的衬衫要比花哨的衬衫的效果好。唯一要注意的是，夹克、衬衣和领带三者的颜色要搭配。另外，白色衬衣是最好的选择。米色或浅蓝色也可以。尖领比带扣衣领显得更为职业化，但均适合商务场合。衬衣不应带有徽章标签。衬衣袖口应比西服袖口长出半英寸。

❑ Ties 领带

For the great majority of men who dress for business, the tie remains the most important of all accessories. Ties should be of good quality and made of 100% silk. Always wear a tie that is darker than your shirt. Tie you tie to fall in the middle of your belt. Regardless of the design, make sure your tie color coordinates with your shirt and jacket.

对于大部分要穿正装上班的商务男士来说，领带是他们最重要的配饰。领带应质地优良且为真丝。领带颜色要比衬衣颜色深，长度以长及皮带扣处为宜。不管领带的设计怎样，只要保证它的颜色和你的衬衫、夹克搭配就行。

❑ Shoes, Socks and belts 鞋袜及皮带

Conservative shoes are the most appropriate. Choose black, brown or burgundy shoes. Shoe color should match your suit or be of a darker color. Shoe should be in a good condition and polished.

Use dark socks for business wear, match them to your pants, and make sure they're high enough not to show your bare shins when you sit down.

Belts should be in good condition and match the color of your shoes.

款式保守的皮鞋最为适宜。鞋的颜色以黑色、棕色和酒红色为佳，应与西装颜色配套

或稍深。鞋子应该有型有款，抛光擦亮。

为配合商业服饰应选择深色的袜子，使袜子和裤子的颜色相搭配，确保袜子足够长以至于在你坐下时不露出你的腿。

皮带质地要好且与皮鞋颜色相配。

❑ Accessories 配饰

Men should limit accessories to 3 pieces. Accessories include watch, ring, hand kerchief and tie tacks. Watch should be worn but avoid athletic styles. Avoid bracelets, necklaces, and visible piercings.

男士身上的配饰不应多于三件，包括手表、戒指、手绢和领带夹等。正式场合应佩戴手表，但要避免佩戴运动表。不要佩戴手镯、项链和显眼的穿孔饰物。

② Women's attire 女士服装

❑ Suits 套装

Choose a classic suit avoiding trendy styles. For a conservative organization, a skirt suit is still considered the most appropriate attire. Hemlines should be knee-length or longer. Choose wool, gabardine or rayon fabric. Color does not have to be limited to dark colors. Make sure the suit flatters your figure and is a good fit, not too tight or too loose. Jacket sleeves should fall 1/2 inch below our wrist.

套装建议选择式样经典的款式，避免过于时尚。对于风格保守的机构，西装套裙仍是首选。裙摆应及膝或稍长。面料选择以羊毛、华达呢或人造丝为宜。颜色不必局限于深色。套装要剪裁得体、松紧适度。衣袖长度应盖过手腕半英寸。

❑ Blouses 衬衣

Blouse should be updated, but neither low cut nor revealing. Do not wear a camisole or see-through blouse.

衬衣款式要入时，但不宜低胸和暴露。不要穿短内衣或过透的衬衣。

❑ Shoes and hose 鞋和长袜

Do not wear shoes with open toes, open heel, or ankle straps. Shoes should be of good-quality leather. Shoe color should be darker than your suit. Heels should be 1-2 inches; higher heels should be saved for after-hours. Hosiery should be worn with a skirt to match your skin tone or suit. Skin-colored hose should always be worn with short sleeve suits to create a balanced look.

女鞋不宜暴露脚趾、后跟或带有鞋襻儿，皮质要好。鞋的颜色应略深于套装颜色。鞋跟以 1～2 英寸高为宜。高鞋跟仅适宜工作以外的场合穿着。穿裙子时，应配颜色与套装或肤色一致的长袜。配短袖套裙的长袜颜色应与肤色一致，以平衡视觉效果。

❑ Accessories 配饰

Jewelry should be kept minimal and conservative. Remove all facial piercing except earrings. Wear no more than 3 accessories; do not over accessorize.

珠宝首饰应尽量少戴，款式应保守。除了耳饰，其他所有在面部穿孔的饰品应摘除。配饰应不多于三件，也不要过于杂乱。

（2）Casual business attire 非正式商务装

Dress code policies have been changing for the last decade. There appeared a casual style in business environment. Dressing mire casually is meant to make life easier, but confusion over appropriate casual attire has caused many employers to adopt some types of business casual standard.

着装原则在过去的十年里不断地发生着变化，在商务领域里出现了休闲的着装风格。着休闲装的目的是为了使生活更简便舒适，但什么是得体的休闲装呢？

① Business casual for men 男士商务休闲装

A sports coat creates a pulled-together look in a business casual environment and eliminates the need for a tie. Pair up the sports coat with khakis or dark pants. Traditional dress slacks, khakis, corduroys, wool flannel and linen slacks are appropriate with or without a blazer. Be sure to press them beforehand. Casual oxford shirts are a great alternative to dress shirts, with or without a tie. Choose basic white, chambray or pinstripe. Oxfords and loafers in brown or black are a good match for khakis or corduroys.

男士在商务休闲场合穿运动衣显得精神，无须打领带。运动装可以搭配卡其裤或深色长裤。传统的宽松式、卡其布、灯芯绒、法兰绒和亚麻宽松式长裤可单穿，也可与便装上衣搭配，但事先要熨烫平整。休闲的牛津布衬衣可以取代西服衬衣，领带可打也可不打。白色、格纹或细条纹休闲衬衫为基础款。棕色或黑色牛津鞋和休闲皮鞋与卡其裤及灯芯绒裤子是很好搭配的。

② Business casual for women 女士商务休闲装

Pantsuit is a wise choice for a business casual event, e.g. information session, tour facility, etc. A classic sheath paired with a cardigan or a blazer in the same fabric and color is a good choice. Crisp, cotton shirts in white, chambray added to dress pants, khakis, or skirts make a casual outfit. Cardigan twin sets are also an easy way to present a more casual look while still looking professional. Jewelry, scarves and other accessories will add a polished finish to an outfit. Remember though, "less is more." Shoes should still be well-made and close-toed—no extremes, flats are appropriate. Hose are not essential for business casual, but recommended for shorter skirts. Socks are suggested with pants.

如果是较随意的商务场合，如信息会议、参观设施等，穿着休闲裤装是明智的选择。

经典的紧身衣配开襟毛衫或相同颜色和质地的便装上衣也不错。两件套的开襟毛衫也是简易的休闲打扮，而仍旧不失职业形象。休闲装加上珠宝、丝巾和其他配饰可以打造近乎完美的形象。但是应该牢记，配饰"以少为佳"。鞋子当然要质地好，不露脚趾——但也不要走极端。休闲场合适合穿平跟鞋。穿商务休闲装不必配长裤，但建议穿短裙时穿上。穿长裤时则最好配短袜。

Situational practice for etiquettes 礼仪口语实景

Make up or search for more situational conversations concerning professional image and put them into practice.

A: Good morning everyone. Thanks for being on time.

B & C: Good morning, Frank.

A: We've got a whole bunch of topics to go over today, but let's start with a simple one: our company's dress code.

B: What exactly does this mean?

A: I've become concerned that we are getting a bit too casual. I was walking through the office the other day and some people were wearing shorts and T-shirts! I don't think that is appropriate office wear.

C: It's true. Our standards have been going down. It used to be that we wore casual clothes only on Fridays, but these days it seems we do it almost every day.

B: But Frank, don't you think maybe this isn't such a big issue? I mean, why does it matter what we are wearing? I think productivity is more important!

A: Actually, I agree with you, Gary. Productivity is the most important thing. But I think what we wear is linked to productivity.

C: In what way are they linked?

A: Police officers wear uniforms, right? It's a symbol to both them and the public that they are serious about what they do.

B: You're the boss, Frank, so of course it's your call...but I have to say, I'm not so keen on this idea. I think neckties cut off blood circulation. I'm much more in favor of a relaxed workplace environment.

A: And for some companies a relaxed atmosphere might work. At Google they let you bring your dog to work! But we are a serious financial company with an image to uphold.

Terminology related 相关礼仪术语

Business casual

Business casual is a term used to describe a type of office dress code or clothing style that is a little more casual than traditional business wear. Many employers adopt this dress code in an effort to allow employees to feel more comfortable on the job and to have more freedom of expression through their choice of attire. Although business casual is casual, it also doesn't mean that anything goes.

商务休闲装是指比传统商业着装略微轻松的办公室着装规范或服装样式。很多公司采取这种着装规范是为了让员工在工作中感觉更舒适自在，通过着装自由地表达自己。虽然商务休闲装是便装，但并不意味着穿什么样式的都行。

Useful expressions for etiquettes 礼仪用语集锦

The followings are appropriate terminology you may use when talking about professional image:

- Always make sure your clothes are wrinkle-free.
  要一直保持着装平整无皱纹。

- Strive for a tailored look with your clothing. Alter if needed.
  要讲究穿着。如果衣服不合体，要去修改。

- Check the weather. Dress accordingly.
  关注天气，根据天气选择合适的衣服。

- Keep hair clean and cut.
  头发要保持整洁有型。

- Remove body piercings.
  去除身上的纹身穿孔。

- Very mild or no fragrance.
  保持香气淡雅或不洒香水。

- Go for the classic and not trendy look if in doubt.
  追求经典，如果对时尚把握不准，不要随意追赶潮流。

- Natural looking make-up and manicure.
  妆容自然，指甲修整得有型不夸张。

- Comfortable clothes that can hide food stains and nervousness.
  舒适的服装能掩饰食物污渍和紧张情绪。

- Always take a portfolio with a pen and some business cards.
  要随身携带公事包、笔和商务名片。

Exercises （课后练习）

I. Questions and answers: answer the following questions according to the information you have got in the previous reading.

1. What does the quotation of Montesquieu imply?
2. How can beauty of cosmetics be achieved?
3. What are the main elements of the dress principles?
4. Have you got any knowledge about the dress code?
5. What are the principles of wearing accessories?

II. Expressions: match the occasions in column A with the dress code in column B.（M for man; W for woman.）

A	B
black Tie	dark suits (M)
	cocktail dress (W)
white Tie	full dress, with white tie, vest, shirt (M)
	long gowns (W)
semi-formal	no jeans or shorts （M/W）
cocktail attire	dark suits (M)
	short, elegant dresses (W)
dressy casual	tuxedos (M)
	cocktail, long dresses (W)
casual	anything

III. Translation: translate the following statements into Chinese to learn about the dress code.

1. Companies often maintain specific administrative policies which set out office dress codes, i.e. what standard of dress is permitted and more particularly what kind of dress does not fit in with the image a company wishes to project to the outside world.
2. The key with regard to your own dress always is the image you wish to present: an impression that conveys professionalism or an impression that may convey a negative attitude toward both the company and the job.

3. Dress codes vary from one company to another. For example, decorum in a state owned corporation may be different from that in a joint venture company. Required dress may also vary from one institution to another, depending sometimes on the number of visitors or foreign customers a company normally receives. Dress codes in international hotels may be much stricter than they are in hotels that cater only to domestic customers or in certain industrial organizations.

4. Dress, grooming, and health tell something about a person. They project an image of you as an individual and you should practice whatever rules will persuade others (management, boss, peers, and outsiders) to see you as you would like to be seen.

5. Not all women are blessed with external beauty but we can all use the attributes we do to have advantage. Sophia Loren, the Italian actress, is credited with the statement that nothing makes a woman more beautiful than her belief that she is beautiful.

6. Men come in different shapes and sizes but they are not usually associated with the idea of being physically attractive or otherwise. Their psychological disposition also differs from that of women. Men become attractive primarily through their male psyche which reinforces the need for their self-reliance and self-esteem, expressed in their behavior among other men and to women. With both sexes, inner beauty is often mirrored in one's face and manner de-emphasizing any unattractive physical features.

7. Women should select their clothing from stores that specialize in dress for business and professional women. They usually have a good selection of women's suits, dresses, and skirts and blouses that are suitable for a professional office environment.

8. Women should dress conservatively and avoid sexy. Stay away from pleats (front, side or back) exposing too much leg, short dresses that barely cover your buttocks, or dresses that show cleavage.

9. Top level secretaries and female executives often prefer traditional fabrics, colors, and styles. In fabrics, woolens and combinations of wool and synthetics are a good choice. Some prefer traditional patterns such as pinstripes, muted plaids, and herring bones. These do not have to be masculine looking or staid, as they can be found tailored in contemporary silhouettes, which allow the wearer to be feminine and stylish.

10. Women must wear clothes that fit properly. Too tight clothes draw attention to one's physique and one's body build. Too loose clothing may look sloppy.

IV.Cloze: Choose the suitable statements from the box and complete the passage.

> A. and we want that image to be proper and professional
>
> B. the first thing will be an impressive appearance
>
> C. Do not challenge the tolerance of the management
>
> D. how you look is a reflection of yourself as a person
>
> E. How you dress is just as important as what you put on your face

_____1_____!

People will not find you attractive even if you put on a nice makeup but dressed sloppily.

We are not asking our staffs to be all dressed like a fashion show or going to a ball, but at least not to be mistaken as cleaners or some delivery men.

Other times,_____2_____. At work, your appearance will be a reflection of our staff and the company they are working for.

How you dress is not just a respect for others, but more important, a respect for yourself. If you like people to respect you and your clients have confidence in your work, before you can demonstrate with your performance, _____3_____.

We are not going to emphasize more on the importance of how you should dress, but as long as you are coming to work or meeting with a client, you represent our company, _____4_____!

Please refer to the dress code and samples provided to you before, dress yourself properly, respect yourself and avoid the embarrassment of being confronted directly by the management on this issue.

Person coming to work in an inappropriate attire will be sent home to change at your own expense and will have to work overtime (without compensation) for making up for the time loss. _____5_____, first time offenders will be given verbal warnings, subsequent offence will lead to more severe action from the management.

On "Casual Friday", only jeans, T-shirts, polo shirts, sport shoes are allowed but NO shorts of any length, hot-pants/skirts, bra-tops, slippers, or any overexposure wear.

V.Case study: study the world's most basic principles (TPO). T represents time, season; P on behalf of place, situation, position; O on behalf of the purpose, object. Pay more attention to the choices of dresses/cosmetics/accessory in various occasions and get ready for the following cases:

1.Christmas party.

2.Meeting with a very important client.

3.The wedding of your colleague.

4.Playing golf with your boss.

 Extension（拓展阅读）

Dress for Work Success: A Business Casual Dress Code

Your company's objective in establishing a business casual dress code, is to allow our employees to work comfortably in the workplace. Yet, we still need our employees to project a professional image for our customers, potential employees, and community visitors. Business casual dress is the standard for this dress code.

Because all casual clothing is not suitable for the office, these guidelines will help you determine what is appropriate to wear to work. Clothing that works well for the beach, yard work, dance clubs, exercise sessions, and sports contests may not be appropriate for a professional appearance at work.

Clothing that reveals too much cleavage, your back, your chest, your feet, your stomach or your underwear is not appropriate for a place of business, even in a business casual setting.

Even in a business casual work environment, clothing should be pressed and never wrinkled. Torn, dirty, or frayed clothing is unacceptable. All seams must be finished. Any clothing that has words, terms, or pictures that may be offensive to other employees is unacceptable. Clothing that has the company logo is encouraged. Sports team, university, and fashion brand names on clothing are generally acceptable.

Certain days can be declared dress down days, generally Fridays. On these days, jeans and other more casual clothing, although never clothing potentially offensive to others, are allowed.

Guide to business casual dressing for work

This is a general overview of appropriate business casual attire. Items that are not appropriate for the office are listed, too. Neither lists is all-inclusive, and both are open to change. The lists tell you what is generally acceptable as business casual attire and what is generally not acceptable as business casual attire.

No dress code can cover all contingencies so employees must exert a certain amount of judgment in their choice of clothing to wear to work. If you experience uncertainty about acceptable, professional business causal attire for work, please ask your supervisor or your Human Resources staff.

Slacks, pants, and suit pants

Slacks that are similar to Dockers and other makers of cotton or synthetic material pants, wool pants, flannel pants, dressy capris, and nice looking dress synthetic pants are acceptable. Inappropriate slacks or pants include jeans, sweatpants, exercise pants, Bermuda shorts, short shorts, shorts, bib overalls, leggings, and any spandex or other form-fitting pants such as people wear for biking.

Skirts, dresses, and skirted suits

Casual dresses and skirts, and skirts that are split at or below the knee are acceptable. Dress and skirt length should be at a length at which you can sit comfortably in public. Short, tight skirts that ride halfway up the thigh are inappropriate for work. Mini-skirts, skirts, sun dresses, beach dresses, and spaghetti-strap dresses are inappropriate for the office.

Shirts, tops, blouses, and jackets

Casual shirts, dress shirts, sweaters, tops, golf-type shirts, and turtlenecks are acceptable attire for work. Most suit jackets or sport jackets are also acceptable attire for the office, if they violate none of the listed guidelines. Inappropriate attire for work includes tank tops; midriff tops; shirts with potentially offensive words, terms, logos, pictures, cartoons, or slogans; halter-tops; tops with bare shoulders; sweatshirts, and T-shirts unless worn under another blouse, shirt, jacket, or dress.

Shoes and footwear

Conservative athletic or walking shoes, loafers, clogs, sneakers, boots, flats, dress heels, and leather deck-type shoes are acceptable for work. Wearing no stockings is acceptable in warm weather. Flashy athletic shoes, thongs, flip-flops, slippers, and any shoe with an open toe are not acceptable in the office. Closed toe and closed heel shoes are required in the manufacturing operation area.

Jewelry, makeup, perfume, and cologne

Be in good taste, with limited visible body piercing. Remember, that some employees are allergic to the chemicals in perfumes and make-up, so wear these substances with restraint.

Hats and head covering

Hats are not appropriate in the office. Head covers that are required for religious purposes or to honor cultural tradition are allowed.

Conclusion

If clothing fails to meet these standards, as determined by the employee's supervisor and Human Resources staff, the employee will be asked not to wear the inappropriate item to work

again. If the problem persists, the employee may be sent home to change clothes and will receive a verbal warning for the first offense. All other policies about personal time use will apply. Progressive disciplinary action will be applied if dress code violations continue.

(http://humanresources.about.com/od/workrelationships/a/dress_code.htm)

After-reading tasks （读后任务）

When you finish reading text above, get into the groups and discuss with your group members about the following tasks and fulfill them.

Task 1

As mentioned in the text: "Your Company's objective in establishing a business casual dress code, is to allow our employees to work comfortably in the workplace. Yet, we still need our employees to project a professional image for our customers, potential employees, and community visitors." What kind of problems do you think will arise if the company sets the standard of business casual dress and follows it?

Task 2

Study the guides to business casual dressing for work, including:

Slacks, pants, and suit pants

Skirts, dresses, and skirted suits

Shirts, tops, blouses, and jackets

Shoes and footwear

Jewelry, makeup, perfume, and cologne

Hats and head covering

Discuss in your groups and allot each a task of looking for the clothing or pictures of clothes satisfying the business casual dress code. When done, show the collections before class and illustrate the different wearing matches. If you like, your group even can make a business casual dress show.

Task 3

Discuss with your group members and decide on what to wear in the following occasions:

A company banquet   A family wedding   A business conference

A business trip   A meeting with a client   A visit in your boss' home

Self-study（自学反馈）

If possible, summarize what you have learned in this unit with the help of the following table.

Focus of this unit:
Guidelines for etiquette: 1. 2. 3. 4. ...
Summary:
Application: 1. 2. 3. ...
Feedback:

Chapter Three
Telephone Etiquette
商务电话礼仪

Objectives (学习目标)

After you have studied this chapter, you should be able to:

❑　Have a command of the etiquette for making and receiving telephone calls
❑　Handle some problem situations in telephone communications
❑　Cultivate the cross-cultural awareness when communicating through phones

Lead-in (导读)

Even in an advanced age of communications, telephone, for many companies, is still a very important medium to do business. With telephones, it is possible to establish business relationships for years without ever meeting the people with whom you are doing business. As a clerk to a busy company, a good portion of your working day will be taken up by placing and receiving telephone calls. Most of people may get the impressions of your company image through the way they are received via telephone. Therefore, it is extremely important to master the telephone skills and etiquettes to communicate effectively over the phone.

即使在通信高度发达的时代，对于很多公司而言，电话仍然是进行商品交易的重要沟通工具。人们甚至不需要见到自己的商业伙伴，通过电话联系，就能建立起经年累月的贸易关系。如果公司业务繁忙，有着大量的业务往来，职员们一天的相当一部分工作时间会花在拨打和接听电话上。大多数人是通过电话里的交流方式来形成对你所在公司的印象。因此，掌握高效电话交流的技能和礼仪尤为重要。

Test yourself (自我测试)

To start with, take a test to see to what degree you have mastered the telephone skills and etiquettes. You can use Yes or No to make responses to the following statements.

1.Remember to avoid making phone calls before 7 a.m., after 10 p.m. or during the meal time.　　　　　　　　　　　　　　　　　　　　　　　　Yes ☐ No ☐

2.Always check the difference in time before making a long distance call abroad.

Yes ☐ No ☐

3.A telephone call usually takes up no more than three minutes.　Yes ☐ No ☐

4.Prepare before making a call in case that important messages be omitted due to the absence of logic.　Yes ☐ No ☐

5.Less senior speaker should wait till the other end hangs up first.　Yes ☐ No ☐

6.It is best to pick up the phone after it rings twice.　Yes ☐ No ☐

7.When answering the calls, glancing over the documents, watching TV, talking to people around meanwhile, or ever eating can be accepted.　Yes ☐ No ☐

8.Talking on the telephone is not face-to-face communication, so facial expressions are not important.　Yes ☐ No ☐

9.It is acceptable to inquire the name of the caller and the matter concerned first, then inform the caller the person concerned is not available.　Yes ☐ No ☐

10.When getting a personal telephone call while your employer is standing by your desk, try to find out quickly what the caller wants and to make the conversation as brief as possible.

Yes ☐ No ☐

Part I　The Guidelines for Handling Outgoing Calls
拨打电话的礼仪

　　Looking closely at telephone situation, people may find the advantages as well as disadvantages in adopting this popular means of communications. Telephones are indispensable to communication between people. As a clear path of communications, making phone calls connects people when they are apart. Telephone lines not only convey information but also glue all relationships. With this convenient tool of modern communication, people may be out of sight, but never out of mind.

　　人们在使用电话这种大众化的交流工具时，可以清楚地看到电话沟通的利与弊。电话对于人与人之间的交流是不可缺少的工具，将分居两地的人们联系起来。电话线不但传递着资讯，也建立了各方联系。有了这种便捷的现代通信工具，人们就算不见面，也能随时交流。

　　However, we cannot ignore the disadvantages of telephone communications. Telephone communications are an indirect contact, quite different from face-to-face communication which lacks visual cues and consequently we are more dependent on tone of voice through which we can learn more information than from language. As estimated, tone of voice accounts for 82%, while wording just 18% for the success of telephone communications. Problems may arise in this situation. Some obstacles may exist in fully understanding the meanings of telephone conversations by each other mostly because the person who is answering your phone can not see any documents you are talking about; or he or she cannot see your facial expressions, your hand gestures and other similar "body language" and vice versa. Therefore, some percentages of understanding may be lost, and even worse, misunderstanding may arise.

但电话交流的弊端也不容忽视。电话交流不同于面对面交流，是间接接触，由于缺乏视觉提示，人们获得信息更多的是通过声音而非语言。据统计，成功的电话交流中，82%的功劳归于语音，而语言只占到18%。这一点导致了问题的出现。沟通障碍产生常常因为接听电话的人看不到对方谈论的文件，以及表情、手势和其他"身体语言"。因此无法完整理解，甚至由此产生误解。

Thus, to improve the situation, we have to focus on the adjustment of non-verbal communication instead of the improvement of the verbal communication. First, never forget that your only means of conveyance is your voice. Once you do get through to the person you're calling, keep in mind that the impression you make depends entirely on your voice and choice of words, not your appearance; this makes it all the more important to sound professional and personable. Your voice should be alert (don't sound as if you just got out of bed); distinct (speak clearly so that callers do not have to ask you to repeat yourself); pleasant (wear a smile over the phone and slow down if you are used to speaking rapidly); cheerful (use a rising inflection and thus leave the impression that you are happy to answer the call).

因此，要改善电话交流，我们要关注的是非语言交际范畴，而非语言交际方面。首先，永远不要忘记声音是信息传送的媒介。当你拨通电话后，要记住给对方留下印象的是你的声音和措辞，而非容貌，因此声音表现出专业化和个性化很重要。声音应该是清醒的（不要听起来像刚从梦中醒来似的）；清晰的（讲述清晰，避免听者要求你重讲）；和悦的（面带微笑，不急不躁）；兴奋的（语调上扬，给听者的印象是你很乐意通话）。

In the following, we shall focus the attention on the specific telephone skills and etiquettes that should be mastered when placing a business call and answering calls.

下面将具体介绍接听电话时应掌握的技巧和礼仪。首先从拨打电话谈起。

1.Before Placing the Call 打电话前

Prepare a desk telephone list for the numbers called frequently on company business.

Check the difference in time before placing a long-distance call.

Plan the call beforehand and know the points you want to make. Write down any question you want to raise, along with the specific topics you want to cover. Then place these notes by the phone so you can refer to them throughout the call. If your phone call involves facts and figures, gather together all data sheets or other reference materials you might need. Also, have a blank pad and pen handy, so you can take notes during the conversation, and a desk calendar, in case you need to set dates.

首先备好公司经常联系的电话名单。

如打长途电话，先查时差。

提前计划并明确通话要点。记下要问到的问题和具体要谈到的要点。将记录放在电话机旁便于通话中随时参考。如通话会涉及事例和数据，备好相关资料。备好纸笔便于记录。预备台历便于标注通话中可能涉及的时间安排。

2.During the Call 通话中

Dial correctly and identify yourself at once and your company also. Give your full name even if you talk with the person fairly often, since he may not be as familiar with your voice as you think. Using your first and last names each time you call will also reinforce your name recognition.

Quickly explain why you've called and ask if this is a convenient time to talk. Failing to ask this question is one of the most common of all telephone errors. If the person you call says talking now is fine, briefly state your business and estimate length of the call. Keep your telephone conversation brief, but not to point of curtness. If the person you call says he is busy, ask when you might call back. Try to avoid having him return the call—this may put you in the awkward spot of not having your thoughts collected or your notes at hand when the call comes out of the blue.

Leave your name and number and arrange for a call-back if you can't reach the party you want.

When your call is to complain about a problem, make sure you speak with someone who has the authority to correct the situation.

准确拨通后，报上公司名和自己姓名。即使是来往频繁的，也须如此。因为对方可能不像你想象的那样熟悉你的声音。重复自己的名字可加深印象。

说明自己打电话的缘由，并询问对方是否方便通话。忘记这一询问是人们常见的失误。

如对方表示方便接听，简要说明主题和预计通话时长。通话应简洁但勿过于草率。如对方表示无暇通话，询问再次拨打的合适时间。避免对方回拨电话，因为在无准备的状态下接听电话，你可能思路不清或无法准备纸笔记录等。

如对方电话未接通，可留下电话号码和名字，安排再次电话联系。

如为投诉电话，务必接通相关负责人。

3. When the Call is Finished 当通话结束时

Don't leave matters hanging. Wind things down with a conclusive statement: "I'll get the final figures to you by noon Friday" or "I think we agree we need more research. Shall we talk again, maybe tomorrow?" Then sign off on a positive note with a polite acknowledgment: "Thank you for calling" or "It's been nice talking with you."

Hang up promptly when your business is finished. A few minutes spent discussing things that have nothing to do with the business at hand are perfectly in order after callers have established a friendly relationship. But don't overdo it: without any visual clues from your phone mate, it's hard to tell when you're wearing out your welcome.

勿让所谈事项悬而不决。对所谈事项作出结论，如："周五中午之前我会告知你方准确数字。"或"我方要研究一下，明天再谈好吗？"最后以礼貌积极的态度结束通话："感谢来电。"或"与你通话很愉快。"

谈完事宜迅速结束通话。与对方建立良好的关系可花几分钟闲聊，但不可过分。因为看不见通话对方，很难判断对方是否已经厌倦了通话。

Part II   Guidelines for Handling Incoming Calls
接听电话的礼仪

1. The Guidelines for Handling Incoming Calls 接听电话的礼仪规范

Then, it's turn to study the guidelines for handling incoming calls. Never underestimate the importance of how you answer the phone. You never know when it may be the first call from a potential client or customer. Your attitude and demeanor, in turn, will form her initial impression of your company, and you want it to be positive, not poor.

再来谈谈接听电话的礼仪规范。永远不要低估接听电话的重要性。你无法预知你的潜在客户何时打来第一个电话，而你的态度和行为将形成对方对你所在公司的第一印象。你希望对方留下的是正面印象。

（1）Answer the phone promptly 迅速接听电话

That is, by the third ring. Answering with your full name is an absolute necessity whenever a call is coming from outside. If you work in a company with several departments, state your department after your name. This saves time for both you and the caller, eliminating the need to ask "Is this Mr. Smith's office?" or "Have I reached the accounting department?"

迅速接听电话是指在电话铃响过三声之前接听。接听外部来电，应报全名和部门名。这样节省双方时间，无需再问"请问是史密斯先生办公室吗？"或"请问是会计部吗？"

（2）Get the caller's name immediately 立即问明来电人姓名

If, on obtaining the name of the caller, you realize your boss would not wish to talk to him, you may offer your help.

得知来电人姓名后，如果意识到你的上司不愿与其通话，你应主动提供帮助，自行处理此电话。

2.Other Details 其他细节

If the caller is waiting on the line for your boss to be free, check frequently with him and deliver a progress update every 60 seconds: "I thought she was almost done with her call, but she's still on the line." At the second or third check, ask whether the person would like to keep waiting or would rather leave a message.

Announce the caller when connecting him with your employer.

Transfer the call to correct person if your boss cannot handle the matter.

如打电话的人在电话另一端等待你的上司从繁忙中抽出时间来与之通话，应和上司保持联系并告知对方进程，如"我想她快打完电话了，不过还未挂断。"通报两三次后，可询问对方是否继续等待或留言。

在与上司取得联系后，要将对方情况通报给上司。

如上司无法处理，可将电话转给相关人士解决。

Be familiar with your employer's wishes and know which calls he expects you to handle with and which calls he wants you to refer to him. Screening calls for the employers and others is an area where touchiness abounds. Make sure to respond with a courteous tone.

了解上司的想法，知道他希望哪些电话你来接，哪些电话要转给他。为上司代接电话时需谨慎，应彬彬有礼。

Always have your pen and paper ready. Take message accurately. In addition to neatness, accuracy, and legibility, a good phone message should include the date and time of the call; the caller's name, company and the caller's telephone number; the message and your signature or initials, so the person for whom you have written the message knows whom to ask for any additional information.

备好纸笔，便于随时记录。电话留言除了应干净、准确、易于辨认外，还应记录通话日期及时间，联系人的名字、公司名、电话号码，留言内容，记录者签名，以便看留言的人知道找谁询问通话详情。

Answer questions pleasantly and cautiously.

In closing the call, review details if necessary. Conclude your telephone conversation with "Thank you for calling. Goodbye." Wait to let the caller hang up first.

Always have a pleasant smiling voice. Try to visualize the caller as if you were speaking to someone in the same room.

接通电话时，应和悦认真。

结束通话时，如有必要可重复通话要点。可以"感谢来电，再见"作结束语。等待对方先挂断。

通话应亲切友好，好像和通话人同处一室面谈一样。

Whenever you pick up the phone, there is something you should never forget: a person may forget what you say, a person may forget what you do, but a person will not forget how you made them feel...

只要拿起话筒，有一件事不能忘记：人们可能会忘记你说过的话和做过的事，但不会忘记你带给他们的感觉。

Situational practice for etiquettes 礼仪口语实景

Make up or search for more situational telephone conversations that may occur and put them into practice.

Model

A: Good afternoon, sales department. May I help you?

B: Could I speak to Mr. Bush, please.

A: I'll see if he is available. Who shall I say is calling, please?

B: John Smith.

A: Hold the line, please. Mr. Bush is in a meeting with the Managing Director at the moment. Can I help you?

B: Well, I want to discuss with him the new contract we signed last week.

A: I don't think the meeting will be much longer. Shall I ask him to call you when he is free?

B: Yes, that would be fine.

A: Could I have your name again?

B: Yes. It's John Smith.

A: And the number?

B: 010-64358796.

A: OK. You should be hearing from Mr. Bush later in the morning, Mr. Smith.

B: Thank you for your help. Good-bye.

A: You're welcome. Good-bye.

 ## Terminology related 相关礼仪术语

Telephone messages

Telephone messages or slips are a kind of notes. They are written for the convenience of the people who are temporarily off. They are not sent through the post, but are left for people to read, or sent to people by hand. They are often written in informal style, except that they are written for a superior to read, when the style may become formal. Telephone slips may be designed and printed as standard office slips or written in a casual way.

电话留言或便条是一种便签笔记。电话留言是为了方便暂时不在的人查看而写的。电话留言不需要邮寄，可直接留给某人，方便他查看，或亲手送交某人。电话留言的书写风格通常是非正式的，如果该留言写给上司，那么应改为正式的风格。电话留言或便条可以设计并印刷成标准的办公室便签或者用随意的风格手写。

Format of telephone message：

电话留言的格式：

From		Tel No.	
To		Department	
Time			
Message			
Handling suggestion			

Useful expressions for etiquettes 礼仪用语集锦

The followings are appropriate terminology used for business telephone communication under various circumstances:

❑   When the boss is away:

"Mr. ... is travelling and will not be back in his office until the week of...Is there anything I can do for you or would you like to speak with someone else." (Never give a specific day because the boss may not be able to see visitors on the first day back at the office.)

"Sir / Madam, I am sorry but I am not at liberty to discuss Mr. ...'s business affairs. If you can let me know the purpose of your call, I may be able to help."

当老板不在时：

"×× 先生正在旅行途中，将在第 × 周回到办公室……有什么事我可以为您效劳？或者您是否愿意联系其他人？"（注意：不要给出具体的回访日期，因为无法确定老板能在回来的第一天安排时间约见打电话方。）

"先生 / 女士，很抱歉我无权告知 ×× 先生的差旅事宜。如果您能告诉我您来电的目的，我或许能帮到您。"

❑   When the boss is talking on another line:

"I am sorry, Sir / Madam, but he is engaged on another telephone line. May I have him call you when he is free or is there anything I can do for you."

当老板在和他人通话时：

"先生 / 女士，很抱歉他正在接听另一个电话。我请他有空时回复您的来电好吗？或者有什么事我可以效劳的？"

❑   When the boss has left instructions not to be disturbed:

"I am sorry, Sir / Madam, Mr. ... is not available at the moment. May I have him call you or is there anything I can do."

当老板留下指示，要求不被打扰时：

"很抱歉，先生 / 女士，×× 先生现在不在。我之后请他回复您的来电好吗？或者有什么事我可以效劳的？"

❑   When the boss is in a meeting:

"I am sorry, Sir / Madam, but Mr. ...is in a meeting and will not be available for about (state approximate length of time). Is there anything I can do for you or would you like him to call you when he is available?"

"I am sorry, Sir / Madam, Mr. ...has left specific instructions that he / she is not to be disturbed due to the importance of this particular meeting. I am sure you understand my position...If you will let me have your telephone number, I will bring your call to his / her attention as soon as he / she is free."

当老板在开会时：

"很抱歉，先生 / 女士，×× 先生现在正在开会，会在……（大约的时间长度）后有空。您有什么事我可以效劳的？或者等他有空再回复您的来电好吗？"

"很抱歉，先生 / 女士，……先生现在正在开会。因为本次会议非常重要，他明确要求不得打扰。请您理解。您是否能留下您的电话号码？等他开完会，我马上转告他您的来电。"

❑　When the caller asks you for information you do not have:

"I am sorry, Sir / Madam, but I do not have that information at hand (or: I cannot immediately answer your question). If you would like to leave your name and telephone number, I will call you back as soon as possible."

当来电者问到你不了解的信息时：

"很抱歉，先生 / 女士，我手边没有您需要的信息（或我目前无法马上回复您的询问）。如果您方便留下您的姓名和电话，我会尽快回复您的。"

Exercises（课后练习）

I.Questions and answers: answer the following questions according to the information you have got in the previous reading.

1.Do you agree that the telephone line is equal to the life line in the business world? Why?

2.Compared to the face-to-face communication, what is the deciding factor in a successful telephone communication and what shall we do to ensure a fruitful telephone communication?

3.Is there anything you have to do before placing a telephone call? What are they?

4.What must be done when the call is finished?

5.How can you handle the telephone call when the boss has no time to answer it?

II.Expressions: match the terms in column A with the Chinese equivalents in column B.

A	B
place a telephone call	转接电话
answer a telephone call	结束电话通话
screen a call	拨打电话
leave a message	接听电话
close a call	留言
transfer a call	替接听人代接电话

III. Translation: translate the following statements into Chinese to ensure to stay away from Phone-call Faux Pas.

1. Don't do other things at your desk while talking on the phone. Typing or shuffling papers suggests that your attention is elsewhere.

2. Eating while on the phone is not only distracting but also subjects the other person to unnerving smacks and crunches. Because sounds are magnified over the telephone, even a cough drop in the mouth can make its presence known.

3. Don't leave a radio playing or office equipment running in the background. These sounds, too, are magnified over the phone.

4. Never chew gum while talking on the phone. While gum chewing may not be offensive to some people, you have no way of knowing whether your phone mate considers it unprofessional and crass.

5. Don't sneeze, blow your nose, or cough directly into the receiver. Either excuse yourself for a moment or turn your head away.

6. If you have to put the receiver down during the conversation, set it gently on the desk to avoid startling your phone meat with a sudden bang.

7. Don't address a business associate by his or her first name in sentence after sentence: it sounds insincere and patronizing.

8. Monitor the volume – ringtones should never be intrusive or cause heads to turn.

9. Don't use text messages to communicate important information or anything that needs a lengthy explanation.

10. Don't pay more attention to your phone than your date.

IV. Cloze: choose the suitable statements from the box and complete the passage.

> A. Return missed calls as soon as possible
>
> B. Prepare for a phone call
>
> C. Place phone calls when you're able to talk uninterrupted
>
> D. Refrain from answering the phone when you are in the presence of clients or other associates
>
> E. Decide what message you want to portray when you answer the phone

_____1_____. Whether you're the company's president or the receptionist directing calls, answer the phone with stated purpose. The standard greeting never fails: "Good morning, thank you for calling XYZ, this is Joann, how may I help you."

_____2_____. If possible, forward your calls directly to voice mail. If you're required to answer your calls, state "Excuse me" to whom you're having a face-to-face conversation and quickly place the caller on hold or take a message to return the phone call when you are alone.

_____3_____. If you have a meeting in 10 minutes, it's unwise to make phone calls to clients on business matters. You're going to feel rushed and may forget to cover an important area that needs your attention.

_____4_____. Have materials related to your call in front of you and available for easy reference. Expect the unexpected and be able to respond to answers directed toward you. If you're unsure of the answer, don't guess, but make a note of the question and ask for permission to get back to the caller on that topic.

_____5_____. What's insignificant to you may be very urgent to someone else, and waiting for your response may be holding up their work. Be conscientious and aware of other's needs.

V. Case study: in business setting, careful consideration should be taken to handle some calls. Special tact will be needed in the following situations. Discuss in groups to find out some suggested procedures for future reference.

1. A call needs information that will take you some time to find.

2. A caller refuses to state his or her names or business, but insists on talking with your boss.

3. A caller demands to talk with the employer when the employer is very busy.

4. An important caller comes in while the executive is at a meeting.

5. The employer is out of town when a person calls.

6. A person who calls continually with important questions but is so disorganized that the call takes forever while she bums and bows through them.

7. Answering machines are built into many business telephone systems these days, but I prefer to talk to a human being. Should I just hang up?

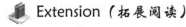 Extension（拓展阅读）

Telephone Manners

Getting Through

Although email and instant messaging are quickly becoming standard forms of office

communication, the telephone still plays an important role in business. Just like a face-to-face meeting, telephone conversations are expected to and should follow certain rules of etiquette to help make the experience pleasant and productive for all those involved.

It's easy to forget manners when talking over the phone. Distractions abound, from impromptu meetings or email notifications blinking on your computer screen. Remember that a conversation over the phone carries just as much weight as a face-to-face meeting, as it is a great opportunity to communicate in real time.

Tuning up your pipes

If your job requires being on the phone most of the day, remember it usually takes a few hours for the human vocal cords to fully warm up after a night's sleep. Eight hours of rest usually leaves them a little rusty. Practice enunciation in the bathroom mirror while you get ready for work, or do some vocal exercises in the shower. Singing in the shower does wonders for a day of cold calling—but make sure you're not disturbing someone else's slumber with your warbling. Deep breathing exercises help condition your stomach and throat for a day's worth of talking, as well as gently clearing your throat and blowing your nose. If you drive to work, you can also sing along with the radio in the car.

Making the call

When making a business call, be sure to first identify yourself and your company. If you're routed to a receptionist or operator, also include the name of the person you're trying to reach. A simple, "Hello, this is Mary Robert from Off the Wall Productions. May I please speak with Mark Grand?" will do.

Be prepared with a one or two sentence explanation of the purpose for your call. When you are connected with the person, state the purpose of your call and then be sure to ask if you are calling at a convenient time. This is one of the most overlooked areas of phone etiquette, and allows the person you're calling the opportunity to better address your needs at a later time. Don't fib about how long your call will take—if you know it will take longer than five minutes, don't say, "It'll be quick." Let the person know what they are getting into at the start of the conversation.

If you get shunted to a receptionist and he or she asks why you are calling, give a concise but informative statement that can be easily relayed. Do not, however, assume that your message will be communicated; when you speak directly with the person you are trying to call, repeat your message in your own words. Don't be insulted if you're asked to leave a message or call back later—previous engagements do take priority.

Answering the phone

People make business phone calls for specific reasons. Very rarely do vendors or clients call just to catch up. Telephone calls usually lead to some action to be taken, so make sure your first vocal impression is a good one by trying to answer the phone as pleasantly and professionally as possible.

Identify yourself and your company when receiving an incoming call. While it's not impolite to say, "Off the Wall Productions, Mary Robert speaking," it might be easier on the listener to say, "Thank you for calling Off the Wall Productions. This is Mary Robert. How may I help you?" Variations on this theme can convey your greeting quite effectively. If you work at a large corporation with many departments, it may also help to include your department or section name, "This is Mary Robert, accounts receivable. How may I help you?"

Hold, please

The hold feature is generally considered a double-edged sword in telephone etiquette. No one is usually available at the exact moment of a phone call, and being on hold simply must be tolerated. However, there are many things the caller and the person taking the call can do to make the experience a pleasant one.

If you must put someone on hold, ask first and—most importantly—wait for their answer. If someone expresses reservation about being put on hold, calmly explain why it is necessary. Perhaps the person they are calling for stepped out of the office and needs to be tracked down, or is on another call. Callers like an explanation for their inconveniences, but don't give away too much information. If Bill from distributing is in the restroom, just tell the caller he is away from his desk.

Remember to keep the person on hold updated on the status of his or her call every 30 seconds. A simple "She's on another call" or "His meeting is running a little late" is sufficient. It's okay to hang up after three minutes on hold. Call back and ask to leave a message instead.

Voice mail and messages

If you have to leave a message or voice mail for someone, make it short and to the point. Speak clearly and slowly and leave your name, phone number, and a brief message. Say your name and number at the beginning and again at the end of the message, especially if you don't know the person you're calling. If the voice mail system allows you to play back your message, consider taking advantage of that feature to make sure your message is clear and communicates your needs.

Returning messages promptly is always appreciated. It's customary to return telephone calls within 24 hours. If you cannot attend to the caller's needs within that time, briefly phone the person to say when you will be available.

Your own voice mail

The message you leave as your outgoing message is an important business tool. Information is critical. The best messages communicate several key things to the person calling you: your name, the organization and/or group you're in, the current date (this tells them you are checking your messages), whether you are in the office or not that day, when to expect a call back, whom to contact if the call is urgent, and how to get to that person.

This seems like an enormous burden, but it just requires a little discipline first thing every morning or last thing every night. If you've ever called someone and gotten a generic voicemail, you know how disconcerting it can be. Is the person on vacation? Will I get a call back? When? So it's especially important for people who travel frequently to attend to outgoing messages.

Of course, you can simplify the approach and perhaps change your message once a week providing an update of the days you'll be out of the office that week. Any useful information in your outgoing message will make your caller feel more comfortable that the message is important and you will respond. Be sure to respond.

On the Call

After establishing contact with the party you're trying to reach, you should be ready to use the time as effectively as if you were in a face-to-face meeting.

The speakerphone? Friend or foe?

Speakerphones are a great tool for communication via the telephone, but they must be used wisely. Some people prefer to use a speakerphone even when no one else is listening in so that they can take notes during the conversation without having to juggle a phone receiver. If you're one of those people, make sure you inform the people on the line with you that you are using a speakerphone, and if they seem apprehensive, explain why it is necessary.

Speakerphones are also useful for conference calls. If you are leading a speakerphone meeting with a number of people, allow each person to introduce himself or herself, to help the listeners match a name to a voice.

"In conference calls, always identify yourself by name and never rely solely on voice recognition," said Lena Bottos, compensation market analyst for Salary.com. "Always preface your comments with an introduction."

Silent partners

Conference calls provide unique opportunities for colleagues to communicate with one another. For example, it is not unusual for conference calls to include one or more silent listeners, who may or may not be introduced. Their objectives vary considerably, from training and monitoring to evaluating and getting strategic insights. Never assume your business telephone call is a confidential conversation between you and the people who introduce themselves on the other line.

Another silent strategy for conference calls is to use email, whiteboards, or instant messaging software to communicate with other participants on the call. This can be advantageous, for instance, when a silent partner wishes to prompt a speaker to say something in particular. If you are using such signals, however, be careful not to distract the other party by the sound of typing, nor to alienate the other party with your surreptitious strategizing.

Tolerant neighbors

When using the telephone at work, don't forget about the people around you who aren't taking part in the conversation. If you can, shut your office door or warn your cubicle neighbors before making speakerphone calls, as a person's speaking voice tends to increase in volume when using remote technology.

Headset etiquette

In many offices, people whose job involves considerable telephone work use a special hands-free headset-type telephone. This technology frees these workers to walk around the office with the ergonomically friendly device.

If you use this type of telephone, be careful not to bring your conversations into parts of the office where they do not belong. Many office workers can relate stories of coworkers walking up and down the halls seeming to talk to themselves. Be sensitive to the acoustics of the area in which you are conducting business, and to your coworkers' work spaces.

If you work with people who use hands-free telephones, develop a way of ascertaining quickly whether they are on a call before beginning a conversation with them.

When to say no

Learn how to use the "do not disturb" function on your phone, or lower the ringer if you to have a meeting in your office that you don't want to interrupt. A ringing telephone can create quite a disturbance in a sensitive meeting. Also, if you want to focus on a particular project—say you've got a deadline and you're not expecting any important calls—you can disable your ringer so that your calls go straight to voice mail.

However, don't hide behind your voice mail. Technology makes it quite feasible to keep

people at bay indefinitely. But if people begin to think you never answer your phone, they will stop calling, which could adversely affect business relationships.

Have a nice day

At the end of each call, thank your caller or the person you called for his or her time and hang up with a pleasant goodbye.

(http://www.salary.com/Articles/ArticleDetail.asp?part=par224)

After-reading tasks（读后任务）

When you finish reading the text above, get into the groups and discuss with your group members about the following tasks and fulfill them.

Task 1

It is of great importance to master the skills of making or receiving a telephone call, especially in a business setting. So practice the skills mentioned above with your group members. Make a telephone conversation and let the other group members to observe your performance and give suggestions.

Task 2

As mentioned in the text, there are many aspects in dealing with a telephone call. So make a list of different situations and corresponding suitable expressions or patterns. When you finish it, compare yours with your group members' to acquire the comprehensive knowledge of telephone manners that you should pay attention to.

Task 3

Communication over phones has been prevailing in western countries for centuries. China has become increasingly familiar this convenient way of communication. Make a questionnaire to get information from people around you after class to collect Chinese telephone manners and finally write an essay to compare Chinese telephone manners with the western ones.

Self-study（自学反馈）

If possible, summarize what you have learned in this unit with the help of the following table.

Focus of this unit:

Guidelines for etiquette:

1.

2.

3.

...

Summary:

Application:

1.

2.

3.

...

Feedback:

Chapter Four
Etiquette For Receiving Guests
商务接待礼仪

Objectives (学习目标)

After you have studied this chapter, you should be able to:

❑ Have a command of the etiquettes for receiving and meeting with the guests
❑ Handle some problem situations during the reception
❑ Cultivate the cross-cultural awareness when meeting with people from different backgrounds

Lead-in (导读)

It takes years sometimes to build a customer relationship—it can take but a moment to destroy it. We never get a second chance to make a first impression.　　*—B. Bader*

建立客户关系需要经年累月——但破坏这层关系只需要一瞬间。永远没有第二次机会去留下第一印象。
　　　　　　　　　　　　　　　　　　　　　　　　　　　　　　——毕·贝德

Business meetings are one arena in which poor etiquette can have negative effects. Comfort, trust, attentiveness and clear communication are results of good etiquette. The purpose of greeting is to establish or maintain friendly contact, and the purpose of manners is to make your guests feel comfortable.

商业会议如同一个舞台，礼仪不佳会产生负面影响。良好的礼仪会产生舒适、信任、体贴、清晰交流等积极效应。问候的目的在于建立或保持友好的交往；礼仪得当可以让你的客户感到舒服。

Test yourself (自我测试)

To start with, take a test to see to what degree you have mastered the greeting skills and etiquettes. Make responses to the following statements by using Yes or No.

1. It's casual Friday, but you'll meet with an important client. Dress yourself as you normally would on Friday—the concept of casual Friday is well understand.
　　　　　　　　　　　　　　　　　　　　　　　　　　　　　　Yes ☐ No ☐

2. You have a business meeting scheduled, but you're running a little late. Your clients have been waiting about 5 minutes already. You should tell your assistant to tell the clients that you'll be there soon. Yes ☐ No ☐

3. If you're managing a meeting when an adversarial relationship is present, try to make sure that the seating is mixed to encourage open dialog and discourage an adversarial dialog and discourage an adversarial environment. Yes ☐ No ☐

4. When you usher a group of people to a lift, you should enter first to ensure the safety, then come out to usher everyone in. On formal business occasions, ladies, the elderly & the people in higher positions walk out of the lift first. Yes ☐ No ☐

5. When exchanging name cards, don't exchange the name card with the clients before your boss or leader. Yes ☐ No ☐

6. In business occasions, once the relationship is established so that the casual usage of first names is expected. Yes ☐ No ☐

7. When being introduced to others, men should rise while women may remain seated. Yes ☐ No ☐

8. Firm handshakes are reserved for men and at the beginning of a meeting while loose handshakes for ladies and at the end of a meeting. Yes ☐ No ☐

9. I'm occupied with paper work and somebody approaches to greet me. It's forgivable for me to offer a handshake across the desk. Yes ☐ No ☐

10. Words such as "Hello" and "Nice to meet you" are more acceptable to respond to an introduction in formal situations than "charmed" or "a pleasure". Yes ☐ No ☐

Part I   Etiquettes for Introduction and Greetings
介绍和问候礼仪

1.Introduction 介绍

（1）How to introduce 如何介绍

In business setting, the rules for introductions are different from those of social introductions. The basic rules in social introductions are:

❑   Introduce your own acquaintances first, guests second;

- Introduce the host first, guest second;
- Introduce the young first, the old second;
- Introduce the man first, woman second.

商务活动场合的彼此介绍不同于社交场合的介绍认识。社交场合介绍他人，通常遵循以下基本原则：先介绍自己的熟人，再介绍来宾；先介绍主人方，再介绍来宾方；先介绍年轻人，再介绍年长者；先介绍男士，再介绍女士。

In business introduction, there is one basic rule: make sure who is the most important person and accordingly determine the order of precedence. It is noted that women are not treated as women but are introduced according to their business rank. When introducing people of equal rank in business situations, social rules apply—a man is introduced to a woman, and a younger person to an older person. The general order of precedence is as follows:

- Introduce a non-official person to an elected official;
- Introduce a person from your own firm to a client or customer;
- Introduce a junior executive to a senior executive;
- Introduce an individual to a group first, then the group to the individual.

商务场合的介绍有一个基本的原则：先明确谁是最重要的人物，再以此决定介绍的先后顺序。值得注意的是介绍中不考虑性别，只考虑职务级别。在商务场合介绍同级别的人时，同样适用社交场合的介绍顺序，即，将男士介绍给女士，将年少者介绍给年长者。商务场合的介绍顺序为：将非官方人士介绍给官方人士；将本公司人员介绍给客户或顾客；将职位低的行政人员介绍给职位高的行政人员；将个人介绍给群体，然后再将群体介绍给个人。

When you are introducing people, you should be careful of how to address them.

- Do not use first names in business introductions, unless it is the office custom with a business client or customer until requested to do so or granted permission and invited.
- If you're introducing someone who has a title "Doctor", for example, include the title as well as the first and last names in the introduction.
- If the person you're introducing has a specific relationship to you, make the relationship clear by adding a phrase such as "my boss", "my wife".
- Avoid using Mrs. unless you are definitely sure she is married and happy.
- Use your spouse's first and last name. Include the phrase "my wife/ husband".

在介绍他人时，应注意以下称呼问题。

- 介绍时不能只叫名字不带姓，除非是某个客户的惯例或者对方要求如此。
- 如果对方有博士（或医生）头衔，介绍时应在姓名前冠以头衔。
- 如果你所介绍的人和你有特定的关系，应在介绍时用诸如"我上司""我夫人"

等表述表明关系。

- □　除非你确定对方已婚而且乐意，否则不要用夫人称呼。
- □　介绍自己配偶时，要介绍全名，并说明"我夫人或我丈夫"。

Don't ignore the need of introduction even if you forget the name of a person. Before an event, use your address book or your "people database" to refresh your memory about the people you are likely to meet. If you forget someone's name, you can sometimes "cover" by introducing a person you do know first, for example, "Do you know Mr. Joe Smith, one of our sales reps?", which will usually get the unknown person to introduce him or herself. If this doesn't work, an admission that you've had a mental block and the name has escaped you is preferable to seeming neglectfulness.

即使忘记某人姓名也不能避而不做介绍。在商务活动前，要用通讯录或"人际资料库"来强化记忆你可能会遇到的人。万一遗忘了某人姓名，可通过先介绍一位熟人给对方来掩饰。例如，"您认识乔史密斯先生吗？他负责销售工作。"通常对方会介绍自己。如果这个方法未奏效，可坦承自己一时想不起来对方姓名。

Here are some tips for manners of introduction that should be remembered: always be gracious; smile; make eye contact; use clear voice; offer a firm handshake; pay attention to names when you meet people; never point at somebody with your index finger, smoke or chew gums while making introduction.

谈到介绍的礼仪，下列技巧应铭记在心：亲切有礼、微笑、眼神交流、嗓音清晰、握手坚定、记住名字，介绍中勿用食指指人、抽烟及嚼口香糖。

（2）The response to the introduction 对介绍的应答

Once you are introduced, you'll attract other's attention. Now, you should respond properly.

- □　Stand up. It is appropriate to do so whether you are a man or a woman. By doing so, you are demonstrating respect to the other person. While at dinner party or negotiation tables, you should nod with smile.

- □　Approach and look at the other person with smile to show respect to the other party.

- □　Shake hands. Shaking hands is to show your trust and respect, and it's also a way to send your greeting.

- □　Greet the other party by repeating the other party's name and making sincere and friendly responses like "How do you do, Mr. Smith?" or "Nice to meet you." Or "I've heard so much about you, I'm looking forward to meeting you."

当被介绍给他人时，对方会注意你，这时应该做出以下几种得体的应答：

- □　起立。无论男女这样做都很得体。这样做可以向对方表达你的敬意。如在餐桌上或谈判桌上，可点头微笑示意。

- ❑ 微笑着走近对方，表明敬意。
- ❑ 握手。握手既是表达信任和尊重，也是问候的一种方式。
- ❑ 和对方寒暄。可重复对方姓名，诚挚友好地说："您好，史密斯先生！"或"久仰大名，期待相见。"

2.Greeting 问候

There are many ways to greet people, which include formal and informal greetings, verbal and non-verbal greetings.

问候的方式有很多种，包括正式和非正式问候，语言和非语言问候。

（1）Verbal greeting 语言问候

Verbal greetings include formal and informal greetings. Informal verbal greetings are usually between close friends. In business situations, formal verbal greetings are appropriate. When you greet the clients, you can say: "Good morning, Mr. Brown. How are you?" "Good afternoon, Dr. Jones." or "Good evening. How about your weekend?"

语言问候包括正式和非正式问候。非正式问候通常用于关系亲密的朋友之间。在商务场合，正式的语言问候是得体的。在问候客户时，可以说："早上好，布朗先生。最近过得好吗？""下午好，琼斯博士！"或"晚上好！周末过得如何？"

（2）Non-verbal greeting 非语言问候

Non-verbal greetings include shaking hands, kissing, bowing, hug and salute with putting palms together.

非语言问候包括握手、亲吻、鞠躬、拥抱和合十礼等。

① Handshake 握手

Now handshaking is the most common international social etiquette, and it is the most popular meeting etiquette in international business settings.

握手在当今国际社交礼仪中最为常见，也是国际商务场合会见中最常用的问候方式。

In business situation, we should know when to shake hands. The good time to shake hands should be:

- ❑ When you are introduced to others and when you say goodbye to others.
- ❑ When the visitor comes into your room or office, you should shake hands to show your welcome.
- ❑ When you go to meet your client.

☐   When others send gifts to you.

☐   When you go to attend the receptions or parties and when you take leave.

在商务场合中，有必要了解何时握手为宜。握手的最佳时机应为被介绍给他人时，和他人告别时，都应握手；会见客户时；当收到他人礼物时；在参加招待会或晚会时和告别时。

The standards for handshaking should be strictly met. First, the order of holding out the hand cannot be messed up. Conventionally, the senior or the person who is in the high position holds out the hand first; women hold out the hand first; the superior holds out the hand first. The host first holds out the hand to welcome guests upon meeting, but before leaving it is the guests' turn to hold out the hand first.

握手时应严格遵守握手规范。首先，谁先伸手是有讲究的。按惯例，年长者或位高者先伸出手；女士先伸手；级别高的先伸手。主人迎客时先伸手，告别时则是宾客先伸手。

The duration of shaking hands generally takes three to five seconds. The handshaking must be firm and the strength is estimated two kilos. Right hand must be used to hold another right one, especially shaking hands with Singaporean, Malaysian, Thai, Arab, and Indian. They think the left hand is used to doing unclean things. Never shake hands with sweaty palms when being introduced. Remember to take off gloves, sunglasses and caps. When shaking hands, we should fix our eyes on each other and smile, accompanied by the greetings "nice to meet you". Cross-shake hands should be carefully avoided.

握手时长应在 3 ～ 5 秒之间。握手应坚定，双方握手力度约在两公斤。应右手相握，这一情形尤其在与新加坡人、马来西亚人、泰国人、阿拉伯人和印度人握手时应注意，他们认为左手是用来做不洁之事的。再则，避免握手时手里有汗。握手时应脱下手套，摘去墨镜和帽子。握手时，应目视对方，面带微笑，伴随问候语"很高兴见到您"。交叉握手现象要避免。

② Bowing 鞠躬

Bowing is always used in Japan, Korea, and South Korea. It is often used for showing respect and greeting to others. In China, we bow after speech, performance and winning an award or when holding a wedding ceremony, attending funeral. In European countries, people do not use it frequently. When do bowing, you should take off your hat and stand at attention, look at the recipient and bend forward. Men's hands should be posted on the sides at his trousers and women's hands place down before stomach. The lower the amplitude of bending, the more respect you show. Generally, bow only once except for attending a funeral that you should bow three times.

鞠躬盛行于日本、朝鲜和韩国，用于表达敬意和问候。在中国，演讲、表演、获奖后或婚礼、葬礼上都会行鞠躬礼。鞠躬礼在欧洲各国很少用。鞠躬时，应脱帽、立正、眼睛看着对方、身体前倾。男士的手应放在裤子两侧，女士的手放在腹部。鞠躬时幅度越大，表示越有敬意。一般鞠躬只需一次，葬礼例外，需鞠躬三次。

③ Kissing 亲吻

Kissing is a very personal way of saying hello, so you have to be careful about using it in business situations. Social kissing—or the peck on the peck—has become so widespread in many places including North America that it has spilled over into the formal business environment. Many people find social kissing awkward and confusing. Both men and women say that they are often unsure about just whom to kiss and under what circumstances. To avoid the awkwardness, secretaries and female managers would therefore be wise not to initiate the corporate kiss, particularly in a cross-cultural environment. When approached, reciprocate only with a peck on one cheek. Take into consideration the occasion and the setting. Kisses exchanged in the context of business meetings that are social in nature, such as banquets and conventions, may be acceptable. Those exchanged in pure business settings such as conference rooms of offices should be replaced with a handshake.

亲吻是一种私人问候方式，在商务场合慎用。社交亲吻是指轻吻面颊，在包括北美的很多地方盛行，也进入了正式的商务场合。很多人面对亲吻不知所措。男士和女士们都表示他们不确定该在何种场合亲吻谁。为避免尴尬，女秘书和女经理们应避免发起亲吻礼，尤其在跨文化场合。当被亲吻时，可在对方脸颊上轻轻一吻作为回礼。此礼节要考虑场合。在宴会或大型会议等社交性会见中亲吻礼是可接受的；但在公司会议室应用握手礼代替。

④ Hug 拥抱

In western countries, especially in Europeans, hug is one of the most popular etiquettes. Hug is also used when people are excited, greet, congratulate to others. In Asian countries, however, except for some minorities, hug is seldom used as etiquette. If you hug a person who you first meet, he will feel that you are too enthusiastic. Also, we consider it as an impolite manner. In formal business occasions, hug is a rare choice. In private meetings sometimes businessmen may hug to build up more intimate relationship.

在西方各国，尤其是欧洲国家，拥抱是常用礼仪之一。当人们感到兴奋、表达问候或祝贺时会拥抱。但在亚洲国家，除了少数民族，拥抱很少用作礼节。如果初次见面，拥抱对方，对方会认为你热情过头了。我们会把这作为失礼的举动。在正式商务场合，很少采用拥抱。商务人士在私人聚会有时会用拥抱建立更为亲密的关系。

⑤ Salute with putting palms together 合十礼

The "salute with putting palms together" was seen as an important etiquette in Buddhism. At present it is still used by Buddhist and worshipers in some Asian countries, even in business occasions.

合十礼是佛教的重要礼节。如今，合十礼在一些亚洲国家仍被佛教徒或信徒使用，甚至用于商务场合。

3.Etiquette about Name Cards 名片礼仪

Name cards are a necessity in business communications. Usually the colors of the business name cards are white, cream-colored, light yellow, blue and light gray. The content of the cards includes the name of the company, the department, the profession/title and the name of the owner. As for the exchange of the name cards, the lower in position should offer their cards first. If many people are involved in the exchange of the name cards, they can do it in the clockwise order.

名片是商务交往中必备的。商务名片的色泽通常为白色、奶油色、浅黄、蓝色、浅灰。名片内容包括公司名、部门、职业、头衔和名字。交换名片时，职位低者应先递出名片。如果多人一起交换名片，可按顺时针方向进行。

In order to show the politeness, it is best to follow the instructions when presenting your business card. Offer your card with the printing positioned so the recipient can read it. When you accept name cards, you should stand up with smile, keep eye contact, use both hands (at least right hand, not left hand), carefully read the information on the card (a very important step), avoid silence, saying "Thanks", give your own back and explain if not carrying with you.

为礼貌起见，递送名片时应注意规范。将印刷面朝上，以便对方查看。接收名片时，应微笑起立，目视对方，双手接过（至少用右手，而不是左手），仔细阅读名片上的信息（这是重要环节），避免沉默，口中道谢，并回赠自己的名片。如未带，可作些解释。

There are some other rules you had better observe in the exchange of the name cards: carry your business cards, or place another person's business card in the pockets of your coats instead of those of your trousers; never play with or fold the name cards of others; don't write some notes on others' name cards; don't exchange the name card with the clients before your boss or leader.

交换名片时还应遵循的礼仪包括：将自己名片或对方名片放在上衣口袋中，而不是裤袋中；不要把玩或折叠他人名片；不要在他人名片上书写；不要在老板或上司面前与客户交换名片。

Part II   The Procedure of Receiving Guests
商务接待具体步骤

1.Preparation 准备

Once you are notified of the date of the guests' arrival, contact the guests before they set out and begin to prepare for accommodations. Then designate the delegates who are going to meet the guests at the airport or the station and inform them the data of the clients or the business partners they are going to meet.

一旦接到来宾到达日期，应在客人出发前与之取得联系，开始着手安排食宿。然后指派接机或接车人员，告知来访客户或合作伙伴的相关信息。

Here rises another question: who receives the guests? To show respect and sincerity, it is acceptable to designate someone in the same business or who has the same or similar rank, title or status. If the designated person cannot go, someone having similar position or a deputy of the designee can act on his behalf.

那么，派谁去接合适？为表示尊敬和诚意，应派出参与这项生意的人员或职位、级别、地位相当的人员。如指派人员无法前往，则相近职位或其代表可担当此任。

2.Reception 接待

（1）At the airport or the station 机场或车站

The effect of welcoming people personally on their arrival in the town or country is highly rewarding compared to the small effort invested. From the moment they arrive, your guests should feel welcome. Remember to book the car(s) sufficiently far in advance to ensure availability. Then, check or ask the information office at the airport or the station for actual arrival time of the flight or the train two hours ahead of the schedule. Wait at the airport or train station ahead of the arrival and greet your guests when the plane lands or the train arrives. During the waiting, you need to get in touch with the porters, confirm the places where the checked luggage will be handed over and where the luggage will be delivered. Meanwhile, inform the hotel of the guests' approximate arrival to try to speed up their check-in. Finally, when you meet the guests, take them to hotel and make sure they settle in comfortably.

相比亲自迎接来宾得到的回报，所花的功夫实在微不足道。接站可以让来访者从抵达的那一刻就有宾至如归的感觉。记得提前定好车。然后提前两小时在机场或车站问讯处核实到达的准确时间。提前在机场或车站等候。等候时，可和行李处联系，确认行李在何处领取。同时可和宾馆联系，通知登记入住的大致时间，以节约时间。最后，接到来宾后，将其护送到宾馆并确保其舒适入住。

（2）On the road 在路上

The etiquette in cars is to remember to give the seat of honor to the guests. The seat of honor is the right one of the second row. The VIP seat is behind the driver as it is the safest.

车上的礼仪要注意的是将贵宾座安排给来宾。VIP 座是后排靠右边座位。VIP 座在司机身后，是最安全的。

On the way it is considerate to inquire whether any help is needed and what is really his concern at the moment—return bookings, exchanging, changing and washing, calling home. When all this has been settled, his or her mind will be much more receptive to your intended tour of the beauties of the town. And schedule for the next day can be arranged on the way to the hotel or when arriving at the hotel. Deliver a small timetable with essential telephone numbers where the visitor can contact someone for help, even outside normal office hours.

在路上应周到地询问来宾是否需要一些帮助，有什么担心的事。如订购回程票、兑换外汇、洗漱、给家中打电话等。这些事安排好了，他或她才会关注你所安排的城市游览观光。在去宾馆途中或抵达宾馆后可安排好次日行程。给宾客一个计划时间表，列上必要的电话号码，以便来宾即使在办公时间以外也能获得需要的帮助。

（3）In the elevator 电梯内

When you usher the guests to a lift, the proper order should be that you enter first to ensure the safety and then come out to usher everyone in. On formal business occasions, ladies, the elderly and the people in higher positions walk out of the lift first. Nowadays, it is not so strict sometimes. Those near the lift door walk out first. When you touch others by chance, an immediate apology will be expected. It is inappropriate to speak or laugh in a loud voice.

当引领来宾搭乘电梯时，得体的做法是你先进入电梯确保电梯的安全，再引领宾客进入。正式商务场合中，出电梯时，应请年长者和位高者先行。如今，这一点没那么严格，靠近电梯门的可先出电梯。如偶然触碰他人，应立即道歉。在电梯中高声说笑是不得体的。

3.Formal Welcome 正式接待

This should take place in reception room or any such venue where tea / coffee / light refreshments can be served. It is best to allow people to wander in and invite them individually to help themselves before the formal welcome is to take place.

正式接待应在会客厅或类似可提供茶点的场所举行。最好在正式接待前让客人在此处自己随意歇息用些茶点。

When the guests arrive at the reception room, where to sit should be taken into consideration. In business negotiation, the participants of both parties sit face to face. In other business occasions, the common rule that has been observed is that the guests will be given the seat facing the door, the seat of honor, as well as the right one. In Chinese tradition, left is more honorable than right.

在会客厅要考虑如何安排就座。商务谈判中，双方参与者应相对而坐。其他商务场合，遵循的共同原则是来宾坐上座，靠右面门而坐。按中国习惯，左边座位较右边更尊贵些。

In many large organizations a receptionist initially greets all office visitors. After obtaining such information as the name of the visitor, his company affiliation, the nature of his visit, and the person he wishes to see, the receptionist notifies the secretary that the caller has arrived. The secretary may go to the receptionist area and escort the visitor to the office and see that they are directed to the proper persons. When escorting the visitor into the boss' office, the secretary introduces him if they have not previously met.

在大的机构，接待员会首先迎接所有来访宾客。在获知来访者姓名、所属公司部门、来访目的以及他要拜访何人等信息后，接待员会通知相关秘书。秘书会来到会客区，引领来访者到办公室，并介绍给相关人员。在引领来访者到上司办公室时，如是初次来访，秘书应将来访者介绍给上司。

4.Seeing Guests off 送别宾客

The guests may be departed from the company. In this case, the host expresses the reluctance and thanks in words, accompanying with the handshake. The host takes the guests to the elevator, see the elevator going down to the first floor, show them to the car, close the door of the car for the guests and wave or see them off.

如将宾客送离公司，接待方应握手，并表示挽留和感谢来访。主人应送宾客到电梯，并陪同至一楼，送到车上，为来宾关上车门，并挥手或目送告别。

If the guests are departed from the hotel, be sure to arrive earlier at the hotel where the guests stay first. Later accompany the guests to the airport, the train station or the port when they are ready; or the host goes directly to the airport, the train station or the port to see the guests off. Before they get aboard, shake hands with and say goodbye to them. Wave hands to the guests when the plane, train or ship begins to move; stay there until the plane, train or ship disappears from your sight.

如从宾馆送别宾客，应先赶到宾馆，待来宾准备就绪后，再陪同来宾到机场、车站或港口。在登机或上车船前，应握手道别。飞机，车窗驶离时，应挥手告别，待在原处直到飞机或车窗消失。

Situational practice for etiquettes 礼仪口语实景

Make up or search for more situational conversations that may occur when receiving the guests and put them into practice.

Model 1 Introductions & greetings

A: Mr. Clarke, this is our Development Manager, Mr Song.

B: Pleased to make your acquaintance.

A: How do you do? Did you have a nice flight, Mr Clarke?

B: Yes. The flight was smooth, and the service was good. Things couldn't have been better.

A: I'm glad to hear that. But you must be very tired after such a long journey.

B: Yes, a little bit. But I'll be all right by tomorrow.

Model 2 Bon voyage

A: It's very kind of you to see me off. I really had a very pleasant stay here.

B: It's shame you haven't got the time to visit all the places of interest.

A: Business trips never leave much time for sightseeing.

B: Perhaps we can make things up the next time you are here.

A: I hope so too. Don't forget to look me up if you and Mr Li are ever in New York.

B: We certainly will.

A: Thank you again for everything.

B: It's my pleasure.

A: Goodbye.

B: Goodbye. Have a nice journey! Bon voyage!

Terminology related 相关礼仪术语

Business cards

Business cards are the most popular marketing tool of small business, and it's no wonder—they're portable, affordable, versatile and people actually expect you to use them! Yet more than 90% of business cards wind up in the trash the day they're received. So Attention should be paid to how to make a distinctive, memorable business card that doesn't cost a fortune and yet won't get thrown away.

Business cards are an internationally recognized means of presenting personal contact details, so ensure you have a plentiful supply. Business cards are generally exchanged at the beginning of or at the end of an initial meeting. Good business etiquette requires you present the card with the recipient's language upward. Make a point of studying any business card, commenting on it and clarifying information before putting it away.

商务名片是小型生意最常用的营销手段，因为方便携带、价廉、风格各异，而且人们希望你能使用它们。然而，每天90%以上的名片送出后都被当作垃圾扔弃。所以，务必确保名片独特、令人印象深刻，关键是不会被扔弃。

商务名片是国际公认的提供个人联系方式的方式，所以一定要足量准备。通常在会议开始或结束时交换名片。良好的礼仪要求递送名片时应将印有对方语言的一面朝上。收到名片后，收起来之前应研究评判它，看清上面的信息。

Useful expressions for etiquettes 礼仪用语集锦

The followings are appropriate expressions that you may use when receiving guests:

❑　　Greetings 问候

Hello!

嗨，你好！

Good morning / afternoon / evening!

早上好 / 下午好 / 晚上好！

Glad to see you here /again. / How nice to see you here /again.

很高兴再次见到您。

Haven't seen you for ages /for a long time. / Long time no see.

多日未见。

How's everything? / How are things with you? / How are you? / How have you been? / What's up/ new?

一切可好？ / 近况如何？

I'm fine/great /Pretty good /Very well, thank you. How about you?

我一切都好，谢谢。你呢？

Can't complain / So-so / Not too bad, thank you.

尚好，谢谢。

Oh, the usual rounds / the same stuff, thanks.

老样子，谢谢。

Still alive / Surviving, thanks.

还活着呢，谢谢。

❑　　Introducing oneself 自我介绍

Hello! I'm...

嗨，我是……

First let/allow me introduce myself.

首先我做个自我介绍吧。

May I introduce myself?

我做个自我介绍好吗？

❑　　Introducing others 介绍他人

I'd like to introduce...

我想给各位介绍……

Let me introduce...

请允许我介绍……

May I introduce ...?

我来介绍……好吗？

It is with great pleasure that I introduce...

我很荣幸给各位介绍……

❑　　Responses to an introduction 回应介绍

Nice to meet you. / Happy to know you.

很高兴认识您。

I've heard so much about you. / I've often heard about you. / I know you very well by reputation. / I have wanted to see you.

久闻大名。一直渴望见到您。

❑   Parting 分别

Good bye! / See you! / See you later/tomorrow! Nice meeting you and talking to you.

再见 / 待会儿 / 明天见！和您见面交谈甚为愉快。

I'd like to say good bye to you. I look forward to see you again.

要和您说再见了，期待再次见到您。

All the very best / I hope everything goes well. / Good luck with your family. /Best wishes.

祝一切顺利。/ 问候您的家人。

Keep in touch.

保持联系吧。

Give my love to your daughter. / Say hello to your uncle for me.

问候您的女儿。/ 请代我问候您的叔叔（舅舅等）。

Exercises（课后练习）

I. Questions and answers: answer the following questions according to the information you have got in the previous reading.

1. What are verbal greeting and non-verbal greeting? How do we apply them to business practice?

2. What are the differences between the social introduction and business introduction?

3. Why do we have to choose a suitable representative to pick up the guests?

4. What are the etiquettes we should pay attention to during the reception?

5. How do we see guests off to show our respect?

II. Match the terms in Column A with the chinese equivalents in column B.

A	B
attorney	教授
certified Public Accountant	牙医
dentist	学院、大学行政人员
physicist	注册会计师
veterinarian	律师
college / University officers	物理学家
professor	兽医

III.Translation: translate the following statements into Chinese to learn about Behavior Guide for the Receptionist.

1.A receptionist should dress conservatively;

2.Wear make-up properly (if a lady) and have hairstyle neatly and conservatively done;

3.Wear little jewelry, and it should be noiseless and unobtrusive;

4.Not eat, chew gum, smoke, or drink at the receptionist desk;

5.Keep hands and fingernails presentable;

6.Keep the desk neat, with everything in its proper placer;

7.Smile when greeting each visitor, try to show gladness to see each other and use the telephone to announce the visitor in cheerful voice;

8.Transmit orders and directions to the visitor in a very clear manner;

9.Never continue a conversation when a visitor approaches the desk unless it is an important one;

10.Not turn back to the visitor when on the telephone;

11.Call to see what is happening and then report to the visitor if a visitor is kept waiting longer than usual;

12.Treat executives, visitors and employees with equal courtesy as they enter or leave;

13.Call everyone by his last name;

14.Fastidiously keep the company directory up to date, with accurate names, numbers and locations of all personnel;

15.Know senior management, their titles, what they do, and how they fit into the hierarchy.

IV.Cloze: choose the suitable statements from the box and complete the passage.

A.during formal introductions

B.a means to contact the business or representative of the business

C.striking visual design

D.whether it gets thrown in the trash or filed for contact later

E.bearing business information about a company or individual

Business cards are cards_____1_____. They are shared _____2_____ as a convenience and a memory aid. A business card typically includes the giver's name, company affiliation (usually with a logo) and contact information such as street addresses, telephone number(s), fax number, e-mail addresses and website. It can also include telex, bank account, tax code. Traditionally many cards were simple black text on white stock; today a professional business card will sometimes include one or more aspects of_____3_____.

Business cards are frequently used during sales calls (visits) to provide potential customers with _____4_____.

Your business card is often the first impression a potential client has with your company. The business card design and message will ultimately determine _____5_____.

V.Case study: Read the profile of the business people below. Choose ways of entertaining them from the following list:

a meal at an expensive restaurant   a round of golf

a shopping trip   a visit to a sports event

a sightseeing tour of the city

1. Tom Peterson, 32, the Sales manager of a British computer software company. This is a new but important customer. He has a two-day stopover on his way to London.

2. A party of five Japanese businessmen in their mid-thirties. They are on fact-finding mission to help them decide whether to offer your company a substantial contract.

3. Frida Mellor, 46, the Managing Director of your company's largest client. He is flying in from Milan to finalize one or two small details concerning a major deal with you. His wife, Andrea, is with him on the trip.

4. Angela Goddard, 36, the Manager of Shirts & Shorts, a manufacturer of fashion sportswear, and her personal assistant, Andrea Meier. Several orders you placed with their company arrived late. As a result, you nearly lost a valued customer.

Extension （拓展阅读）

Guide to Social Kissing

It can happen to anyone. You want to give more than a business-like handshake as a greeting, and a hug seems disconcertingly personal. You lean to bestow the compromise—a peck on the cheek—and the person turns her head, and suddenly you're bumping noses or even brushing lips and teeth.

That's what happened to Margery Colloff, a Manhattan lawyer, when she was introduced to a more senior lawyer at a dinner party.

"I went for a peck on the right cheek, but he was zooming in from the left," she recalled. "And I literally crashed into his teeth."

The social kiss is unpredictable, agreed R. Couri Hay, the society editor at Hamptons magazine.

"I never kiss on the first meeting," he said, "but if someone offers a kiss, I feel I have to be polite and take it. Generally, I really don't want to be covered in lipstick."

The kiss "has been dumbed down," Hay said. "It is supposed to be a sign of affection, but I've seen people recoil when they see someone they don't even know coming in to lick their cheek."

Despite the awkwardness, the cheek kiss is displacing the handshake, once the customary greeting in North American social and business circles.

It may be a growing Latin influence, an aping of European manners, and the influx of women in the workplace or just a breakdown of formality: no one seems to know. It's not just celebrities smacking the air or diplomats puckering up with the European-style double kiss or Soprano family wannabes mimicking a sign of forced fealty.

If being bussed on the cheek is way too intimate, some advice that sticking your hand out firmly—keeping a straight elbow—is the best way to show yourself willing to shake hands and nothing more.

That's what Hay did at a nightclub opening in February, and then added his own follow-through.

"A woman was coming in for the kiss, so I took a step back and then put my hand out in front of me," he said. "I turned left and kept going in one continuous movement, like a dance step, to escape."

While the handshake still holds sway in big corporations, said Barbara Pachter, who heads an etiquette-training firm in New Jersey, the kiss has migrated into areas like sales, where it can denote a warm relationship that encourages buying. Still, figuring out where the limits are can present problems.

"I had one pharmaceutical saleswoman client—young and attractive—who would kiss and hug her clients," Pachter said. "Then she saw one doctor at dinner and gave him a kiss and hug. His wife didn't appreciate that, and it was not appropriate."

The kiss is "happening more and more," agreed Peggy Post, a spokeswoman for the Emily Post Institute founded by the doyenne of etiquette. "We're much more informal in everything from the clothes we wear to how we greet people."

Post advocates the handshake and agrees that it's better "to steer clear of kissing people of the opposite sex, which can be misconstrued in some cases."

This is especially true on first meetings. Later, kissing as a greeting depends on the relationship, she and others said. Still, it doesn't always go smoothly.

Sarah Felix, 27, a features editor at Good Housekeeping, remembered a cheek-and-lip collision with a former boss, which she found unsettling because, she said, "there is always a certain amount of tension in that gesture between an older man and a younger woman."

P. M. Forni, a professor at Johns Hopkins University, who wrote Choosing Civility: The 25 Rules of Considerate Conduct (St. Martin's, 2002), said, "You can use the kiss to overpower a person."

But, Forni said, "In an age when there are all these prohibitions on physical contact, such as putting an arm around someone's shoulder, we are looking for a way of physical contact that is beyond reproach."

He added: "The social kiss is a gentle reminder that we are physical beings. It is face-to-face encounters that make us human."

Even so, confusion often reigns because there is no set formula for social kissing.

The French, for example, kiss on both cheeks—one kiss each—although in a few regions it is the double-double kiss with two on each cheek. The Belgians, the Dutch and even the dour Swiss go for the triple kiss. If you can't keep that straight and need a refresher, the lip balm company Blistex has a rundown of kissing customs on its website, www.blistex.com, under the heading Global Lip Customs.

In most countries, the social kiss begins with the right cheek, probably because most people are right-handed and, according to a German study in 2003, most people tilt their heads to the right when heading for a lip kiss. So it follows that they would lean right for a cheek kiss.

Pamela Eyring, who served as chief of protocol for the U.S. air force Materiel Command at Wright-Patterson Air Force Base for 23 years and owner of The Protocol School of Washington, offers these suggestions for social smooching:

Whom to kiss: though social kissing is appropriate among friends and family, it still must be consensual. I do not recommend a social kiss with the boss, especially if you are of the opposite sex.

As for kissing your host and hostess at a party, it matters what type of relationship you have. Determine if you have been invited for professional reasons or social.

When to kiss: wait for the other person to go first.

Where to kiss: if you kiss a friend socially, always do so on the cheek. Lips are too intimate.

How to avoid the kiss: if you want to avoid a social kiss, put your hand out and offer a handshake.

When your kiss isn't wanted: if you kiss someone socially, watch for nonverbals that might tell you if it's all right. If a person becomes stiff, you will know immediately.

Bottom line: if a good friend gives you a social kiss, return the gesture so as not to embarrass him or her.

(http://www.001bbs.net/thread-208693-1-1.html)

After-reading tasks（读后任务）

When you finish reading the text above, get into the groups and discuss with your group members about the following tasks and fulfill them.

Task 1

Social kissing can happen to anyone. Read about the cases mentioned in the text.

"I went for a peck on the right cheek, but he was zooming in from the left," she recalled. "And I literally crashed into his teeth."

"I never kiss on the first meeting," he said, "but if someone offers a kiss, I feel I have to be polite and take it. Generally, I really don't want to be covered in lipstick."

And add more examples to illustrate your attitudes towards it and how you feel about it.

Task 2

The text has given the guides to social kissing. And use the framework to create your own guides and. Then introduce your creation to your group members and try to convince yours can achieve the best effects in business interaction.

Whom to kiss	
When to kiss	
Where to kiss	
How to avoid the kiss	
When your kiss isn't wanted	
Bottom line	

Task 3

Greeting can be the first step in the business interaction, thus, we must never ignore its importance. As one of greetings, social kissing must be familiar to business people. Since guides to social kissing vary all over the world, it seems not easy to handle. Now get into groups and each group should focus on one country to find out the local customs of social kissing. When that is done, share the information that has been collected in class to enlarge the knowledge of customs of social kissing. Pay attention to the way of presentation and try to make it lively and let us have fun.

Self-study（自学反馈）

If possible, summarize what you have learned in this unit with the help of the following table.

Focus of this unit:
Guidelines for etiquette: 1. 2. 3. ...
Summary:
Application: 1. 2. 3. ...
Feedback:

Chapter Five
Business Dinner Etiquette
商务宴会礼仪

Objectives（学习目标）

After this chapter, you should be able to:

❑ Have a command of the etiquettes for business dinner
❑ Handle some problem situations in entertaining guests
❑ Cultivate the cross-cultural awareness when doing business over dinner

Lead-in（导读）

In a fast food world where most of us have more experience eating from bags rather than fine china, the prospect of a formal business dinner can evoke more than a little anxiety!

—Lisa Smith Klohn

在快餐盛行的世界，我们大多数人从快餐袋中取食的经验远比用精美瓷器进餐的经验丰富。因此，一提到正式的商务宴会，就难免会令人陷入焦虑。

——莉萨·史密斯·科勒恩

Imaginably, there is a lot to worry about in preparing for a business dinner, including how to navigate the place setting, butter your bread, make peace with your napkin, and manage messy foods and much more! You can have your cake and eat it, too. Just be sure you are using the right fork! Remember: there's no such thing as a free lunch. In a business situation, table manners may well be the key factor that differentiates you from your competitors. Doing business over dinner is a good way to build relationships and seal the deal. However, it is not an easy thing. Get it right, and it's duck soup. Get it wrong, and you're dead in the water. Undoubtedly, you will be thirsty for a full menu of strategies that will have your clients eating out of your hand. Manners do matter, so take your steps now to learn how to confidently increase your bottom line every time you sit down with a customer, potential client, supervisor, board member or anyone who has influence on your career or business.

可以想象，在准备商务宴请的时候要考虑方方面面，例如：如何指引宴请地点；如何给面包抹黄油；如何摆放餐巾；如何料理棘手的餐点等。虽然你可以独自享用自己的蛋糕，不过，要先确定是否用对了叉子！时刻记住：天下没有免费的午餐。在商务场合，餐桌礼仪足以成为区分你和竞争对手的关键因素。在餐桌上谈生意是建立商业关系和成交贸易的好方式。然而，实施起来却并不容易。行事正确，回报丰润；行事错误，则有可能陷入困境。毋庸置疑，你急于找到一系列策略，来让客户最终进餐愉快。在这个用餐过程中，礼仪至关重要，因此我们有必要学会如何提升自己的餐会礼仪水平，自信地和客户、潜在客户、上司、董事会成员或任何影响事业或生意的人坐下来进行商务交流。

Test yourself（自我测试）

To start with, take a test to see to what degree you have mastered the business dinner rules and etiquettes. You can use Yes or No to make responses to the following statements.

1. If you want to go to the bathroom during a meal, you must leave the table quietly.

Yes ☐ No ☐

2. Things that are not eaten, like bones, should be put on your plate.

Yes ☐ No ☐

3. You should stand up to get the salt if it is out of your reach. Yes ☐ No ☐

4. If you do not want a certain food, give a clear explanation to the host why you can't have it. Yes ☐ No ☐

5. Watch how fast others are eating. Try to keep up with their pace. Yes ☐ No ☐

6. It is appropriate to ask for a doggy bag to avoid the waste for the host when you are a guest. Yes ☐ No ☐

7. If you need something that you cannot reach easily, you'd better not bother others to pass it to you, just quit it. Yes ☐ No ☐

8. Signal the servers that you are still eating by placing your fork and knife in an inverted V on your plate from the 10 to 4 o'clock positions. Yes ☐ No ☐

9. If it's fifteen to twenty minutes after the appointed time and your lunch or dinner date hasn't shown up, keep waiting, don't phone her office. When the no-show phones to explain, simply accept his apologies and reschedule the meal. Yes ☐ No ☐

10. For a large group of guests, it would be appropriate for the host to precede his/her guests into the dining-room so that the host can indicate where each guest is to be seated.

Yes ☐ No ☐

Part I Forms of Business Entertaining
商务宴请的方式

Business meals (essentially meetings with food) can take many forms, from casual to more formal. Obviously, the decision whether to meet over lunch, breakfast, or dinner depends mainly on which of these meals best fits the time constraints of the participants. Also, take into account what you wish to accomplish.

商务餐形式多样，有较为随意的，也有较为正式的。至于选择早餐、中餐或晚餐宴请主要取决于双方的日程安排，也取决于宴请想要达到的效果。

Even a breakfast meeting has real benefits, many people are at their sharpest early in the morning; as with lunch, the timing of a morning meeting helps it stay short and focused; unlike lunch, it barely interrupts the workday, if at all; plus, breakfast is less costly than either lunch or dinner.

商务会见即使安排在早餐时分，好处也有很多。早餐会见时间和午餐一样，不会过长。商谈的主题也会更集中；和午餐会见不同的是，早餐会见基本不会影响全天的工作安排；另外，早餐会见比起午餐和晚餐会见来讲成本更低。

A business breakfast can be held at any location that is handy to both host and guest, a restaurant or coffee shop, a hotel dining room, or perhaps a private club. If it's convenient for all concerned, guests can even be invited to breakfast in the host's office. Putting out a selection of cookies or muffins and coffee or tea requires little preparation and lends the meeting the affable touch of an away-from-the-coffee meal.

商务早餐可在主客方便的任何场所进行，如餐厅、咖啡厅、酒店餐厅或私人俱乐部。如果参与者方便的话，甚至可设在邀请者的办公室里。准备曲奇饼、松饼、咖啡或茶饮简单易行，却可让会见亲切放松。

Lunch is the traditional workhorse of business meals. Because the participants have to return to the office, the meeting stays relatively short and focused. There are other advantages as well: unlike a business dinner, lunch is faster-paced, it doesn't cut into someone's personal time, and it doesn't raise the issue of the inclusion of a spouse or partner.

午餐是传统的商务聚餐。因为参与者饭后要返回办公室，所以会见相对简短，会谈主题也相对集中。其他优点包括：不同于商务晚宴，午餐节奏快，不占用参与者的私人时间，而且也不涉及配偶和伴侣的参与。

Dinner also proceeds at a more leisurely pace because no one has to get back to work. At the same time, dinner's longer time span can be an advantage when doing serious business is the goal. The aim is usually the strengthening of relationships, with an eye on mutual rewards to be gained in the future.

因为没人急着赶回办公室，商务晚餐通常节奏舒缓。晚餐充足的时间适合谈重要的生意。晚餐的目的在于加强彼此的联系，关注双方长远的利益回报。

Part II　Preparations for the Business Meals
商务宴请的筹备

In order to seek the confidence of a client or prospective client, or celebrate a newly closed deal, even to get to know each other better, in many cases, we want to extend an invitation to entertain clients or co-workers. As for a business meal, a little careful preparation will build up an image that can only serve to help your professional life.

为了取得客户的信任或发展潜在的客户，庆祝交易会谈成功，或加深彼此了解等很多情况，我们都会发出邀请宴请客户和合作者。花点心思认真准备商务宴请将展示出一个极其有助于你事业生活的良好形象。

1.Seating Assignments 座位安排

As a guest, you'd better look to the host for seating assignments as the host may have a specific seating arrangement in mind. As a host, how you seat your guests from the start can assist in making the occasion more successful, so put some thoughtful effort into this decision. Thus, everything should be taken into consideration beforehand: Do they have a need to discuss business together? Do they have hobbies or interests in common? Do they have professions in common? Do they like one another or not? Be careful of seating people you know have an animosity towards one another unless you want a dampener on the occasion.

作为客人，应考虑到主人对座次的排定有具体的考虑，按主人示意就座即可。作为主人，如何在最初安排好座位关系到宴请是否圆满，因此应周详考虑。应预先考虑到：他们是否愿意一起谈生意？他们有共同的兴趣或爱好吗？他们职业相同吗？他们喜欢彼此吗？如果不想有不愉快事件，应避免将有敌意的双方安排在一起就座。

Seating etiquette rules should be observed, even in recent years, to symbolize the formality of the occasion. In formal business setting, there is a standard protocol regarding who sits where.

近年来，遵守座次礼仪仍被看作是正式场合的象征。在正式商务宴请中，座位安排有标准的规范。

When there is but a single table, the host and hostess usually sit at opposite ends, or occasionally in the center of the table facing each other. When multiple tables are needed, the host and hostess may be at separate tables in which case you may wish to opt for a co-host and co-hostess.

如只有一桌，男女主人通常坐在餐桌两端，有时会坐在餐桌中间的座位，相对而坐。如有多桌，男女主人则分桌而坐或宴请方安排人招呼其他桌。

Generally, when the event involves both men and women, guests are seated alternating man and woman. The place of honor is to the right of the host if the guest is a woman and to the right to the hostess if the guest is a man. Namely, the highest ranking male generally sits to the right of the hostess. The wife of the highest ranking man or the highest ranking woman herself sits to the right of the host. Guests are then seated alternating left to right from the host and hostess after the honored guest is seated. The second ranking male will usually sit to the left of the hostess. Now the seating should be arranged such that no two women sit side by side and no two men sit side by side.

通常宴请中有男女宾客，则交叉就座。对于女宾，上座为男主人右手边座位，对于男宾，则为女主人右手边座位。即，职位最高的男宾坐在女主人右边，其夫人或职位最高的女宾坐在男主人右边。在贵宾就座后，其他宾客从男女主人处从左到右交叉就座，即，职位第二的男宾坐在女主人左边。不应安排两位女宾或男宾坐在一起。

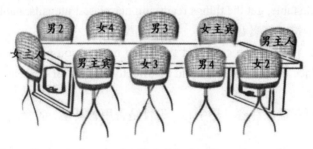

When the number of guests is evenly divisible by four, the male guest of honor may sit across from the host in the hostess' seat. The hostess then sits to his left.

如果来宾人数是四的倍数，男宾中的贵宾应坐男主人对面的女主人座位，而女主人则坐在他的左边。

When men and women are not equal in numbers, for example, gatherings of business persons of either sex from two or more companies or different countries, it is acceptable to arrange the host's seat facing the door and then "alternate host and hostess", that is to say, each guest sits next to the host or a representative of the host so that they can communicate. Besides, diners' rankings should also be taken into consideration.

如宴请多家公司或不同国家的男士或女士，男女来宾人数不对等时，主人面门而坐，然后主客双方交叉就座，即，每位来宾和宴请方代表相邻而坐以便交谈。当然，同时要考虑到职位高低。

2.Table Setting 餐桌摆设

The knowledge of established etiquette rules when setting the table prevent confusion during the meal and help diners avoid embarrassing situations, like sipping from a companion's water glass. There are slightly different rules for the placement of specialty dishes and utensils depending on the formality of your meal, but the basic table setting does not vary. The placement of utensils is guided by the menu, the idea being that you use utensils in an "outside in" order, working in toward the dinner plate. The typical order of the menu is: appetizer and soup—the salad course—the main course—dessert.

熟悉规范的餐桌摆设礼仪可避免餐桌上的混乱和尴尬的局面，诸如拿错了邻座的水杯等。应宴请的规格不同，餐具的摆放会有差别，但餐具的摆放还是有基本规范可循的。餐具的摆放以菜单为准，基本原则是按由外往内的顺序，逐步靠近餐盘。菜单一般的顺序为：头盘、汤—沙拉—主菜—甜品。

Before setting the table, get the things ready: dinner plates; utensils; napkins and glasses.

摆设餐桌前，应准备好餐盘、餐具、餐巾和酒杯。

Place the dinner plate in the center of the place mat, if you are using one. Regardless of whether you use a place mat, the plate should be directly in front of the seat, about 6 inches from the edge of the table.

如用餐具垫，将餐盘放在餐具垫中心。不管是否用餐具垫，餐盘应摆放在座位正前方，距离桌边六英寸。

Place the dinner fork to the left of the plate. If you are serving salad, place the smaller salad fork to the left of the dinner fork.

将主菜叉放在餐盘的左边。如上沙拉，将较小的沙拉叉放在主菜叉的左边。

❑　Fold the napkin and place it to the left of the forks. Alternatively, you can place the folded napkin on the dinner plate.

折叠餐巾，并放在叉子的左边。或将折好的餐巾放在餐盘上。

❑　Place the knife to the right of the dinner plate. Be sure that the knife's blade faces the plate.

将餐刀放在餐盘的右边。刀锋应朝向餐盘。

❏ Place the spoons to the right of the knife. If you are serving soup, place the soup spoon to the right of the dessert or coffee spoon.

将勺子放在餐刀的右边。如上汤，可将汤勺放在甜食勺或咖啡勺的右边。

❏ Place all glasses to the right of the dinner plate, above the knife and spoons. For a formal meal, offer a water glass and a wine glass. If you have room on the table, you can also set a cup and saucer for coffee or tea with dessert above the utensils.

将酒水杯放在餐盘右边，刀勺的上方。正式宴请时，摆放水杯和酒杯各一。如桌上有空地，可在餐具上方摆放盛咖啡或茶的杯碟。

❏ Place the bread plate and butter knife to the left of the dinner plate, above the forks. This step is optional.

将面包盘和黄油刀放在餐盘的左边，餐刀的上方。这个步骤可以省略。

❏ Place the salad plate to the left of the forks and napkin. This plate is also optional. If you are serving salad with dinner, you may serve it on the dinner plate if the main meal does not include gravy or other sauces.

将沙拉盘放在餐刀和餐巾的左边。此盘也可省略。如随餐上沙拉，主食中无卤汁或其他调味汁，可将沙拉上在餐盘里。

❏ As an alternative, you can place the dessert spoon horizontally above the dinner plate, with the handle facing right. If you are also setting a dessert fork, place the fork on the table horizontally, below the dessert spoon with the handle facing to the left. In formal table settings, bring dessert forks and spoons out with the dessert.

如需要，将甜食勺水平放在餐盘上方，勺把朝右。如放置甜食叉，水平置于甜食勺下方，叉把朝左。在正式宴请中，甜食叉和勺随甜食一起送上。

Notice: In general, etiquette rules dictate that there should be no more than three of any type of utensil on the table at one time. If you plan to serve more than three courses before the meal, bring out the utensils for the fourth course with the food. When confronted with a place setting of three or four forks and spoons that confuses you, a good rule of thumb is to start with the outermost utensil and work your way in with each course. In general the dishes for liquids are on the right, while dishes for solids are on the left.

注意：一般餐桌上任何餐具一次不可出现超过三种。如要上的菜超过三道，可将第四道菜用的餐具随餐送上。如果分不清餐桌上的第三、四把叉子和勺子，一个重要的原则是从最外面的餐具开始用起，一道道菜往内取用。一般来说流质菜式的餐具在右边，固体菜式的在左边。

bread（b）is on your left; drink (d) is on your right.

Part III Etiquettes for Business Dinner
商务餐会礼仪

Although business dinners take different forms, what they all have in common is a measure of sociability over and above that of an office-bound appointment. Your own behavior at business meals is every bit as important as the fellowship they foster. Remember: these are the only times when your conversational abilities, your self-possession, and your table manners are all on display at once. Bear in mind, too, that your manners reflect on the company you represent. The desire to make a good impression hardly means rehearsing your across-the-table banter or becoming a wine connoisseur. It does mean knowing how to use the cutlery, eating your food with civility, and conveying the sense of being at ease with those around you.

商务宴请尽管形式多样，其共同之处在于都是基于公务范畴的社交方式。你个人在餐会上的举止与在此建立的交情同样重要。记住：这是展现你善于辞令、沉着从容、优雅举止的难得的机会。记得你的举止代表的是你所在的公司。想留下良好印象并不意味着笑惊四座、品酒入微。良好的印象来自于正确地使用刀叉、礼貌优雅地用餐，以及为四邻营造轻松的氛围。

1.Dress Appropriately 着装得体

Show respect for your host or guests by dressing appropriately. When an invitation specifies a certain type of dress, you should follow it. "White tie" is the most formal evening wear — white tie, wing collar and tailcoat. This is almost never required today, except for official and diplomatic occasions and a rare private ball. For a woman, "white tie" indicates a long gown should be worn. "Black tie" or "formal" is a tuxedo with a soft shirt and bow tie. Jackets may be white in the summer and black the rest of the year, or are available in patterns and many other colors. Women usually wear long dresses, but a short or cocktail-length dress is acceptable. "Semiformal" means women wear dresses or good slacks and men wear sports shirts and slacks. Neither should wear T-shirts or jeans. In some areas, "Semiformal" means dresses for women and suits and ties for men. If in doubt, it is perfectly acceptable for you to check with your hostess.

向主人或来宾表达敬意的方式之一即着装得体。当请柬中特别要求你穿某类衣服时，你应该照做。"整套燕尾服"是晚会上最正式的服装——白领带、尖翻领以及燕尾。现在除了官方、外交场合和极少数家庭舞会之外，几乎不要求此类装束。对于女士来说，与"整套燕尾服"配合的应当是长礼服。"夜常礼服""正式着装"是指无尾夜常礼服，配软质地衬衫，蝴蝶结。在夏天上衣可以是白色的，其他季节可以是黑色的，或者是可供选择的其他式样或颜色。女士通常穿长裙，但是短裙装或鸡尾酒会裙也可以。"半正式服装"是指女士穿的裙装或者合适的便装裤，男士穿的运动衫和便装裤。但绝不能穿 T 恤衫和牛仔裤。在某些地方，"半正式服装"是指女士穿礼服，而男士穿西装打领带。如果你不清楚如何着装，可以打电话向女主人咨询。

2.Be Punctual 准时出席

The impression you make on your business meal companions starts when you first arrive at the restaurant, well before you lift your first utensil. The first rule of table etiquette is to be punctual. Arriving even five or ten minutes late leaves a bad impression; any later than that sends a clear message of carelessness and thoughtlessness.

你留在就餐者心中的印象始于你抵达餐厅的那一刻，早于坐下拿起餐具进餐之时。进餐礼仪的首要规则就是守时。迟到五分钟或十分钟都同样会给对方留下恶劣的印象；迟到时间越长越暴露你的粗心和轻慢。

3.Eat Gracefully 优雅进餐

（1）Posture 身姿

Proper posture at the table is very important. Sit up straight, with your arms held near your body. You should neither lean on the back of the chair nor bend forward to place the elbows on the table. When you are not eating, keep your hands on your lap or resting on the table (with wrists on the edge of the table). Elbows on the table are acceptable only between courses, not while you are eating. It is permissible to lean forward slightly every now and then and press the elbows very lightly against the edge of the table, if it is obvious that you are not using them for support.

在餐桌上保持正确的身姿很重要。坐直，手臂靠近身体。不要向后靠在椅背上，或向前将双肘支在桌上。只有在进餐时才允许手肘接触桌面。偶尔微微向前，手肘不支撑地轻靠桌缘，是被允许的。不用餐时，可将手置于腿上或手腕靠桌放置。

（2）Placing order 点餐

When placing orders, it is best to order food that can be eaten with a knife and fork. Finger food can be messy and is best left for informal dining. Be careful about ordering alcoholic beverages. Becoming tipsy or drunk is inappropriate behavior at business dinners.

点餐时，最好点能用刀叉进食的菜式。手抓食物不雅，最好在非正式宴会中享用。点酒应谨慎。在商务宴请中微醉或大醉是不得体的。

（3）When to start 何时开始进餐

If water is on the table as you are seated, it is appropriate to sip your water after everyone is seated and after you have placed your napkin in your lap. For other beverages and foods, wait until everyone has been served, and do not eat until your host/hostess has begun; when your host picks up his/her fork, this is an indicator that you may do so. Do not help yourself to the bread basket and other communal foods until your host has indicated you may do so. If you pick up the bread basket, hold the basket and offer to the person to your left, then serve yourself, and then pass the basket to the person on your right. (Same applies to butter, salad dressings, and other condiments that are passed.) The host/hostess may ask you to start eating and you should comply with the request.

如就座时餐桌上有水，在所有宾客就座，腿上铺好餐巾后，可先喝水。至于其他饮料和食物，则要等到所有宾客的菜上齐，主人开始进食时才可享用；主人拿起叉子，表明你可照做。在主人示意前，不可拿取面包和其他公用食物。拿面包篮时，应先递给左手边的人，再自己拿，之后递给右手边的人（这种拿取食物的顺序同样适用于黄油、色拉调料及其他调味品的传递）。如果男主人或女主人请你开始进餐，照做。

（4）Bread 面包

Bread/rolls should never be eaten whole. Eat rolls or bread by tearing off small bite size pieces rather than bringing a big piece of food to your mouth and then tearing a bite off with your teeth. Butter only the piece you are preparing to eat. When ready for another piece, repeat the same process.

面包 / 面包卷等不应整块食用。吃面包等时，应撕成小块，而不要送大片面包到嘴边再用牙齿撕下一片。只在要吃的那片面包上涂黄油。吃下一片时，再重复同样程序。

（5）Salad 色拉

It is suggested to cut the salad if the lettuce pieces are too large. Cut a few bites at a time; don't slice and dice the entire salad at once. It is preferable to cut large salad pieces than to attempt to stuff large bites of food in your mouth.

如生菜叶较大，可切分。每次切几片，不要一次将整个生菜切分完。将大块的生菜切成小块，而不要将大块的菜塞入嘴中。

（6）Soup 汤

When eating soup, think of making a circle: spoon away from you, bring around to your mouth and back to the bowl. Soup is taken from the side of the soup spoon—it is not inserted into your mouth. Do not slurp or make noises when eating soup. Rest your spoon periodically. When a service plate under the soup bowl is provided, always place your spoon on the service plate behind the bowl. If no service plate is provided, obviously you rest your spoon in the soup bowl. Used utensils are never placed on the table. Sip quietly. If your soup is too hot, wait until it cools; do not blow on it.

喝汤时，想象在画一个圆：舀汤时勺子离开自己，再送回嘴边，再回到汤碗里。从汤勺一侧喝汤，不要放到嘴里。喝汤时，不要喷喷作声或发出声响。不时地放下勺子。如汤碗下有辅助餐盘，将勺子放在餐盘上。如无餐盘，将勺子放在汤碗里。用过的餐具是不能放在餐桌上的。喝汤不要出声。如汤太烫，待冷却再喝，不要吹。

（7）Main course 主菜

Cut only one or two pieces of meat at a time to prevent cooling or losing the flavor. Resist the temptation to cut up the whole thing all at once.

吃肉时，每次只切一两块，以免肉变凉，失去原有风味。不要一次将肉全部切完。

（8）Common sense of dining etiquette 餐饮礼仪常识

It is important to know how to conduct oneself properly at the table. The rules of dining etiquette are fairly straightforward and mostly require common sense.

知道如何在餐桌上举止得体是很重要的。餐饮礼仪通常是直白的，要求的是常识。

① Napkin 餐巾

When dining with others place your napkin on your lap after everyone at your table has been seated. Do not open your napkin in mid-air. As you remove your napkin from the table, open it below the table level and place it on your lap. If you must leave a meal, do so between courses, and place your napkin on your chair or to the left of your plate. When a meal is completed, place your napkin to the right of your plate—never on the plate.

一同进餐时，等各位宾客就座后，可将餐巾铺于腿上。不要在空中展开餐巾。从桌上拿起餐巾，在桌面以下展开，铺于腿上。如在用餐中途离开，应选在两道菜之间，并将餐巾放于座椅上或餐盘左边。当用餐完毕时，将餐巾放于餐盘右边，不要放在餐盘上。

② Passing 传递

Pass "community food" such as the breadbasket, salt and pepper, and salad dressing to the right. Always pass the salt and pepper together. When passing items such as a creamer, syrup pitcher or gravy boat, pass it with the handle pointing toward the recipient.

向右传递像面包篮、盐、胡椒、色拉调料等共用食品。盐和胡椒一定要一同传递。在传递乳罐、糖罐或调味瓶时，应将把手朝向接受者。

③ Seasoning 调味

Always taste your food first before using any seasonings. Do not assume it needs to be seasoned as it is disrespect for the cook.

应在品尝过食物后再用调料。勿自以为是地调味，这是对厨师的不尊重。

④ Utensils 餐具

Be careful how you hold your utensils. Many people tend to make a fist around the handle of the utensil—this is the way a young child would grasp a utensil (not an adult). There are two acceptable ways to use the knife and fork: continental fashion and American standard. Continental fashion—the diner cuts the food usually one bite at a time and uses the fork in the left hand, tines pointing down, to spear the food and bring it to the mouth. American standard—a few bites are cut, the knife is laid across the top of the plate, sharp edge toward you, and the fork is switched from the left hand to the right hand, if right-handed, tines up to bring the food to the mouth. Do not cut more than two or three bites at a time.

拿餐具时应小心。很多人会把手指捏成拳头握住餐具——这是儿童抓餐具的方式，而非成人。使用刀叉时，有两种方式可以接受：欧式和美式。欧式——用餐者每次只切一块肉，一直左手持叉，叉齿向下，叉中食物，送至嘴中。美式——每次切下几块肉，然后将餐刀放在餐盘顶部，刀齿朝自己，如果是惯用右手的，将叉子从左手换到右手，叉齿朝上，将食物送至嘴中。每次切肉不要超过两三块。

When you're taking a break, signal the servers that you are still eating by placing your fork and knife in an inverted V on your plate from the 10 to 4 o'clock positions. When you are finished, put them diagonally on the plate, side by side. The knife blade should face the center of the plate, not point out toward another guest.

用餐间歇时，可将刀叉按10点到4点方向摆成"八"字形，示意你还在用餐。如果已结束用餐，则将刀叉并排按对角线摆放。刀锋应朝向盘子中心，而不要对着旁边的宾客。

4.Talk Pleasantly 愉快交谈

An experienced and thoughtful host realizes that the key point is that the bonds forged at a meal can last long after the check has been paid. One of the benefits of a business meal is the chance it offers participants to get to know each other better, personally as well as professionally, and so leaves plenty of time for non-business talk as well. As a co-founder *Zagat Survey Restaurant Guides*, Nina Zagat is a skilled guide to the unwritten rules of business meals. She draws no rigid boundaries when it comes to conversation. "Start off with a nice conversation, find out what people are interested in," she suggests. "Be careful of coming across as pushy. If there are points you want to discuss, don't throw them on the table right at the beginning," she says. Therefore, when you are dining do make small talks so that your guests feel comfortable and at ease.

富有经验、考虑周详的主人意识到，饭桌上重要的是促进双方友谊延续长久。进餐的一个好处是让进餐者从生活上或工作角度增进了解，因此大量的时间应花在非商务的谈话上。作为《查格餐厅调查指南》的共同创始人，妮娜·查格熟知商务餐不成文的法则。她认为商务餐桌上的话题没有死板的规定。"展开一个愉快的话题，找到来宾的兴趣所在。"她建议，"切忌过于急迫，如果有事要商谈，也不要在刚开始用餐时就摆到桌面上。"因此，用餐时，要用闲聊的方式让宾客愉悦放松。

Determining what topics of conversation are appropriate for which situations, with which people, is an important element of successful business communication. Topics are likely to be the weather, sports, common interests and acquaintances, and current affairs. Steer clear of topics relate to religion, sex or personal problems when you make social conversations. Remember the sharing of gossip and crude jokes should not be practiced in such situations.

选择在何种场合和谁谈什么话题，对成功的商务交流很关键。话题可以是天气、体育、共同的爱好和熟人，以及时事。社交谈话中避免涉及宗教、性、隐私。这种场合也不适合聊八卦和开粗俗的玩笑。

5.Chinese Banquet Etiquette 中国餐饮礼仪

Through thousands of years of evolution, Chinese dining etiquette has continued to develop, albeit always with one foot in the traditions of the past.

经过几千年的演变，中国的餐饮礼仪虽然仍在不断发展，但一直带有古老文化的印记。

（1）Seating 座次

In China, it's necessary to know how to pick up your seat at the table. Different from the western, tables in China are usually round. Normally, seat facing the door is for the host or the hostess. At a small table, the seat right across of the host seat, the back which is facing the door, is the seat for the main guest. But when it's a bigger table, the host or hostess and main guest can just sit side by side to make it easier for them to talk.

在中国，座次是很有讲究的。不同于西式餐桌，中式餐桌通常是圆桌。面向门的座位一般是给男女主人的。如果餐桌较小，主人对面背对门的座位要留给贵宾。如是大餐桌，男主人或女主人和贵宾可并肩而坐，这样便于交谈。

（2）Tea 茶

Before dinner, you'll be served by a cup of tea. Tea is for rinsing the mouth, which means making your mouth ready for eating.

进餐前，会为每位来宾奉上一杯茶。以茶漱口，准备好用餐。

（3）Tableware 餐具

Different from the west, Chinese food is usually cut into proper sizes when cooking, so you don't have to use folks or knives to eat them. As a result, you'll use different tableware when you enjoy Chinese food. Chopsticks are the main tool for eating. Chopsticks should always be held correctly, i.e. between the thumb and first two fingers of the right hand. Chopsticks are traditionally held in the right hand only, even for the left-handed. One explanation for the treatment of such usage as improper is that within the confines of a round table this may be inconvenient.

不同于西餐，中餐烹饪时已将食物切割成便于进食的大小，所以不需要再用刀叉分切。因此，中餐会使用不同的餐具。筷子是主要的餐具。筷子的拿法要正确，即用右手的拇指和两根手指夹住筷子。筷子通常只用右手拿，惯用左手者也须遵循。这是考虑到围坐圆桌，避免相互打搅。

（4）Food 菜品

If you are being treated by a Chinese host, be prepared for a ton of food. Chinese are very proud of their culture of food and will do their best to give you a taste of many different types of cuisine. If it is a business dinner or a very formal occasion, there is likely to be a huge amount of food that will be impossible to finish. A typical Chinese meal consists of: cold dishes, main courses, soup, the starchy "staple" food, snack and dessert, fruit.

如果参加中式宴请，应该做好迎接丰富菜品的准备。中国人以饮食文化自豪，会尽可能让来宾品尝到各种中餐菜式。如果是商务宴请或隆重庆典，很有可能所上的菜品根本享用不完。典型的中式宴席包括冷盘、主菜、汤、主食、甜点和水果等。

（5）Table manners 餐桌礼仪

Generally, Chinese table manners are more informal than the West, although there are more rules concerning interactions with other guests. People in China tend to over-order food, different from the west, for they will find it embarrassing if all the food is consumed. When you have had enough, just say so, or you will always overeat.

相对而言，中餐餐桌礼仪没有西方那么严格，更多考虑的是便于宾客之间交流。不同于西餐，中餐人们喜欢菜肴丰富，如果餐桌所有食物已吃得荡然无存，主人就会感到尴尬。所以如果你在中国就餐，如果已吃饱，一定要说已经吃好了，否则饮食一定会过量。

（6）Drinks & Toast 饮酒和敬酒

Drinks play an important role in Chinese food culture. Usually, both hard drink and beverage are served throughout the meal. It is customary for the host to insist that guests drink to show friendship. If the guests prefer not to drink, they may say, "I'm unable to drink, but thank you." The host may continue to insist that the guests drink, and the guests may likewise continue to insist upon being "unable" to drink. The host's insistence is to show generosity. Therefore, refusal by the guests should be made with utmost politeness.

酒在中国饮食文化中有着重要的地位。一般，中餐桌上会同时上酒和饮料。主人会劝酒，以增加情谊。如果来宾不欲饮酒，可说："谢谢，我不会喝。"主人会继续劝酒，客人可同样拒绝。主人劝酒是出于好客，所以来宾拒绝时也应礼貌周全。

During the meal, we make toasts to make a friendly atmosphere. Toast means clink the rim of each other's glasses and saying "gan bei". Usually, the hosts propose a toast to all the guests and every one "gan bei" together.

席间为营造友好氛围，可以为宾客敬酒。敬酒时，轻碰杯缘，齐道"干杯"。一般，敬酒由主人发起，用餐者一起说"干杯"。

Situational practice for etiquettes 礼仪口语实景

Make up or search for more situational conversations that may occur during the business dinner and put them into practice.

Model

(President A invites the foreign guests B to a dinner as a welcoming ceremony.)

A: Please take your seats, ladies and gentlemen, and make yourselves comfortable. For honored guests, we usually arrange the menu in advance and we hope that our selection of dishes this evening will be to your liking.

B: We have heard a great deal about the famous Chinese dishes and we are looking forward to tasting them.

A: This is Shaoxing Huadiao wine, one of our favorite wines in China. We are quite proud of its quality. I hope you like it.

B: It tastes good. While we were in Beijing last summer, I had the chance to taste Maotai. It was really wonderful. I can still smell it.

A: I'm so glad that you like Chinese wines. Here, let me propose a toast to our future co-operation and to our guests' health.

B: Thank you very much for preparing such a sumptuous banquet for us today. I propose a toast to the health of everyone here and to the future success of our negotiations.

A: Here are the Chinese cold dishes. Please help yourselves and choose what you like.

B: Every time I came to China, I was greatly impressed by the Chinese people's hospitality.

 Terminology related 相关礼仪术语

Business Dinner Invitations 商务宴请邀请

Whether you're inviting colleagues to a business dinner, or have received an invitation for such an event, it's important to know how etiquette can help you to make a good impression with co-workers. Submitting and responding to the invitations in a timely manner is essential.

无论你是邀请同事参加商务宴会，还是收到类似邀请，都有必要了解怎样才礼貌得体，以给同行们留下好印象。及时发出和回复邀请也是基本礼节之一。

RSVP

请即回复

It is proper etiquette to respond to the business dinner invitation on or before the date indicated on the invitation. It is also important to confirm attendance in the matter that is detailed on the invitation. Even if no RSVP is requested on the invitation, it is best to confirm attendance via phone or e-mail.

礼貌的做法是在受邀时或之后回复。如邀请卡上注明，应确认出席。即使邀请卡上未注明"请即回复"，最好也用电话或电邮的方式确认出席。

Changing Attendance Status

更改出席状况

Once a guest has confirmed his or her attendance for the business dinner, it is acceptable to respectfully decline the invitation if there is illness or death in the family. If there is another emergency on the same evening as the dinner that the guest can not get out of, it is proper etiquette to notify the host as soon as possible, and to offer apologies for not being able to attend.

来宾确认出席后，如果又因家庭成员生病或过世而谢绝邀请，是可以接受的。如果在受邀请当晚，来宾有其他急事无法脱身，应尽快告知主人，并为自己未能赴宴致歉。

Information to Include

应注明的信息

When inviting colleagues to a business dinner, inform them the entire address of the location where the dinner will take place. This will make it easier for guests to find driving directions to the location, so that the proper amount of time can be allotted for travel (it is considered impolite to show up late for a business dinner). The time and date of the dinner stated be clearly stated on the invitation (usually in the center), as well as the company that is hosting the dinner, if applicable.

在邀请同事赴宴时，应告知宴请的详细地址。这样方便来宾明了驱车方向，以合理安排路上的时间（商务宴请迟到会被认为不礼貌）。时间、地点以及举办宴请公司名应清楚地标在邀请卡上（应位于中心）。

Addressing Invitations

邀请卡上的称呼

It is proper etiquette to send hand-written addressed envelopes to colleagues with the invitation inside—this is the case even if the invitation has been professionally printed. The address should ideally be written in cursive and should acknowledge everyone who is invited to the dinner. For instance, if you have invited a colleague and his wife, it is best to address the invitation "Mr. and Mrs. John Smith." When inviting doctors or judges to the dinner, using the person's honorific, Dr. or Honorable, is appropriate.

信封上称呼应该手写，并内置邀请卡——这也适用于专业印刷的邀请卡。地址可用草写体，而且要向每一位来宾致谢。例如，邀请同事和他的妻子，即在邀请卡上写道："约翰史密斯先生及夫人。"当邀请医生或法官时，应用敬语。

Sending Invitations

发送邀请

Business dinner invitations can be sent to the home of the colleague who is being invited, particularly if the colleague's spouse also has been asked to the dinner. It is also acceptable to mail the invitation to the colleague's place of work, especially if the professional has a private mailbox. If a co-worker is inviting everyone in his or her department to the dinner, it is appropriate to hand-deliver the invitations.

商务宴请卡可寄送到被邀请人家中，这种情况适合对方的妻子也在被邀请之列。寄送到对方的工作场所也可以，如果对方是专业人士，可寄到他的私人邮箱。如果邀请部门所有同事赴宴，最好亲手递交邀请卡到他们手上。

Useful expressions for etiquettes 礼仪用语集锦

The followings are appropriate expressions you may use during the business dinner:

❑ Inviting 邀请

Would you like to come to my housewarming party tomorrow night?

您是否方便参加明晚在我家举行的乔迁晚会？

I was wondering if you felt like spending the holiday with us?

我冒昧邀请您和我们一起度假。

❑ Accepting or declining 接受或拒绝邀请

It's a pleasure. /I'd love to. /That sounds terrific.

乐意参加。/ 听起来不错。

It's nice of you to ask, but I don't think I can.

感谢您的邀请，但我恐怕难以赴约。

I'm awfully sorry. But can't we make it another time?

我很抱歉不能前去。我们可以再约个时间吗？

❑ Persisting with invitation 坚持邀请

Are you sure you can't? I promise it'll be fun.

您真不能来吗？ 我保证一定会很有意思的。

❑ Reserving or finding a table for dinner 预约或找餐位

1.A: Have you got a table for seven, please?

请问，有七人桌吗？

B: I'm sorry, but the restaurant is full now. There will be a wait of about half an hour. Would you care to have a drink in the lounge while you wait? I'll let you know the moment we have a vacant table.

抱歉，本店现已客满。您需要大约半个小时的等位。等位期间您在休息区喝杯饮料好吗？一有空位我会立刻通知您的。

2. A: Waitress, is this table free/taken？

服务员，我们可以坐这张桌吗？

B: Sorry, this table has been booked. Would you mind sharing the table with that man?

抱歉，这张桌已被预订。您介意和那位男士同桌就餐吗？

A: I'd prefer sit alone.

我还是一个人坐吧。

❑　Offering help with a menu 点餐服务

Would you like me to explain some local dishes to you?

我为您介绍一些地方菜好吗？

Would you like me to help you with the menu?

您需要我给您介绍菜单吗？

❑　Recommending food 推荐菜品

1.A: What do you suggest/recommend?

您有什么推荐的吗？

B: What about/you could try Mapo Douf. It's very delicious.

您可以品尝一下麻婆豆腐。非常美味。

A: What is it?

麻婆豆腐是什么？

B: It's beancurd cooked with minced beef in chili sauce.

是用辣椒酱浇上牛肉末烧豆腐。

A: OK, I'll try that./No, I think I prefer something sweet.

好吧，我就尝尝这个吧。/ 我还是来点甜品吧。

❑　Taking orders 接受点餐

May I take your order now?

您现在可以点餐吗？

Would you like to order?

您现在点餐吗？

❑ Ordering food 点餐

1.A: What shall we order?

我们点什么菜呢?

B: How about some local specialties ?

吃点地方特色菜如何?

2.A: I'd like a steak and a chicken soup.

我想来份牛排和鸡汤。

B: How would you like your steak cooked/done?

牛排几成熟?

A: Medium/rare/ well-done, please.

六成熟。/ 三成熟。/ 九成熟。

3.A: You aren't a vegetarian, are you?

您是素食者吗?

B: No, I love meat.

不是，我喜欢吃肉。

❑ Commenting on dishes 评论菜品

1.A: How is the taste?

味道如何?

B: It smells good/looks great/tastes delicious.

闻起来香。/ 看起来诱人。/ 吃起来美味。

2.I've never had such tasty food before.

我从没吃过如此美味。

3.Sichuan food is too hot for me. My mouth is burning.

川菜对我来说太辣了。我吃的嘴火烧火燎的。

4.This dish tastes kind of salty/sour/greasy/stale.

这道菜有点咸 / 酸 / 腻 / 不新鲜。

5.The soup is too heavily seasoned.

这道汤味太重，放料太多了。

6.The beef is too tough and the fish is too raw.

这道牛肉太老，鱼太生。

❑ Proposing a toast 祝酒

1.Cheers!

干杯!

2.I'd like to propose/ May I propose a toast to our friendship and friendly cooperation/to our distinguished American guests?

这杯酒敬我们尊贵的美国来宾。祝我们相处愉快，合作顺利。

3.Let's drink to your health/promotion/success/a pleasant trip to New York/a successful new year.

为您的健康 / 晋升 / 成功 / 纽约之行愉快 / 新年进步干杯!

❑　　Asking for the menu/bill 要菜单 / 账单

1.Waitress, can you please bring me the menu/bill/check?

服务员，请把菜单 / 账单 / 发票拿来。

2.A: What is it for?

这是什么费用?

B: Service charge, 10% of the total amount.

服务费。餐费的 10%。

❑　　Paying for the meal 付账

1.It's on me./It's my treat./You are my guest./Let me get the bill./Let me do the honors.

我请客。

2.Let's go Dutch./Let's split the bill.

我们各付各的吧。

❑　　Dinner talks 餐桌闲谈

1.Make yourself at home./Help yourself to whatever you like.

把这儿当家好了。 / 想吃什么自己来，随意。

2.Would you like to try some? / Would you like some more to drink?

你想喝点什么?

No. thanks. I'm a bit tipsy.

不用，谢谢。有点醉了。

3.I've had (more than) enough./ I'm too full to eat any more./Oh, I'm so full. I have no room for dessert.

我吃饱了。甜食吃不下了。

4.I can't reach that dish. Could you turn around the turn table?

那道菜我够不着。方便转一下转盘吗?

5.She's a vegetarian while he's a teetotaler.

她是素食者，而他是禁酒者。

❑ Talking about cooking 谈论烹饪

1.Chinese food is characterized by its color, aroma and flavor.

中国菜以色、香、味著称。

2.Guangdong, Sichuan, Shandong and Jiangsu cuisine are the four most famous Chinese cuisine.

粤菜、川菜、鲁菜、苏菜是中国四大菜系。

3.Cantonese cuisine is noted for/known for/famous for raw, lightly-cooked foods preserving the original flavor.

粤菜以清淡生食著称，力求保存原味。

❑ Explaining the ways of cooking 介绍烹饪方式

1.Mix the minced pork with the chopped cabbage, garlic and onion, and add a spoonful of sugar, a little salt, a bit of gourmet powder and pepper.

将肉末和白菜末、蒜末、葱末搅拌在一起，加一勺糖、少许盐、味精和胡椒粉。

2.Cut the meat in small pieces.

把肉切成丝。

3.Marinate the fish in cooking wine and soy sauce for ten minutes, then sprinkle salt and white pepper on it.

先将鱼在料酒和酱油中浸泡十分钟，然后用盐和白胡椒腌上。

4.Rub the chicken all over with honey for several minutes.

在鸡肉上抹上蜂蜜，持续几分钟。

5.Stir-fry the beef with celery for about five minutes.

旺火炒牛肉和芹菜大约五分钟。

6.Simmer the spare ribs over low heat for half an hour.

用文火炖排骨半小时。

7.Slice the duck, add the chopped garlic and serve with the sauce.

片好鸭肉，加上蒜末，浇上汁。

Exercises（课后练习）

I. Questions and answers: answer the following questions according to the information you have got in the previous reading.

1.What is the purpose of business dinners? What do we do to ensure the success of a business meal?

2.Is breakfast a suitable time to discuss the business? Why?

3.Why do we pay attention to the table manners? What are the general ones?

4.How do we arrange the seats in a western business dinner? Are there any differences from Chinese dinner?

5.Are there any rules we can observe when setting a tale in a western business dinner?

II. *Expressions: match the terms in column A with the chinese equivalents in column B.*

A	B
service plate	鱼刀
butter plate	牛排刀
dinner fork	沙拉叉
fish fork	黄油刀
salad fork	主菜用叉
dinner knife	汤匙
fish knife	鱼叉
soup spoon	黄油盘
butter knife	座席盘或辅助盘
water goblet	红酒杯
champagne flute	高脚水杯
red wine glass	雪莉酒杯
sherry glass	餐巾
napkin	香槟杯

III.*Translation: translate the following statements into chinese to ensure to stay away from bad table manners.*

1.It is inappropriate to ask for a doggy bag when you are a guest. Save the doggy bag for informal dining situations.

2.Sit up straight at the table. It makes a good impression.

3.When eating, never chew with your mouth open or make loud noises when you eat. Although it is possible to talk with a small piece of food in your mouth, do not talk with your mouth full.

4.If food gets caught between your teeth and you can't remove it with your tongue, leave the table and go to a mirror where you can remove the food from your teeth in private.

5.Do not smoke during a meal or when others are eating.

6.You should not leave the table during the meal except in an emergency. If you must go to the bathroom or if you suddenly become sick, simply excuse yourself. Later you can apologize to the host by saying that you didn't feel well.

7. Never spit a piece of bad food or tough gristle into your napkin. Remove the food from your mouth using the same utensil it went in with. Place the piece of food on the edge of your plate. If possible, cover it with some other food from your plate.

8. Do not use your napkin to wipe your nose. If you wipe your nose, don't put the used tissues on the table.

9. If a piece of your cutlery falls onto the floor, pick it up if you can reach it and let the server know you need a clean one. If you cannot reach it, tell the server you dropped a piece of your cutlery and ask for a clean one.

10. If food spills off your plate, you may pick it up with a piece of your cutlery and place it on the edge of your plate.

IV. Cloze: choose the suitable items from the box and complete the passage.

A. vegetables	B. red wine	C. liqueur	D. main course
E. appetizers	F. soup	G. cheese with bread	
H. salad	I. beer	J. dessert	

In United States, for dinner, I'd like to take our customers out to a nice steak restaurant. Generally, we'll start with a cocktail. Recently, _____1_____ has become quite popular before-dinner drink. When ordering, in addition to the _____2_____ and dessert, I like to order one or two _____3_____.

One of my favorites is deep-fried squid. Usually the main course comes with a _____4_____ and salad and one or two _____5_____. I usually have white coffee with _____6_____ although sometimes I'll have a _____7_____ or some brandy.

In England, We usually take visitors out for a "pub lunch" somewhere near the office. It's an old-style pub and it's very popular with visitors to England. The food, like most English food, is generally not very good, I'm afraid, but the "Ploughman's lunch" isn't bad. It's _____8_____, pickles and _____9_____. It tastes delicious in summer with a pint of __10___, especially if the weather is nice and we are able to sit outside.

V.Case study:Study the following talk to find out how to behave properly in a business dinner and discuss with your partners.

Situation: Chen Hao (C) works in a USA Company in Beijing and chats with his American colleague (A) during having afternoon tea.

A: Chen Hao, you've been attending a lot of business dinners lately. Didn't your team go out again last night with the clients?

C: Yeah. My boss, Mr. Brown entertained the clients in the newly-opened French restaurant nearby.

A: How did it go?

C: The dishes were tasty. But one of the clients behaved inappropriately.

A: What do you mean?

C: First, the dishes she ordered were the most expensive ones on the menu.

A: What did the others do?

C: The rest people ordered moderately priced ones. So did I.

A: This client sounds as if she could take some business etiquette training. Unless Mr. Brown suggested that you all order certain pricey dishes, she should have chosen something moderately priced.

C: I agree. Unless the host insists, people usually don't do this.

A: It's rude to take advantage of your host like that. This client is not very savvy about business dining.

C: What does savvy mean?

A: Savvy means having knowledge and experience.

C: The client is impolite. It's more than that.

A: So there is more to this story?

C: That guest not only ordered the dearest one, but didn't miss any course.

A: Like what?

C: Start with the soup, then the starter, salad, main course and dessert all.

A: What did everyone else do?

C: Mr. Brown ate little, but finished one course after another with her.

A: He was doing the correct thing as host by ordering the same as the client.

C: Does a host have to do like this?

A: When someone orders appetizers or other dishes in addition to the entrée, it is polite for others to order the same courses.

C: Why?

A: That keeps the pace of the dinner even and avoids the awkwardness of one person eating a course by herself.

C: So it would be embarrassing for her to have soup if others didn't order the same course.

A: At an informal dinner, some people have soup while others may select a different appetizer to have at the same time. Everyone should have an equal number of courses.

C: What can a host do to help?

A: Simple. The host can say, "Why don't we all have an appetizer?" Or he could ask, "Would anyone like something to start with?"

C: Then you can see whether you are the only one to have the starter.

A: Right. If no one else has a starter course, then you don't either.

C: It seems that the guest has a lot to learn.

 Extension（拓展阅读）

How to Charm and Do Business over Dinner

Navigating a business dinner can be complicated, but a successful evening out will solidify any business relationship. Nina Zagat, who co-founded Zagat Survey restaurant guides, has dined out several times a week at New York's best restaurants for more than 30 years, and she is a skilled guide to the unwritten rules of such meals.

The main goal for Ms. Zagat is for the person with whom she is dining—whether it's a colleague or a potential business partner—to leave the meal knowing more about who she is as a person. "The feeling that (all) people should come away with at the end of the business dinner is one that they've had a really nice conversation, met interesting people and had a good time," says the 68-year-old, who owns the restaurant-guide business with her husband Tim. "That's sort of the home run."

Before choosing a restaurant, Ms. Zagat finds out about her fellow diners' food and location preferences. "Think about who your guests are going to be," says Ms. Zagat, who often visits restaurants like Jean Georges near her Midtown office.

Since restaurant dining rooms can be loud, she suggests seeking out places where diners don't need to strain to carry on a conversation. Look for restaurants with tables placed far apart or with several smaller dining rooms, instead of one large space.

For larger groups, Ms. Zagat likes round tables, which feel "inclusive", and prefers not to sit at the head of a very long table. When being seated, the host or hostess should ask the guest of honor or business partner to sit on his or her right side, she says. And when dining a deux, she says, just ask your dining partner which seat he or she would like.

When ordering, Ms. Zagat has one key rule: "At a business dinner, you're not trying to draw a lot of attention to yourself and what you're eating," she says. A pet peeve she cites is when others are not discreet about their food allergies or other dietary restrictions when eating or ordering.

Since food shouldn't become the focus of the evening, she avoids dishes that are complicated to eat such as lobster and spaghetti, and she says it's all right, if you're not hungry, to request half-portions or to offer to share appetizers or dessert.

In a similar vein, if she is the first person to finish her entree, she won't let a waiter take the plate until her dining companions are finished. If the other diners aren't ordering tea or dessert, she'll skip the last course. And if she leaves the room momentarily, Ms. Zagat discreetly leaves her napkin on the chair, rather than displaying it—and its possible food spots—on the table.

Ordering the most expensive bottles of wine could also draw unwanted attention, coming off as showy, Ms. Zagat says. Asking the sommelier to recommend a low to midrange bottle is your best bet. "Even at dinner last night," we said "Can you recommend a wine that's not more than X' and gave some other qualifications," she says.

She draws no rigid boundaries when it comes to conversation. She even talks about politics, as long as the conversation doesn't get heated. One kind of communication, however, is discouraged. While she believes taking out a mobile device to read notes or refer to an email is acceptable, she never leaves her phone on the table or lets it ring.

Ms. Zagat likes to chitchat until she's well into a meal, rather than turning to business-related topics right away. Start off "with a nice conversation, find out what people are interested in," she suggests. Be careful of coming across as pushy. "If there are points you want to discuss, don't throw them on the table right at the beginning," she says.

At the same time, Ms. Zagat never waits until dessert to bring up serious business matters. She wants the night to end on a casual note: "The most important thing is to have a relaxed time," she says.

(http://cn.wsj.com/gb/20110207/trv100112_ENversion.shtml)

After-reading tasks（读后任务）

When you finish reading the text above, get into the groups and discuss with your group members about the following tasks and fulfill them.

Task 1

After you have finished reading this article, you must have benefited a lot from the practices mentioned. To facilitate the application of the principles scattered in the passage, it is best to make a table to take notes. Do it now and share with your group members to see who has got the most efficient way to transform the information got from reading.

Task 2

To ensure a successful business dinner, the host has to do a lot of preparations and pay much attention to the details and manners as we can see from the text. Think of your past experiences, have you got any successful or frustrating ones? Share with the group and the group leader tend to get the group to discuss about them and learn from them.

Task 3

Ms. Zagat assumes that food shouldn't become the focus of the evening and she gives more suggestions about the food choice. Imagine you are going to entertain some foreign guests, what will you choose from a variety of Chinese food. Try to work together with your group members and make the menu for the dinner you have to get ready for. If you like, you can pick out some local dishes of your hometown and explain why you think they are suitable.

✎ Self-study（自学反馈）

If possible, summarize what you have learned in this unit with the help of the following table.

Focus of this unit:
Guidelines for etiquette: 1. 2. 3. ...
Summary:

Application:

1.

2.

3.

...

Feedback:

Chapter Six
Job Application And Interview
求职与面试礼仪

Objectives（学习目标）

After this chapter, you should be able to:

❑ Have a command of the writing skills of resumes and application letters
❑ Define the differences between chronological resumes and functional resumes
❑ Understand how to be more appropriate while we are attending an interview

Lead-in（导读）

If you are an interviewee, surely you want to get help from this chapter and succeed in the coming interviews. However, have you experienced or heard about these? How many times are candidates kept waiting in the lobby only to be interviewed by someone who hasn't even reviewed their resume yet? Or, the phone rings during the interview or they're interrupted constantly making the interviewer clearly distracted? A well-prepared interviewee deserves a professional interviewer. So before we instruct the interviewees what to do first, we would like to send a few words to the interviewers and remind them that employers should be selling the candidate as much as they're being sold. The interview is a time for the company to make an impression on a candidate, as well. A candidate is like a guest in your home or a customer—whether you hire them or not. Candidates are members of our communities, consumers and even potential customers. In addition, they have taken time out of their day to consider employment with your company and deserve the respect of your attention and professionalism. Think about the common guidelines for candidates and turn them around to apply to the employer: dress professionally; be on time; be prepared; greet the interviewer; respond to interview questions; follow up.

Finally, when the interviewer rolls out the red carpet and puts his or her company's best face forward, it is the interviewee's turn to come to the stage and try to be at your best and win what you deserve to have. If both are ready, let's begin.

作为一名面试者，通过对本章的学习，肯定能获得帮助，从而成功通过面试。不过，你经历过或听说过以下场景吧？求职者经过长时间的等待，终于等到面试机会，而面试官连简历都没看就草率收场；或是面试期间电话突然响起，面试者的介绍被不断打断，注意力分散。一位有准备的面试者应该面对一位专业的面试官。因此，在我们指导面试者如何为面试做好准备前，我们想对面试官说几句话。面试官应该像求职者一样推介自己。求职者通过面试对公司形成印象，因此，从商务礼仪角度讲，不管是否雇用对方，公司都应该把求职者当作客人或客户来对待。从某种角度讲，求职者是社会成员、消费者或潜在的客户。求职者拿出时间来公司求职是应该得到公司的尊重和专业对待的。适用于求职者的准则也适用于雇佣方：着装得体；守时；做好准备；问候面试官；回应面试问题；跟进。

当面试官铺好红地毯，展现出公司最佳的形象时，就该面试者登场了。拿出最好的状态，赢得你意向中的职位。如果双方都准备好了，那么我们开始学习吧。

Test yourself（自我测试）

When finishing reading the interview conversation, please use Yes or No to make responses to the following statements to see whether you have mastered the successful interview skills.

1. It is rewarding to spend a few minutes taking care of the details before attending an interview.   Yes ☐ No ☐

2. Non-verbal communications can be the deciding factor in leaving the first impression.   Yes ☐ No ☐

3. Small talk can be omitted as it is a waste of time during an interview.   Yes ☐ No ☐

4. It is not wise to disclose your weaknesses, so try to steer clear of the questions   Yes ☐ No ☐

5. To show your respect and politeness, never be an initiator during the interview   Yes ☐ No ☐

Part I　Resumes and Application Letters
个人简历与求职信

As you prepare to fax, e-mail, or post your resume to the company which you apply for, face up to a blunt reality: in today's time-conscious world, people are looking for reasons to dispose of it. The person who receives your resume is under no obligation to actually read it or respond—and is all the less likely to if it's not well presented or contains a misspelled word. To lessen the chance of your resume being directed toward the wastebasket or deleted with the click of a mouse, you should make it easy to read, to-the-point, and error-free.

The cover letter you send along with your resume should also be limited to a single page.

This cover letter is actually a letter of application—and it needs to be a well-crafted piece of salesmanship that separates you from the pack. While your resume effectively telegraphs the bare bones of who you are and what you are seeking, the letter allows you to expand on how your background makes you a good fit for a specific company or job.

在你准备把简历通过传真、电子邮件或邮局发送到你申请的公司时，一定会面对这样一种残酷的现实：在今天这个时间就是金钱的世界里，人们都是在千方百计地以最快的速度把事情处理掉，收到你的简历的人实际上没有义务来阅读或回复——如果你的简历没有表达清楚或其中有错别字，就更不可能使对方产生兴趣。所以为了减少简历被直接扔进垃圾桶或是鼠标一点就被删除的可能，一定要让自己的简历容易读懂，直奔主题，同时要避免一切错误。

随同简历一起发送的信件应该限制在一页纸的范围之内，这实际上是一封申请信——必须艺术地组织语言，这是一种推销术，使自己的简历从千万份简历中脱颖而出。如果你在简历上已经清楚地说明了你是谁，在寻找什么样的工作的话，申请信可以让你扩展自己的经历和背景，这些经历和背景决定着你是否能够胜任这份工作。

1.Preparation of the Resume 准备履历

（1）Basic requirements 基本要求

① Be brief and easy to read 简练易读

For all the attention that goes into creating a resume (ideally, it should be tailored to the desired job), the end product should be short and concise—one page or, if you have extensive work experience, two. A "quick take" shows consideration of the reader's time, a fundamental of business etiquette.

制作简历的时候一定要调动起自己的全部注意力（理想的简历应该是为自己想要申请的工作岗位量身定做，精心设计），最终的作品应该是简短精悍的——最好是一页，如果你的经历很多的话，可以写两页。一览无余的简历其实正显示了你对阅读者时间的考虑，这是最基本的商务礼仪。

② Be to the point and attractive 切中要点，引人注意

Illustrate your skills and abilities by relating your specific accomplishments instead of merely listing the jobs you held.

用具体的作品来阐述你的技术和能力，而不要仅仅列出以前做过的工作。

③ Be honest 要诚实

Make certain your resume and cover letter are completely accurate and a true reflection of your experiences. This is a cardinal rule for the job applicant. Don't even think of lying or exaggerating anything in a resume or cover letter. Assume that the truth will come out and have severe, even lifelong, consequences.

确保简历和信件完全准确并真实地反映你的工作经历。这是职业申请中的一条最重要的规则。不要在简历或信件中撒谎或夸大什么事情。要知道真相总有一天会被揭示出来的，这会带来严重的甚至是影响一生的后果。

④ Be error-free 确保没有错误

Making sure that it's free of any grammatical or spelling errors. It shows you as not only meticulous but also respectful—the compositional equivalent of not slouching in your chair.

保证没有语法和拼写错误，不但显示了你的细心，而且还显示着你的礼貌和尊敬——意味着你没有采取应付的态度。

（2）Structure of resumes 个人简历的结构

Typically a resume consists of personal information, job objective, qualifications, work experience, education background, special skills/ key skills/ technical qualifications, publications and patents, social activity, honors and awards, references, conclusion/ summary/ personal statement.

个人简历通常由以下几个步骤组成：个人信息，工作目标，任职资格，工作经验，教育背景，专业技能／主要技能／技术资格，出版物和专利，社会活动，荣誉与奖励，证明人，结论／总结／个人陈述。

（3）Two types of resumes 两种个人简历的类型

After you've identified job vacancies, you can begin to prepare a resume. This is a historical account of your education, work experience, skills and other job-related personal information.

The two classic resume styles are the reverse chronological resume, which lists the jobs you've had going backward in time, from the current one to your first, and the functional resume, which describes your skills, abilities, and accomplishments as they relate to the job you seek. Employers are most accustomed to the chronological style, but if you have little work experience or some gaps in employment, a functional resume shows your skills and talents in the best light.

在确定了该找什么样的工作后，你便可以着手准备自己的简历了。简历是以年代为顺序，对你所受的教育、工作经历、技能及其他与工作相关的个人情况的记述。

简历有两种传统的形式：一是按照逆时间排列，即按照时间顺序列出自己以前所做过的工作，按照从现在的工作到第一份工作的顺序。二是按照功能排列的简历，即列出与自己现在所寻找的工作相关的技术、能力和相关成就。大部分雇主倾向于接受按照时间顺序排列的简历，但是如果你的工作经历比较少或者是工作过程中有某些空缺的话，按照功能排列的简历可以更好地展示你的技术和能力。

在此要特别强调的是，针对缺乏工作经验的应届毕业生来说，应选择功能型简历。着重强调自己的教育背景以及在校参加的一些课外活动和参与实习、合作性教育活动或其他特殊活动项目。

The Chronological Resume

SARA WANG

No. 125, Xi'dan Street

Beijing, China 100000

010-87042576

Objective

A challenging and responsible product promotion position，with a foreign company in which I may contribute my strong background in marketing and advertising.

Summary

Keen insight into identifying each product's attributes and qualities, and visualize how it should be effectively promoted in the market place.

Always maintain a creative and progressive outlook on promotional concepts and techniques which stimulate new ideas, designs, and opportunities.

In-depth knowledge of all stages for promotion process from product research, idea conception, market entry to feedback analysis.

Experience

2009-present   Marketing Planner, Dante Glass Products, Inc., Beijing

Be Responsible for designing and creating advertisements for interior decoration and other related magazines and publications. Planning and coordinating product displays and merchandising public exhibitions. Participate in marketing research and concept design. Be Recognized as outstanding employees of the year, 2010.

2006-2008   Advertising Assistant, Playland Toys, Inc., Beijing

Responsible for designing and producing the outline, and copyright for the annual products catalogue featuring all the company's toy products. Coordinated all photographic work and carefully detailed each product's description in order to present the most attractive image from both a parent and child's perspective.

2004-2005　　　　Executive Assistant to the General Manager, Universal Import

Performed various secretarial and administrative duties including handling and preparing for correspondence, contracts, and other legal documents; scheduling and arranging all meetings and domestic and international business trips, and all other duties accordingly.

Key skills

Experienced in promoting products

Exceptional writing and speaking skills of English

Proficient in use of Internet and Excel, Word, and PowerPoint

Education

Bachelor of Arts in English & American Literature, Jili University

Using the chronological resume style, this employee is looking for a more challenging position in a foreign company. Because she is quite experienced, she focuses his resume on her work and then lists her educational background at the end. Her track record shows her to be a laborious and industrious person who continues to advance.

通过这份按照时间顺序排列的简历可以看出，这位求职者正在寻找一家外国公司的一个更具挑战性的职位。由于她经验丰富，所以她只是把简历的制作聚焦到工作上，然后在末尾列出自己的受教育背景。她的生活轨迹显示了她是一个刻苦、勤奋的人，可以获得更大的发展。

The Functional Resume

THERSA MONTALVO

211 Elmwood Drive

Houston, TX 77110

(713) 555-1212

Objective

Entry level position in accounting, where exceptional math skills, mastery of applicable software, attention to detail, a willingness to work hard, and a positive attitude are required.

Education

Currently enrolled in night classes as University of Houston, work toward degree in accounting that will enable me to reach my goal of becoming a CPA.

Graduated in 2002 from Hillsboro Junior College, top about 15 percent of class.

Experience

2003 to present   Assistant Bookkeeper, Moonbeam Computers, Katy, TX

- ❑ Created linked spreadsheets to track travel and entertainment using Excel
- ❑ Maintained an Access database to record additions to fixed assets
- ❑ Downloaded mainframe queries to Excel for account analysis
- ❑ Designed an information systems improvement that made cost reports available 20 percent sooner

Summary

Creative problem solver who works well with people.

Be Fluent in Spanish.

In junior college, awarded Moore Math Medal two years in a row.

Using the functional resume style, this aspiring accountant shows she's serious by including her eventual goal in her resume—to become a CPA. Because her experience is thin, she first details her education, then specifies her duties in bulleted entries, with the last showing her as the kind of person who does more than is required.

The inclusion of her math award backs up her claim to superior math skills.

通过这种按照功能排列的简历，这位有抱负的会计人员在简历中严肃地展示了他的最终目标——成为一名注册会计师。因为他的经历比较单薄，所以他首先细化了自己的教育水平，然后突出了自己虽然是入门水平，但是其实会很多东西，最后说明自己是那种实际做的比要求的更多的人。

对自己的数学获奖情况的总结显然支持了自己数学水平更好的声明。

2.Preparation of the Application Letter 准备求职信

（1）Basic Requirements 基本要求

The goal of your cover letter—technically an employment application letter—is to successfully apply for an interview. A good application letter, supported by a concise resume, should make the reader want to meet the writer in person. It doesn't necessarily mean, however, that you will get the job.

求职信，实际上就是申请某个雇用岗位的信件，它的目标就是成功地获得与对方的会面机会。一封有明确简练的简历支撑的求职信，应该使读者想与作者进行个人会面，但这并不意味着可以获得这个岗位。

① Firm in purpose 明确目的

As you compose your application letter, keep firmly in mind what you're selling—your abilities, your skills, your experience, and your education as they relate to the employment needs of the company. You have to convince the reader that you are the best person for the position; do this by stating what you can do for the company, not what the company can do for you.

在写作求职信的时候，一定要在心里牢牢地记住你要推销什么，即与公司的招聘要求相关的你的能力、技术、经验和受教育程度。你必须使读者相信你就是最适合这个岗位的人，要说明你可以为公司做什么，而不是公司要为你做什么。

② Make every letter an original 确保原创

You may be sending out dozens of resumes, but each cover letter should be individualized. It shows respect to the reader.

你可能会发出很多份简历，但是每一封求职信都必须是个人化的。这样显示出你对读者的尊重。

③ Keep it short 保持信件的简短

Never write more than one page. Use your cover letter to point out and expand on information that is directly applicable to the job you're seeking. You'll also want to briefly explain specific experiences or capabilities, such as overseas service and fluency in a foreign language, so long as they are relevant.

不要超过一页信纸，只要简单明确地说出与工作要求直接相关的信息就可以了。当然你可能还想简单地说明一下自己的特殊经历或能力，例如，海外服务的经历，精通某种外语，只要它们与工作有关就行。

④ No apologies necessary 不必抱歉

Remember that you're seeking a job, not begging for clemency. Even if you're a first-time job applicant, your cover letters should reflect self-confidence and competence. You don't have to humble yourself or plead—and never apologize.

记住你是在找工作，而不是在乞求怜悯。即使你是第一次求职，求职信也要显得很自信，相信自己可以胜任这份工作。不必让自己卑躬屈膝或恳求别人——永远不要感到抱歉。

（2）The content of application letter 求职信的内容

① Opening paragraph 开头

In the opening paragraph, you should state the purpose of writing and capture readers' interest. Strong opening sentences make the readers want to continue reading. Name the job for which you are applying for and tell what you learned about it. Mention the name of a person (if any) who referred you to the organization. Perhaps pose a question that attracts the employer.

在第一段中，应陈述写信目的，抓住读者兴趣。开头务必要吸引读者读下去。明确你要应征的职位并告知你所学的相关知识。如果有的话，应提及推荐你到该公司的推荐人的姓名。或可提一个雇主感兴趣的问题。

Useful expressions:

❑　Having heard that the situation of salesman in your company is vacant, I wish to offer my services for it.

据悉贵公司推销员一职空缺，特备函应征。

❑　In reference to your advertisement in the newspaper for an accountant, I believe that I have the qualifications to fit your position.

阅读日报上贵公司的广告，得悉贵公司招聘会计，我深信符合该项职务所列条件。

❑　I have learned from the newspaper that there is a vacancy in your firm, and I wish to apply for the position.

从日报获悉贵公司目前尚有空缺，故本人拟应征。

❑　I wish to apply for the position of editor advertised in the newspaper.

我拟应征贵公司在日报上刊登的招聘编辑一职的工作。

❑　Replying to your advertisement in today's *China Times* for an administration assistant, I tender my services.

拜读今日《中国时报》上贵公司招聘人才广告，本人特此应征行政助理一职。

② Body paragraph 主体

Body paragraph is a critical section in the application letter. It is intended to convince the reader of your skills. First of all, you should acknowledge the skills required by the vacant position. Then, state the skills/ strength you will bring to the job and that parallel those needed to fill the position. Give examples of skills, achievements and explain how they will benefit the job. At last, comment on your knowledge of the company (their products, services, or special projects) and why you are interested in working for them.

主体是求职信中关键的一个部分，目的是使读者能够相信你的技能。首先应确认空缺职位所需要的技能。然后说明你将带给这份工作中所需要的相匹配的技能或者优点。针对技能、业绩举例说明，并讲明将带给这份工作的好处。最后，就自己的理解对应征公司（他们的产品、服务或者特殊项目）发表你的看法，并说明你为什么对该公司感兴趣。

③ Closing paragraph 结尾

Ask for interview—identify next step. Refer to enclosed resume firstly. Then, inform your linkman of the date that you will call. Alternatively, state that you are available for a personal interview at his/ her convenience. Make it easy for the person to contact you: list your phone number and time you would be available. Even if it is on the resume, list it here again.

结尾应申请面试，即明确下一步。首先让其查询附件中的简历。其次告知联系人你将于某日打电话，或表明你能在他 / 她方便的时候进行个人面试，使他们能够方便地联系到你：列出你的电话号码及方便接听的时间。即使简历上有，也要重新再写一遍。

Useful expressions:

❑ If you would like to know more about my ability, I would be available for an interview at any time convenient to you.
倘若阁下愿意接见本人以了解我的能力，我将随时候教。

❑ If you desire an interview, I shall be happy to call in person, on any day and at any time you may appoint.
如贵公司有意面试，本人一定遵照所指定的时日，前往拜访。

❑ Should you entertain my application favorably, I would spare to trouble acquit myself to your satisfaction.
假如本人之应征能够为贵公司服务，本人必以排除万难之决心，为贵公司工作，以期厚望。

❑ I would be very happy to work under your supervision if it is possible. Thank you very much for your kind attention. Please send me an answer at your earliest convenience.
如能为贵公司效力，本人将不胜荣幸。阁下耐心读完这份申请，本人至为感激，并请尽速回函示知。

❑ I wish to assure you that, if successful, I would endeavor to give you every satisfaction.
如蒙不弃，惠予录用，本人将尽最大努力工作，争取诸事满意。

（3）Sample letters of application for a position 求职信模板

Dear Sir or Madam,

I wish to apply for the position of personnel director, which you advertised in *21st Century* of April 6.

My courses at Suzhou University were specially planned to prepare me for a career in personnel management. I believe that my studies have given me the foundation of knowledge from which to learn the practical side of personnel management.

I have been serving Shanghai Toys Import & Export Company as a managerial staff member of the personnel department for three years. I have conducted extensive interviews to clarify the way employees perceive their roles, concerns and priorities. This practical experience has given me more complete understanding of the importance of good human relations. It has also inspired me to further develop my abilities to manage personnel.

I have been very happy with my work at Shanghai Toys Import & Export Company, but I am anxious to assume broader responsibilities in a growing company. The enclosed resume about details of my background which, I believe, qualifies me as the personnel director of your organization.

May I have an opportunity to talk with you in person about my desire to work in your organization? Self-addressed envelope is enclosed, but if you prefer to call me, you may reach me at 1375****108 from 5: 30 p.m. onwards any day.

Sincerely yours,

×××

敬启者：

我想应聘贵公司在 4 月 6 日《21 世纪报》上登广告招聘的人事主管一职。

我在苏州大学所修的课程为我特别规划了从事人事管理方面的事业，我认为我的学业给我提供了去了解人事管理的实践知识的基础。

我在上海玩具进出口公司从事人事管理工作已有 3 年之久。我曾经做过广泛的访谈，了解员工如何看待他们自身的作用，了解员工所关心的及优先考虑的事情。这种实际经验使我对良好人际关系的重要性有了更完整的了解，同时还激发了我进一步培养自己人事管理的能力。

我很满意在上海玩具进出口公司的工作，但我渴望能在一家正处于发展壮大中的公司承担更大的责任，附寄的个人简历详细说明了本人的情况，我相信这些使我能胜任贵机构人事主管的工作。

我可否获得机会亲自与您进一步谈谈我想在贵机构工作的愿望？随信附寄了有我联络地址的信封，但如果您愿意打电话给我，请在任何一天晚上 5 点半之后拨 1375****108 联系我。

××× 敬上

Part II   The Job Interview 面试

Congratulations! Your job skills—all those abilities and all that experience that you wrote about in your resume and application letter—have gotten you in the door. Now it's time to sell yourself and to stand out from the other interviewees. Your expertise and experience are vital, but your attitude, your appearance, and how you handle yourself can either clinch or ruin your chances. Remember: The interview is your opportunity to start building the best relationship possible with the interviewer. And that is what etiquette really is all about—building great relationships.

祝贺你！所有的个人能力以及书写简历和求职信的技巧使你获得了面试机会。现在是你展示自己并脱颖而出的时候了。你的专长和工作经验是最重要的，而你的态度、外表及得体的礼仪既能把握这来之不易的求职机会又能毁灭它。记住：面试是和会见者开始建立良好关系的机会。这也是礼节的真正内涵，即建立良好的关系。

1.Before Interview 面试前

（1）Do some research 做一些调查研究

Some interview questions you can anticipate, others you can't. The best way to stay calm is to recognize what you can control and prepare for that. Improve your odds with some research and self-examination.

有的面试问题你能预料到，有的就不能。保持冷静的最好方法是事前意识到哪些是你掌握和准备的。做一些调查研究和自我测试来增强你的优势。

① Acquaint with the background of enterprise 了解公司背景

Resources such as business magazines, the company's annual report, and its website will fill you in on the company's profile and its general attitude. Collecting information not only helps you anticipate the qualities your interviewer is looking for, but also gives you ideas for questions to ask the interviewer. Ideally, you'll be able to talk about the company's chief products, prime markets, and even plans for future growth. If you are applying for a specific job, ask the firm's human recourses department for the job description beforehand so you'll be able to answer questions in that context, highlighting any skills that directly apply.

商业杂志的报道、公司的日常报道以及网页等资源会使你充分了解公司的一些概况。收集这些信息不仅能帮助你预料到会见者所看重的品质，还会为你向会见者询问提供参考。实际上你还能了解公司的主打产品、主要的市场以及将来的发展计划。如果你申请一个具体的岗位，可事先向公司的人力资源部了解岗位的细节以便面试时回答相关问题。要重视这些直接运用于面试中的技巧。

② Know yourself 了解你自己

Because you'll be asked about your strengths, aptitudes, and experience, it's essential to have a concrete idea of your strengths before articulating them to your interviewer. Spend some time reviewing your resume, refreshing your memory of dates of employment and exact job titles and, if necessary, revising it to highlight the most relevant areas of your experience. Know your resume by heart. During the interview, having it firmly in your head enables you to point out or discuss certain parts of it without consulting a hard copy.

正因为面试时有关个人能力、才能及工作经历会被询问，所以在向面试官清晰表述之前，应对自己的能力要有具体的看法，这点非常重要。花点时间回顾一下自己的工作简历，想想被雇佣的每个阶段和确切的工作职衔，如有必要，反复记忆最相关的几段工作经历。对自己的简历若能熟记于心，就可以在面试时明确谈论简历中的内容，不需要去照搬复制它。

③ Dress one notch up 着装得体

Dress smartly but conservatively. Your appearance is the first impression an interviewer notices about you, so it should be as favorable and professional as possible. The most important factors about appearance are neatness, cleanliness, and appropriateness. Grooming should be immaculate, with hair and nail clean. Buttons should not be missing, hems and cuffs should not be frayed. Shoes should be clean and shining. It is inappropriate to wear excessive jewelry or make-up and elaborate, dressy, tight, sheer or transparent clothing.

打扮要适当得体。主考官对你的第一印象就是你的仪表，因此应尽可能留下一个好的印象，并给人一种很职业的感觉。仪表中最重要的是整齐、清洁、合体。穿戴应得体，头发指甲要干净。衣服不缺纽扣，折边袖口无磨损。鞋子保持干净明亮。佩戴过多珠宝或使用过多化妆品，穿着过于精致、华丽、紧身、透明的服装是不合适的。

（2）Practice 练习

After you received an invitation to an interview formally, you can try to ask yourself the questions which you're likely to be asked and practice answering them aloud.

在正式接到面试邀请后，你可以尝试着问自己可能会被问及的问题，并大声地练习回答。

There are so many questions which may be asked in the interview. However, three kinds of questions are usually asked in all interviews. Let's go to practice.

在面试中有很多问题都有可能被问到。然而，其中有三种问题通常在所有面试中都会被问到。那么我们就来练习一下吧！

① What are your strengths?

This question can be answered in two ways: with a list of your virtues or with concrete examples of your good points at work. The latter is far more effective in making a lasting impression: the interviewer is more likely to take note of your anecdote.

"你的强项是什么？"这种问题可以以下面两种方式来回答：列出你所有的品质；用工作中的具体事例来证明自己的优点。后面这种方式最有可能给面试者留下深刻的印象，因为面试者一般更易于记住你的奇闻轶事。

② Why do you want a job, and why with us?

Put a positive spin on this one. For example, if you're currently employed, avoid saying you feel your talents aren't sufficiently appreciated, you dislike your boss, or anything else negative; instead, say you've gained enough experience in your current job to make you ready to tackle new challenges, and you believe this new position could give you the chance. Back this up with your knowledge of how the company operates (something you've learned in your earlier research).

"你为什么想换一份新工作？为什么会选择我们公司呢？"回答这种问题的时候，要采取一种积极的态度。例如，如果你最近一直在工作的话，一定不要说你觉得自己的才能没有被上司欣赏，你不喜欢你的老板，或者其他消极的事情，而是要说你觉得在现在的工作中你已经积累了足够的经验，有能力迎接新的挑战，你相信这份新工作可以让你充分发挥自己的聪明才智。同时还要用这家公司是如何运作的知识（当然是你在此前的调查中得来的知识）来支持你的观点。

③ What was the hardest thing you ever faced in a job?

This question demands prior preparation. The idea is not to recount the story of a disastrous situation, but to talk about a problem that you were instrumental in solving. This shows that you are ready and able to cope with difficulties that may come your way.

"工作过程中你发现最难做的事情是什么"这种问题需要提前准备。其实最好的回答不是重复你以前遇到过的棘手的问题，而是要讲一个你可以解决的问题。这会显示你不仅乐于而且有能力解决工作过程中遇到的任何难题。

2.During Interview 面试中

（1）Be professional 要专业

During the interview your most important task is to act professionally. Thus, try to answer all questions both thoroughly and accurately. Be natural, too. When you have the opportunity, expand your responses to incorporate ideas you have wanted to include in the conversation.

在面试过程中，最重要的任务是你要表现得很专业，很在行。能够既准确又认真地回答所有的问题，表情也要自然。当有机会的时候，可将谈话内容扩展到一些你所想谈及的想法。

（2）Be calm 要冷静

Whatever happens, try to maintain your composure. The best way to accomplish this is to realize your own value: you can handle the job and you are perfectly capable of explaining why. If, however, you start feeling nervous or anxious, take a deep, silent breath.

无论发生什么，都要试着保持镇静，做到这点的最好办法就是要意识到你的自我价值：你可以胜任这份工作，而且你能很好地解释出原因。如果你还感到紧张或焦虑的话，那么就做一个深呼吸吧。

（3）Be punctual 要准时

No choice here. Late means late, even if you're just one minute late. Your best bet is to be sure you know how long it takes to get there. Then add an extra ten to twenty minutes to your schedule as margin for error. Once there, visit a coffee shop or wait outside so you can enter five minutes early. Knock at the door before you enter the interviewing room. Walk to the desk and shake hands with in interviewer.

在这里没有选择的余地，即使你仅仅晚到了 1 分钟，迟到就是迟到。最好弄清楚到面试地方需要多长时间，然后留出额外的 10 ～ 20 分钟时间提前到达，以防出现意外。到达指定地点后若时间充裕，可以在附近的咖啡厅转转或者在面试地点外面等候，这样就可以提前 5 分钟进入。进门前先敲门，走到桌前与主考官握手。

（4）Be confident and modest 要自信并谦虚

Engage the interviewer, and let your personality shine through. You are showing her that you will represent her company well, and that you are a confident, can-do person.

Especially when answering questions, you should be not only in a clear manner but also in a confident manner. However be careful not to come off as a know-it-all. Start your statements with "I think…" or "I imagine…" or "As far as I can tell…" instead of "There's no doubt that…" or "Everyone knows that…" or "It's clear that…" Don't talk nonsense if you don't know the answers. It is better to tell him or her that you don't know.

把注意力集中到面试官身上，让自己的个人魅力充分散发出来。要给对方一种这样的印象：你可以胜任这份工作，你是一个自信的、战无不胜的人。

尤其在回答问题时，不仅要讲话清晰，还要表现得很自信，但是也不要做出一副无事不通的姿态，最好用"我觉得……"、"我猜想……"或"我现在只能说……"这种表达方式，而不要说"无疑这是……"、"任何人都知道……"或"这是很清楚的……"这种话。如果不知道答案，不要胡言乱语，最好告诉面试官你不知道。

3.After Interview 面试后

After you accept the interview within a day or two, send a thank-you letter—even if you don't think you will be offered the job. Not only is this good manner, but it helps the interviewer keep you in mind when he or she is making a decision as to whom to hire.

在你接受面试后，在一到两天内寄出你的感谢信，即使你认为你不会被录用。但这不仅是礼貌之举也会使面试人在做决定之时对你有印象。

（1）The format of thank-you letter 感谢信的格式

You can use the following three-part format for the letter.

Paragraph 1: State your appreciation for the interview and, if appropriate, request that similar appreciation be extended to others who participated in the interview.

Paragraph 2: Review your qualifications or provide additional information.

Paragraph 3: Say that you look forward to hearing from the prospective employer.

Verify the spelling of the names and titles of various people.

With this letter, you have completed the job-finding process. Now you have only to wait for a response.

你可使用下列三段式的格式来写感谢信。

第一段：对予以面试机会表示感谢，如果你认为合适的话，也应向参加面试你的其他人员表示感谢。

第二段：总结你的资历或者提供新的信息。

第三段：表明你期待着得到雇主的答复。

最后核对有关人员的姓名、职务的拼写是否正确。

有了这封信，你已完成求职的全部程序。现在，你只需等待答复了。

Sample letter:

Dear Sir or Madam,

I wanted to thank you for taking the time yesterday to meet with me and for sharing information on your company and the career opportunity available. I found this interview very informative and useful as a tool for exploring my career opportunities with ABC Company.

As we discussed yesterday, it is my belief that my educational background and expertise would prove to be a valuable asset to your company. I am looking for a career that will utilize my extensive knowledge and current skills, while allowing me to grow and learn more working with an industry leader who is progressive in the marketplace. After meeting with you and learning more about ABC Company, I believe this would be a successful match for both of us.

Again, it was a pleasure meeting you. I look forward to hearing from you regarding the next step in the recruiting process.

Sincerely yours,

× × ×

敬启者：

我想感谢您昨天抽出宝贵的时间面试我，并感谢您与我分享贵公司的信息且提供就业机会。作为探索自己在 ABC 公司工作机会的一种方式，我发现这次面试内容是非常丰富和有益的。

正如我们昨天讨论过的，我认为我的教育背景和专业知识对贵公司将是一个优势。我期待的职业生涯是能够充分运用上我的知识和当前的技能，并让我在和有市场先见的行业领导的工作中学习到更多。与您交谈并更多地了解 ABC 公司，我相信这对于我们双方来说都将是一个成功的选择。

再次表达我见到您的高兴心情。我期待着听到您关于招聘程序的下一步指示。

× × × 敬上

（2）Waiting for results 等待消息

Waiting to hear whether you've been accepted for the job is one of the most stressful parts of the job search. But face up to the fact that you must do just that: wait, and be patient.

等待看自己有没有被录取是求职过程中最让人紧张的时刻。但是一定要勇敢面对现实，而且你必须要做的就是：等待，而且要有耐心。

Usually, there will be two results. One is that you get the opportunity, while the other is failure. For both cases, how to respond?

通常会出现两个结果，一个是你获取了这个机会，而另一个就是失败了。针对这两种情况，该如何应对呢？

① Responding to an offer 回应对方提供的机会

All your preparation has paid off; you've obtained a job offer. No matter how thrilled you may be about it, however, don't succumb to pressure to give an answer right away. Instead, say something to the effect of, "Thank you for the offer. This is very exciting! I'd like some time to consider it. Can I have a couple of days to respond?" Use this time to consider carefully your salary range and benefits needs.

When you meet again with your prospective employer or call to give your response, be aware this is the time when you have maximum leverage. Be sure to hammer out the details of your benefits package and salary before formally accepting the job. Now is also the time to ask about the potential for upward mobility and growth. Then, if everything is satisfactory to you, accept the offer with enthusiasm.

如果你所有的准备工作都得到了回报，获得了这一工作机会，无论你对此多么兴奋，一定要抑制自己，不要立即做出回应。而是要对对方说："谢谢你们提供的这次机会，这真让人兴奋。但是我想再考虑一下，你们能不能再给我一两天的考虑时间？"利用这段时间仔细考虑一下你的工资范围和福利要求。

在跟未来的老板见面或打电话告诉对方你的回答之前，一定要知道这是你可以提出最高要求的时间，因此一定要保证在接受这份工作之前想出所有关于工资和福利的细节问题。同时这也是询问未来的升迁和在公司中成长等问题的时间。然后，如果你对一切都很满意的话，就可以热情地接受这份工作了。

② Responding to a rejection 如何回应拒绝

If you didn't work out this time, sending a brief note acknowledging that you've been rejected is better than just slinking off and acting as if you'd never had personal contact with a company. Thanking the company for considering you will show that you are a person of substance and good manners. There's always the chance that you missed being hired by a hair and could be considered for a job in the future.

如果求职没有成功，写一张简单的便条告知对方你知道被拒绝了，这要比只是销声匿迹，就像根本没有与这家公司有过个人接触好得多。在便条中要感谢公司考虑过你，这会让对方觉得你是一个很有礼貌和有教养的人。落选通常只是因为一些微小的原因，而如果你以这样的方式回应的话，公司会对你有一定的印象，将来一旦有工作机会，首先会考虑你。

Situational practice for etiquettes 礼仪口语实景

Make up or search for more situational conversations that may occur during the job interview and put them into practice.

Model 1

I : Good morning! I'm David Smith from Personnel. Sit down please.

A: Thank you. I know that you have an opening for an assistant.

I : Yes. Who referred you to this company?

A: I saw your newspaper ads in *Wuhan Evening Daily*.

I : Now, have you brought your resume with you?

A: Oh, yes, here it is. There are three copies.

I : Ok. Why are you interested in working for our company? You know we are rather small and young.

A: I believe I would have better opportunities with a small but rapidly expanding company like yours.

I : All right, we will keep your application in our active file. If anything turns up, we'll contact you.

A: Thank you.

Model 2

I : I think you are the right person for the job. Do you have any questions you want to ask?

A: Yes, I'd like to know if there would be any future opportunities for specific training.

I : If necessary there will be. Is any other questions?

A: Could you tell me the benefits of the company?

I : Yes. We provide medical insurance and retirement pension. And we also have vacations and sick leave. Is anything else?

A: When will I know your decision?

I : We'll give you our decision in a few days. How can we get in touch with you?

A: I can be reached at my office during work hours and at home in the evening. My office phone number and home phone number are in my resume.

I : Thank you for your interest in our company.

A: Thank you, sir. I expect to hear from you as soon as possible.

I : Would you please let the next applicant come in on your way out?

A: All right. Goodbye.

Model 3

Here is an example interview that can give you ideas about how you can present yourself in the best possible light. Greg is good at interviewing. He is likeable, and he is liable to get a job offer after this interview.

(Greg arrives ten minutes early, checks in with the receptionist, and fills out his name card. He adjusts his tie, buttons his suit jacket, and sits in the lobby. Five minutes later a secretary brings him into a conference room. Several minutes later he stands to greet his interviewer.)

Interviewer: Hello, I am Robert Miller, a director of marketing at Gateway.

Greg: Hello, it's very nice to meet you.

(Greg shakes his hand firmly, smiles, and looks him in the eye with respect. As they take their seats, Greg sits straight and pays close attention to his interviewer, and they chat briefly about the weather.)

Interviewer: So, why don't you tell me about yourself?

Greg: Okay. I grew up in Ohio and studied engineering at Georgia Tech. In my first job at Compaq, I learned a great deal about managing the flexible assembly of computers. After that I implemented improvements in the logistics department at Dell, where I also put a lot of effort into improving my writing skills. More recently, I've been negotiating with corporate clients on large orders. It's been fascinating learning about the sales side of the business. Outside of work I play basketball in several local leagues, and I also tutor adults in the local library for Project Read.

(They talk briefly about writing at work and about teaching people how to read.)

Interviewer: What are you looking for in a position at Gateway?

Greg: I would like an opportunity to help Gateway grow its sales of computers. At the same time I want to improve my understanding of the industry and to find new challenges in managing teams of people who work in marketing.

Interviewer: We all have weaknesses. Could you describe one of yours?

Greg: In the past I've had trouble being organized. But now it's much less of a problem. I constantly use checklists. And I use note cards to write myself reminders. I've found this a great help—just by developing the habit of writing things down.

Interviewer: Where do you see yourself in 5 years within the company?

Greg: I can see myself as a manager in a marketing or sales department, leading teams of people to accomplish such things as improving customer feedback, growing corporate accounts, or launching new advertising campaigns.

Interviewer: Are you willing to relocate?

Greg: Yes, of course. I've enjoyed experiencing new environments in the past. I'm sure it would be fun to see other parts of the country, or the world for that matter.

Interviewer: Do you have any questions for me?

Greg: Yes, actually. I often get a good feel about a company by learning from the people who work there. Could you tell me why it was that you first accepted a job at Gateway? And how has it been fun and challenging?

(The interview continues very nicely.)

 Terminology related 相关礼仪术语

Interview Etiquette for Employers 面试官礼仪

The interview is a time for the company to make an impression on a candidate, as well. The interviewer should be selling the candidate as much as they're being sold. A candidate is like a guest in your home or a customer—whether you hire them or not. Candidates are members of our communities, consumers and even potential customers. In addition, they have taken time out of their day to consider employment with your company and deserve the respect of your attention and professionalism.

Think about the common guidelines for candidates and turn them around to apply to the employer:

- ❑ Dress professionally
- ❑ Be on time
- ❑ Be prepared
- ❑ Greet the interviewer
- ❑ Respond to interview questions
- ❑ Follow up

同样公司也通过面试给求职者留下印象。面试官应该像求职者一样努力推荐自己。无论雇用对方与否，求职者都如同客人或客户。求职者可能是同一个社区的成员、消费者，甚至是潜在客户。求职者抽出时间来你公司面试，你理应关注对方，专业地接待他们，来表示他们的尊重。

求职者遵循的求职指南同样适用于面试者：

穿着得体

守时

"有备而来"

问候面试官

回应面试中的问题

面试后反馈

Useful expressions for etiquettes 礼仪用语集锦

The followings questions are commonly asked in the interviews:

❑   About yourself 谈论自己

Would you tell me what educational background you have?

请问你的教育背景如何？

What's your major?

你的专业是什么？

What subject did you minor in?

你辅修的科目有哪些？

What led you to choose your field or major study?

你为什么选这个领域或专业深造？

How do you think the education you've received will contribute to your work in this institution?

你所受的教育会对这份工作有何帮助？

How about your academic records at college?

你大学的成绩如何？

Did you get any honors and awards at college?

你在大学是否获过奖？

What are your educational goals for the future?

你未来的教育目标是什么？

How do you rate yourself as a professional?

你如何评价你的专业水平？

What is your strongest trait?

你的强项是什么？

Can you tell me some of your strengths and weaknesses?

你能说说你的优点和缺点吗？

What kind of people do you find difficult to work with?

你觉得和哪种人难以相处？

What kind of people do you like to work with?

你愿意和哪种人一起工作？

What goals have you set and how did you meet them?

你制定过什么目标并如何实现的？

Could you project what you would like to be doing five years from now?

你能否展望在以后的五年你在做什么？

What are your short-term/long-term goals?

你的短期 / 长期目标是什么？

What is most important in your life right now?

你现在生活中最重要的事是什么？

How do you normally handle criticism?

你一般是如何对待批评的？

What do you find frustrating in a work situation?

在工作中什么会让你沮丧？

How do you handle your failure?

你如何对待失败？

What provides you with a sense of accomplishment?

什么能带给你成就感？

❑　 About your current/previous job 谈论你现在 / 之前的工作

Give me a summary of your current job description.

简述一下你现在的工作职责。

What contribution did you make to your current (previous) organization?

你对现在（之前）就职的单位作出过哪些贡献？

Have you received any honors or rewards?

你获过奖吗？

Do you do a second job in addition to your full time job?

你在全职工作以外做过兼职吗?

What have you learned from jobs you have held/had?

你从你做过的工作中学到了什么?

How did you get along with your boss in your last job?

你在上一份工作中和上司相处得如何?

How do you feel about your progress to date?

你认为你到目前为止的进步如何?

What was your reason for leaving?

你离职的原因是什么?

Could you explain why you have changed jobs so often?

为什么你经常更换工作呢?

❑   About the job which you applied 谈论所求职位

What are your plans if you were hired?

如被聘用,你有何计划?

Why do you want to work for us?

你为什么想加入本公司?

What do you consider important when looking for a job?

在求职时,你认为什么最重要?

Why do you consider yourself qualified for this job?

你为什么认为自己胜任这份工作?

What do you think you are worth to us?

你认为你对本公司的价值何在?

Why should I hire you?

我们为什么应该聘用你?

Exercises（课后练习）

I.Questions and answers: answer the following questions according to the information you have got in the previous reading.

1. What are the basic requirements of the resume?

2. What shall we do before attending an interview?

3. Are there any principles we should follow during the interview? What are they?

4. Can you think of anything positive we can do after the interview to make the success?

5. Do we have to respond to a rejection? Why or why not?

II. Expressions: match the terms in Column A with the Chinese equivalents in Column B.

A	B
chronological resume	资历
functional resume	求职信
application letter	福利
qualifications	按时间顺序排列的简历
benefits package	按功能排列简历

III. Translation: translate the following statements into Chinese to learn about the Importance of Appearance on a Job Interview.

1. First Impression

How you appear is essentially the first impression you will make on the person who will interview you. If your appearance is appropriate and well put together, you instantly gain credibility as someone who cares about making a good impression, and who has respect for the company and the interview process. If it is not, you now have extra ground to make up with the interviewer.

2. Grooming

A survey of employers carried out by the National Association of Colleges and Employers looked at various external attributes in interviewees, and how much these would influence a hiring employer. The results indicated that the state of an interviewee's grooming would have the strongest influence on the employer's attitude, with 73 percent of respondents saying it would have a strong influence. This means it's worth getting a good haircut and manicure before your interview, brushing your teeth and polishing your shoes to ensure that your appearance is clean and pleasant.

3. The Role

If the job itself is one that requires you to meet with clients, you need to demonstrate to the hiring manager that you can represent the company appropriately. In this situation it's even more crucial that you meet the company's expectations on appearance, as this will be seen as one element of your aptitude for the position.

4. Dress Code

Some industries may have a more casual dress code, and it may not be appropriate to come to the interview in a conservative, formal suit. If you have contacts at the company, make inquiries about expectations and culture at the company and try to fit with the tone. If you don't have any personal contacts, it's acceptable to call the human resources department and ask what the appropriate interview dress code might be. But remember, it's always safer to err on the side of being too formal than not formal enough.

IV. Cloze: choose the suitable statements from the box and complete the passage.

> A. Why has there been such a large gap between your jobs
> B. Why were you fired
> C. Why are you switching careers
> D. Why did you leave your last job

Q1: _____? The correct answer should be positive and should be directed towards what you know about this position. In an interview for a job where you'd be dealing with customers or public relations regularly, you might answer, "Although I enjoyed my previous job, I wanted to seek out a position that would give me more chances to work with the public."

Q2:_____? A good answer might be the following: "I was fired because there was a miscommunication from the beginning about my job responsibilities. The employer needed someone who had access to a vehicle during the day, and I did not. I should have stated from the beginning that, while my transportation was reliable, I would not be able to run errands outside of the office." In the response, the individual briefly explains the situation and accepts responsibility for her share of the miscommunication. She doesn't speak negatively about the past employer.

Q3:_____? If the interviewer asks about these gaps, then your best strategy is to be honest. For example, you might say "I took some time off to stay home with our new baby, but now that he's settled in pre-school I feel comfortable accepting the responsibilities of a full-time position" or "After I was displaced from my Acme where I'd worked for eight years, it took me a while to regain my confidence. It happened quite suddenly, and I admit I wasn't prepared to make a change. It took me a while to feel comfortable getting back out in the job market."

Q4: _____? Here's a sample answer: "After I spent ten years in advertising, I wanted a change that would give me more opportunities to work with customers directly. That's the main reason I considered sales. I did some research into the field and discovered that the best salespeople have strong interpersonal skills, a genuine desire to help others, and an ability

to recognize the needs and wants of customers. These are all traits I've developed through my experience in advertising so I thought this would be a great fit for me."

V.Case study: imitate the interview with your classmates in front of the class. Before your performance, you should discuss about the following aspects in groups:

As an interviewer, what should be taken into consideration?

As an interviewee, what can be done to ensure a successful interview, verbally or non-verbally?

 Extension（拓展阅读）

Ten Time Saving Tips to Speed Up Your Job Search

Is your job search off to a slow start or getting stuck? Here are some quick time-saving job search tips that will help your hunt for a new job go smoothly.

Be Prepared.

Put your mobile phone number on your resume so you can follow up in a timely manner. This job search toolkit will help you get everything you need set for your job search.

Be More Than Prepared.

Always have an up-to-date resume ready to send—even if you are not currently looking for work. You never know when an opportunity that is too good to pass up might come along.

Don't Wait.

If you are laid-off, file for unemployment right away. You may be able to file online or by phone. Waiting could delay your benefits check.

Get Help.

Utilize free or inexpensive services that provide career counseling and job search assistance such as college career offices, job fairs in universities and job centers in society.

Create Your Own Templates.

Have copies of your resume and cover letter ready to edit. That way you can change the content to match the requirements of the job you're applying for, but, the contact information and your opening and closing paragraphs won't need to be changed.

Use Job Search Engines.

Search the job search engines. Use the job search engine sites to search the major job banks, company sites, associations, and other sites with job postings for you.

Get Jobs by Using Application Websites.

Let the jobs come to you. Use job search agents to sign up and receive job listings by email. All the major job sites have search agents and some web sites specialize in sending announcements.

References Ready.

Have a list of three references including name, job title, company, phone number and email address ready to give to interviewers.

Use Your Network.

Be cognizant of the fact that many, if not most, job openings aren't advertised. Tell everyone you know that you are looking for work. Ask if they can help. This tip isn't a time saver, but, it will broaden your online job search resources.

Don't Stop.

Don't limit your job searching to the top sites like Monster or Career Builder. Check the smaller niche sites that focus on a particular geographic location or career field and you will find plenty of job listings.

After-reading tasks（读后任务）

When you finish reading the text above, get into the groups and discuss with your group members about the following tasks and fulfill them.

Task 1

Have you got the experience of looking for a full-time or part-time job? What are the usual problems you have encountered during the job research? After you have gone through the Ten Time Saving Tips to Speed Up Your Job Search, what do you think of the tips? Do you consider they or at least some of them valuable? Illustrate your judgment. If possible, use your own experience of job search to give more specific details to tell people how to speed up your job hunt.

Task 2

The text has listed different resources we may turn to, for instance, job search engines, application websites or network. According to your own experiences and successful examples you have heard about or around you, which can be more reliable, by searching online or turning to the people around you? Or which resource have you made best use of in your life? What are the advantages or disadvantages of these ways of job search?

Task 3

The author asks the applicants to "be more than prepared", because "you never know when an opportunity that is too good to pass up might come along". Do you agree with the statement above? If you do agree, then how are you prepared? Besides the preparation mentioned in the text, have you paid attention to more aspects that may affect the effects of job search?

Self-Study（自学反馈）

If possible, summarize what you have learned in this unit with the help of the following table.

Focus of this unit:
Guidelines for etiquette: 1. 2. 3. ...
Summary:
Application: 1. 2. 3. ...
Feedback:

Chapter Seven
Correspondence Etiquette
商务信函礼仪

Objectives（学习目标）

After this chapter, you should be able to:

- ❑ Have a command of the basic elements of a more professional business letter
- ❑ Apply the basic writing skills into practical business letters writing
- ❑ Cultivate the cross-cultural awareness in the international written communication

Lead-in（导读）

In our so-called Information Age, information is the medium of exchange. All the transactions are relying on the exchange of information. Because of today's highly developed and toughly competitive society, communication between individuals and groups has become increasingly frequent and important. Business letter is the most frequent instrument which has been employed by companies in daily business communication. So, the etiquette in business writing arouses more and more people's attention. In view of this point, this chapter will systematically and thoroughly expound the etiquette of business letter.

当今可谓信息时代，信息已成为商业贸易的工具。所有的交易都依赖于信息交换来完成。因为社会的高度发展，竞争的激烈，个人之间和公司之间的交流变得越来越频繁和重要。商业信函是各国公司在日常商务交流中使用最为频繁的工具。所以，商务信函写作中应遵循的礼仪规范引起了越来越多的人的关注。鉴于此点，本章将系统、全面地介绍商务信函写作中应遵循的礼仪规范。

Test yourself（自我测试）

Child-rearing books advise readers to communicate positive messages to children. They counsel parents to avoid the negative "Don't slam the door" and to say instead "Close the door gently." Adults are grown-up children. They need positive messages too. If you want to get an affirmative response from your readers, try these tips for focusing on the positive. Following are some sentences which are usually used in business writing, Please use Yes or No to manifest which one you think is right and state why you think so.

1. Always process orders within two days.   Yes ☐ No ☐

   Never take more than two days to process an order.   Yes ☐ No ☐

2. We can meet first thing Monday morning.   Yes ☐ No ☐

   We can't meet now. It has to wait until Monday morning.   Yes ☐ No ☐

3. Let me clarify what I meant.   Yes ☐ No ☐

   You misunderstood what I said.   Yes ☐ No ☐

4. At this company we value natural resources.   Yes ☐ No ☐

   At this company we don't waste natural resources.   Yes ☐ No ☐

5. Thank you for your letter.   Yes ☐ No ☐

   We have received your letter.   Yes ☐ No ☐

Part I   The Format of Business Letters
商务信函的格式

Writing for business purposes requires the adherence to a more rigid structure than is present in personal correspondence. Business writing, whether in the form of a letter, report, proposal, or other document, is bound by certain accepted standards. The presentation of a business document is of the utmost importance and it is for this reason that a uniform standard exists for most types of business correspondence.

相比私人信件而言，出于商业目的的信函写作需要遵守更为严格的结构。无论是信函、报告、提议还是其他文件形式的商务写作均为某些公认的标准所约束。商务文件的结构布局尤为重要，因此，大多数类型的商务信函有其统一的标准。

1.The parts of Business Letters 商务信函的组成部分

（1）The basic parts of business letters 商务信函的基本组成部分

① Letterhead 信头

Letterhead includes the sender's name, postal address, the company's logo, telephone number, telex number, cable address and E-mail address, etc. Letterhead occupies the top first page, and may be positioned at the left margin for full block style or at the center for indented style.

信头包括发件人的姓名、发件地址、公司的标志、电话号码、电传号码、电报地址、邮箱等。信头占据第一页的顶端，位于齐头式的左边或缩进式的中间。如下：

Shanghai Huali Imp. & Exp. Co., Ltd.

Room 606 Plaza Building,	Fax: 86-21-64253378
1302 Meilong Road, 200237	Tel: 86-21-64255578
Shanghai, People's Republic of China	E-mail: huali188@alibaba.com.cn

In some countries the letterhead contains other details. For example, in the U.K. the director's names of a company is given.

在一些国家，信头包含其他细节。例如，在英国，信头包含了公司董事长的名字。

Director Edmond Halley

Capital Food Co., Ltd.

15 PARKGTE ROAD, LONDON SW12 4NQ. U.K.

② Reference 编号

In business communication, when a firm writes to another, each will give a reference for use in further correspondence about the subject discussed in the letter. The reference may include a file number, departmental code or the initials of the signer followed by that of the typist of the letter. These are marked "Our ref:" and "Your ref:" to avoid confusion.

They are often placed two lines below the letterhead. If desired, the reference initials can also be placed at the lower left margin two lines below the name of the signer.

在商务交流中，当一方写信寄予对方时，每一封信都会有一个编号，便于以后就该信内容继续进行讨论。编号包括文件编号，部门代码或信件打字员签名的缩写。为了避免混淆，编号通常注明为"我方编号："和"贵方编号："。

编号通常置于信头下两行。编号缩写如果需要的话，也可以写在签名的下两行，置于左下角。

③ Dateline 日期

The dateline consists of the month, day, and year. The month should be spelled out in full, never use the short form of the month (e.g. Jan. /Feb. /Oct.). All numbers should be written as numerals, either cardinal numbers or ordinal numbers can be used (January 1, 2011, not Jan. 1).

It is usual to show the date in the order of day/month/year (English practice), or month/day/year (American practice). Both of the following styles are acceptable: 1 January, 2011 (English practice); January 1, 2011 (American practice).

The date is typed two to six lines below the letterhead, usually on the right side of the page, although flush-left and centered datelines are also perfectly acceptable.

日期应包括月、日、年。月份应该全部拼写出来，不要使用月份的缩写形式（例如：Jan., Feb., Oct.）。所有的数字都需要用数词来书写，基数词和序数词都可以使用（January 1, 2011, 不是 Jan. 1）。

通常是按照日、月、年（英式），或者月、日、年（美式）来写的。以下两种写法都是正确的：1 January, 2011（英式）；January 1, 2011（美式）。

日期应该写在信头下面 2～6 行之间的位置，通常写在页面的右边，当然在齐头式置于左边或在缩进式置于中间也是可以接受的。

④ Inside name and address 信内收信人姓名及地址

The name and address of the receiver is typed at the left-hand margin at least two lines below the date.

Precede the address's name with a courtesy with title (such as Mr., Ms. or Dr.). If you do not know whether a person is a man or woman, and you have no way to find out, omit the courtesy title and give the full name.

信内收信人姓名及地址通常写在日期下方至少 2 行以下的左边空白处。

收信人姓名前需有尊称（例如：Mr., Ms. or Dr.）。如果实在无法辨别对方的性别，并且也没有其他办法得知的情况下，放弃尊称，直接写出全名即可。

The title of a person's position within an organization may be included and typed below the person's name. For example:

收信人的职衔可以涵盖进去，写在收信人姓名下方。例如：

Mr. Thom Collins

Assistant Vice President

The Hercules Engineering Co., Ltd.

Brazennose Street,

Manchester M60 8AS

*Englan*d

If the title appears on the same line, place a comma between the name and the title. For example:

如果姓名和职衔出现在同一行，需在它们之间加上逗点。例如：

Mr. George Russell, Director

164 Bay Road, Liquorland Oklahoma City,

OK 73125

U.S.A

If the name of a specific person is unavailable, you may address the letter to the department, followed by the name of the company. For example:

如果具体的收信人名字无法获得，可以写上公司名直接将信寄予公司，例如：

Customer Service Department

Acme Construction Company

In order to avoid ambiguity, when you write letters to other countries, always include the name of the country, even if the city mentioned is the country's capital. See the example below:

为了避免含糊不清，当你的信件要寄往国外时，通常收件人地址要涵盖国家名、城市名，即使这个国家名与其首都的名字一致。例如：

Mrs. Ann Meadows

Warner - Thompkins Company

210 Tracy Avenue Spokane,

Singapore 99202

Singapore

⑤ Salutation 称呼语

The salutation is the complimentary greeting to the receiver. Place it two lines below the inside address, flush with the left margin. Its form depends on the writer's relationship with the receiver.

称呼语也就是对收信人表示尊敬的问候。写在信内地址下方 2 行的位置，与左边线对齐。它的格式取决于写信人与收信人的关系。

The customary formal greeting in a business letter is（在商务信函中通常正式的问候）：

❑　for addressing one person 称呼一个人

Dear Sir,

Dear Madam,

❑　for addressing two or more people 称呼两个或以上的人

Dear Sirs,

Dear Madams,

Gentlemen:

If the receiver is known to the writer personally, a less formal and warmer greeting is used as follows:

如果写信人与收信人互相认识，会使用非正式、更加亲切的问候，例如：

Dear Ms. Katherine Black,

Dear Dr. Harry

⑥ Subject line 事由 / 主题行

Subject line is actually the general idea of a letter. It is inserted between the salutation and the body of the business letter either at the left-hand margin for fully-blocked letter form or centrally over the body of the letter to call attention to the topic of the letter. Some companies often use the Latin term in "re" or "Re" in place of "Subject".

主题行实际上是信件的内容大意。位于称呼语与正文之间，在齐头式中，位于信件的左边，或者位于正文上方的中间位置，用来强调信件主题。一些公司通常使用拉丁语的 "re" 或者 "Re" 代替 "主题" 二字。

The following forms are commonly used (以下是通常使用的格式)：

❑　Dear Sir or Madam,

Subject: Annual Trade Fair

❑　Dear Sir,

Re: Sales Contract No.2216 for 200 Metric Tons of Walnuts

⑦ Body 正文

Whether your letter consists of a single paragraph or several, the chief rule here is brevity. Business letters should never go beyond one page unless absolutely necessary. The trick is to be concise and to the point, but never discourteous.

It is best, even for a short letter, to divide the body into at least two or three paragraphs, confining each paragraph to one topic. A typical plan for a three-paragraph letter includes:

Paragraph One: Refers to any previous correspondence or introduces the purpose of the letter.

Paragraph Two: Supports the opening and provides what service or information you have to offer.

Paragraph Three: Ends the body of the letter with the action or idea that you want the reader to consider or with the results you would like to have.

不管信件是包含一段还是几段，最重要的原则就是简短。除非十分有必要时，商务信函最好不要超过一页信纸。正文写作的诀窍就是简洁并直奔主题，但是永远都不要失礼。

为了写一封简洁的信函，最好的办法是将正文分为至少两个或者三个段落，每一个段落突出一个内容。典型的方案就是分为三段：

第一段：承上启下，提及上一封信函所涉及内容或表达本次信函意图。

第二段：支撑开头段落并指出要提供的服务或信息。

第三段：结尾部分就是你希望读者采取的行动，希望他们所考虑的方面，或你想拥有的结果。

⑧ Complimentary close 结尾敬语

The complimentary close is merely a polite way of ending a letter. A complimentary close is used on most letters, typed two lines below the last line of your message and usually positioned flush left on the page. In most business letters, you want to end on a friendly but not too familiar note. Use variations of "sincerely" ("Most sincerely," "Very sincerely," "Sincerely yours," "Sincerely,").

结尾敬语只是用来结尾的一种礼貌的方式。大多数的商务信函最后都会有赞美性的敬语，这要放在正文结尾下方两行的位置，通常是在信纸的左边。商务信函的结尾要友好但不要太随便。用"真诚的"各种变体就可以了。

The most commonly used sets of complementary close are (最常用的结尾敬语):

	Formal	Less Formal	Informal
Complimentary	Yours faithfully,	Yours sincerely,	Sincerely,
	Faithfully yours,	Sincerely yours,	Cordially,
	Truly yours,	Cordially yours,	Best regards,

⑨ Signature 署名

The signature is the signing of the sender's name. Type the name below complimentary close, leave enough blank lines to sign your name by hand in black or blue ink. Never "sign" with a rubber stamp.

If your letter is on plain paper and you want to emphasize that you are legally representing your company, you may type the company's name in Capital letters below the complimentary close and place the title of the message sender on the same line with or below the typed name.

签名是发信人姓名的签署。在结尾敬语的下面写出姓名，并留出足够的空白行，用黑色或蓝色的钢笔签署您的姓名。不要用印章代替签名。

如果你的信件是用普通信纸，并想强调你是你公司的合法代表，那么可以在结尾敬语下用大写字母写出公司名称，并将发信人的头衔放置于同一行或写出的名字下面。

The following are examples of different ways of signing a business letter （以下是商务信函中不同署名方式的例子）：

❑   An official signing for his company（行政官员为公司的署名）：

Yours faithfully,

MAINRICH INTERNATIONAL CO., LTD.

Nancy

Nancy

❑   A partner signing for his firm（合作伙伴为公司的署名）:

Sincerely yours,

Dennis Brown

Dennis Brown

（2）Additional parts of business letters 商务信函的其他组成部分

① Enclosure 附件

An enclosure notation should be added to the business letter, when such documents as brochures, catalogues, samples, price lists are attached to the letter. The enclosure notation follows two lines after the signature block. Type the word "Enclosure", or its abbreviation written as "Enc." or "Encl." with the number of enclosures.

当要在信件中附加例如小册子，目录，样品，价目表等文件时，商务信函中需涵盖附件标记。附件标记与签名相隔 2 行。写上附件的号码，标明 "附件" 二字，或其缩写形式 "Enc." 或者 "Encl."。

Here typical enclosures might read (典型的附件写法):

❑   Enclosure 4 samples

❑   Encl. Price List

② Carbon copy notation 抄送

Carbon copy notation indicates that your letter is to be distributed to other people. Type "CC" or "cc" with the names of the persons who will receive the copies of the letter, usually positioned two lines below the signature block at the left margin.

抄送表明这封信件是要抄送给其他人的。在 "CC" 或 "cc" 后面列出所有收信人的姓名。通常将其放置于签名 2 排以下的左下方。

Many companies are now using "PC" (for photocopy). (现如今很多公司使用 "PC" ， 意思为影印本)For example:

❑   Margaret Ruth

❑   CC: The Chamber of Commerce for Metal and Minerals.

❑   c. c. Mr. Green

③ Postsript 附言

If the writer wished to add something he forgot to mention or for emphasis, he may add his postscript two lines below the carbon copy notation, and flush with the left margin.

如果作者希望补充一些在正文中遗漏的内容，又或者是为了强调，可将附言写在抄送两排以下的位置，与左边线对齐。

For example:

P.S. The catalogue will be sent to you tomorrow. 目录明天将会发送给您。

The adding of a P.S. should, however, be avoided as far as possible, since it may suggest the writer failed to plan his letter well before he typed it.

然而，应尽量避免在最后添加附言，因为这暗示着作者在写这封信时没有提前计划安排好。

（3）Example of formal business letters 正式商务信函的范例

The following letter is designed to illustrate the position of each part mentioned above (下面这封信将上面提及的所有部分细致的列举出来了):

Letterhead	Inytatex Middle East Ltd. P. O. Box 2216 Jeddah 12641, SAUDI ARABIA
Our ref: TF001 **Your ref:** FP/t3	
Dateline	August 5, 2011
Inside address	Milan International Trade Corp. Via Piccolomini 5 20151 Milan, Italy
Salutation	Dear Sirs,
Body	We visited your stand at Milan fair last October. We were interested in your leather boots. We are wholesalers in Jeddah and we think your articles could find a promising market in our area. We would be very pleased to receive your catalogue and price list.

Complimentary close	Yours faithfully,
Signature	*John Carter*
	John Carter
	Purchasing Manager

Encl. Price List

P.S. The covering samples will be transported to you by airmail today.

2.The Formats of a Business Letter 商务信函的格式

The format of English business letters usually becomes a part of the image of a company. There are four formats of a business letter in use at present: Indented Style, Full Block Style, Semi-block Style, and Simplified Style. In the four styles, the indented one of the most traditional and the simplified style is the least formal.

英语商务信函的格式已经成为公司形象的一部分。目前，总共有四种格式可供使用：缩格式、齐头式、改良齐头式、简化式。在这四种格式中，缩格式最为传统，而简化式最不正式。

（1）Indented style 缩格式

The indented style is a traditional British practice with the letterhead usually in the middle and the date line on the right-hand side. The complimentary close may be in the center or commence at the center point. The indented style takes 4 or 5 letters in the first line of each paragraph in the body of the business letter. It looks attractive and makes for easy reading, but it is not convenient to type.

缩格式为传统的英式，信头通常在中间，日期在右边。结尾敬语在中间或者是以中间点为基准开始写。在缩格式中，正文每一段的第一排需要空 4 个或 5 个字符。这样能够引起读者的注意，并方便阅读，但不方便书写。

Specimen Letter

London Trading Co., Ltd

Black road, Hammersmith W5 3DT

Tel: 41 23895563 Fax: 41 23895887 E-mail:lc@msn.com

May 15, 2008

Beijing Garments Imp/Exp Corporation

812 Jianguo Road, Beijing, 100088

China

Dear Mr. Chen,

Your letter of November 1, 2007 has been received. As we are anxious to finalize this transaction, we have been exerting ourselves to persuade our clients to accept your prices. Eventually, they have decided to accept. We are glad to have been able to conclude the business with you.

Await your sales confirmation.

Yours faithfully,

Colin Ryan

（2）Full Block Style 齐头式

The full block style is an American style, which has now come to much more widely used than before. In the block form, every part of a letter is typed from the left margin. It is convenient to be typed with typewriter but the layout looks somewhat crowded and imbalanced.

齐头式为美式，现如今该格式相比以前被广泛使用。在齐头式中，信函每一个部分全部从左边线开始写。用打字机打比较方便，但是整体布局看起来有些拥挤和不平衡。

Specimen Letter

21 CENTRURY TRADERS

77 COOPER ST # 4H

LONDON 2039, UK

9 October 2007

National Geographic Society

475 Kenwood St.

Duluth, MN55811

U.S.A

Dear Mrs. Mason,

Thank you for your letter of 12 August, concerning your forthcoming visit to my company.

I'll be glad to meet you at the time of your visit. Please confirm your flight number, so that my assistant, Helen, We will meet you at the airport.

I look forward to seeing you.

Yours sincerely,
Johnson Morgan

（3）Semi-block Style 改良齐头式

Semi-block style is a combination of the indented style and the block style. It is also called modified block style. In the Semi-block style all the parts starts from the left margin, except the date. The complimentary close and signature are positioned from the middle little toward the right.

改良齐头式是缩格式和齐头式的结合版。它也被称为改良式齐头式。在改良齐头式中，除了日期外，所有部分都是从左边线开始写，结尾敬语和署名写在中间靠右的位置。

Specimen Letter
Capital Electrical Products Co., Ltd
15 Parkagate Road, London SW12 4NQ U.K.
Tel: 44-35987048 E-mail:capital@hotmail.com

25 July 2007

The Commercial Attache
British Embassy
Beirut

Dear Sir,

For a number of years we have imported electric shaves from the United States, but now learn that these shaves can be obtained from British manufacturers. We wish to extend our present range of models and should be glad if you could supply us with a list of British manufacturers likely to be able to help us.

If you cannot supply the information from your records, could you please refer our enquiry to the appropriate quarter in London?

Yours faithfully,

Fred Johns

（4）Simplified style 简化式

Simplified style is somewhat like Full Block style. But some parts omitted, such as salutation and complimentary close.

简化式有点像齐头式。但是有些部分省略了，比如说称呼语和结尾敬语。

Specimen Letter

SHANGHAI LIHUA IMP. & EXP. CO., LTD

Rm.9012 Union Building, 1202 Hingham Road

Shanghai, China 20026

TEL: 86-21-64257881   E-mail: lihua129@yahoo.com.cn

August 28, 2008

Global Trade Group Ltd.

56W 39th ST #3

New York, NY

U.S.A

In compliance with you request in your letter dated August 28, 2008, we have sent you our latest brochure, by separate airmail, for your reference.

If you are interested in any item of our products, please let us know as soon as possible. We are looking forward to your specific enquiry.

Henry Lai

3.Addressing Envelopes 信封的书写

Business Envelopes usually have the return address already printed in the upper left corner. The receiver's name and address should be typed about half way down the envelope. The postmark or stamps should be placed in the up right-hand corner, while the bottom left-hand space is for post notation like "By airmail", "Confidential", "Printed Matter", etc. The format of address on the envelope can be in blocked or indented style, but it is better to keep the same format with the inside address for the letter.

商务信封通常要在左下角写上回信地址。收信人的姓名以及地址应写在信封的中下方。邮戳或邮票应贴在右上角，而在左下角写上邮件标记，例如"航空邮件""秘密邮件""印刷品"等。信封上的书写格式可以分为齐头式或缩格式，但最好是与信内书写格式一致。

Specimen Envelop (Block style)

ASIA SUNHAND CO., LTD
Suit 3B, Galore Building,
28-30, On LAN Street, Central

BY AIRMAIL

Mr. Ali
Imitate Middle East Ltd.
P. O. Box 2216 Jeddah 12641
Saudi Arabia

Specimen Envelop (Indented style)

Jack Simpson
Central Business Consultants
Hyde Towers
Hong Kong

Dr. David Zhang
No.305 Jinxing Building
Naming Rd. Shanghai, 20026
China

Part II   Principles of Business Letter Writing
商务信函写作原则

A good business letter can promote the sale of the products, keep a good impression of the company and enhance the work efficiency. Business letter writing is one of the necessary business activities. The following are a few general principles that are applied to business letter writing.

一封优秀的商务信函可以促进产品的销售、保持良好的企业形象，并能够提高工作效率。商务信函写作是必要的商务活动之一。下面是一些可以应用于商务信函写作的原则。

1.Courtesy 礼貌

Courtesy plays a considerable role in business letter writing as in all business activities. Courtesy means to show tactfully in your letters the honest friendship, thoughtful appreciation, sincere politeness, considerate understanding and heartfelt respecting.

在商务信函书写中，乃至整个商业活动中，礼貌起着相当大的作用。礼貌是指在信函中巧妙地表达诚挚的友谊、周到的赞赏、真诚的礼貌、体贴的谅解和发自内心的尊重。

Compare:

Your letter is not clear at all. I can't understand it. (Impolite)

❑ *If I understand your letter correctly,* (polite and tactful)

You should give us more details on your products. (Impolite)

❑ *Will you give us more details on you products?* (Courteous)

In order to make a business letter courteous, try to avoid irritating, offensive, or belittling statements. Under circumstances when you want to pint out your reader's mistakes but don't want your message to sound accusing, or you want to tell your reader what to do but don't want your message to read like an order, use passive voice, which helps you avoid using the word "you" and make your message sounds more courteous.

为了使商务信函更为礼貌，应尽量避免令人不悦、带有攻击性或贬低意味的表达。当回信要指出来信人的错误，但又不希望对方读起来带有指责意味，又或者你想要读信人去做某事，但又不想让你所写的内容似命令，便可以使用被动语态语句来表达。这样可以避免你在句子开头使用"你"，使信函内容看起来更为礼貌。

Compare the following sentences.

You must correct all these documents by noon. (Sentence with "you")

❑ *All these documents must be corrected by noon. (Sentence without "you")*

You shouldn't load this kind of goods on deck. (Sentence with "you")

❑ *This kind of goods cannot be loaded on deck. (Sentence without "you")*

Courtesy also involves a prompt reply after receiving a business letter. Please do remember not to keep your reader waiting.

礼貌也包括收到信件后及时地答复。请千万记得不要让您的读者等待。

2.Consideration 体谅

Consideration emphasizes You-attitude rather than We-attitude. When writing a letter keep the reader's request, needs, desires, as well as his feelings in mind. Put yourself into reader's shoes and plan the best way to present the message for the reader to receive.

体谅强调了"站在对方角度考虑"，而不是"站在自己角度考虑"。当写信函时，应考虑到读者的要求、需求、愿望以及内心的情绪。站在读者的角度考虑并使用最佳的方式组织信函内容，继而发给读者。

Compare the following pairs of sentences:

We allow 5 percent discount for payment within 10 days. ("We" attitude)

❑ *You earn 5 percent discount if you pay within 10 days.* ("You" attitude)

We offer T-shirts in different colors and styles. ("We" attitude)

❑ *Select your T-shirts from different colors and styles.* ("You" attitude)

As the saying goes "Every cloud has a silver lining", focus on the positive side rather than on the negative. Stress what can be done rather than what cannot be done so that the reader may feel you are sincere and considerate.

正如老话所言：黑暗之中总有一丝光明。书写信函时，与其关注消极的一面，不如多关注于积极的一面；与其表达现在不能做什么，不如强调什么是目前可以做的，这样让读者从中体会你是真诚、体贴的。

Compare:

It is impossible to fulfill your order this month. (Negative)

Your order will be fulfilled next month. (Positive)

3. Completeness 完整

A business letter is successful and functions well only when it contains all the necessary information. To achieve this, see to it that all questions are answered and all the matters are discussed.

一封成功并能起到一定作用的商务信函必须涵盖所有必要的信息。要做到这一点，需看其是否所有的问题和所有的事项都回答并进行了讨论。

Compare:

We have arranged to ship the goods within this week. (Incompleteness)

❑ *We have arranged to ship the goods by S.S "Virgin Mary" which is scheduled to sail for you port on October 25.* (Completeness)

4.Concreteness 具体

What the letter comes to should be specific, definite rather than vague, abstract and general, especially for letters calling for specific reply, such as offer, enquiry, etc. Concreteness is always stressed in business letter writing. For example, some qualities or dimensions of goods should be shown with exact figures and avoid words like short, long or high immediately.

信函书写应该是具体的、明确的，而不是模糊的、抽象的、笼统的。特别是针对那些要求明确回复的信函，如报价、询盘等。"具体"在商务信函写作中较为重要。例如，一些产品的质量和规格应用精确的数字罗列出来，避免使用例如"短"、"长"或"高"之类较模糊的字眼。

Compare:

We have drawn on you as usual under you L/C.

❑ *We have drawn on you our sight draft No.123 for the Invoice amount, USD500, under your L/C 211 of the Bank of China.* (Rewriting)

5.Correctness 准确

Correctness refers not only to correct usage of grammar, punctuation and spelling, but also to standard language, appropriate tone, proper statement, and accurate figures as well as the correct understanding of commercial jargons. It is likely to convey the real message in a way that will not cause offence even if it is a complaint or answer to such a letter.

准确性不仅仅是指语法使用、标点符号、单词拼写无误，还应正确使用标准的语言、恰当的语气、正确的语句、精确的数据以及对商业术语的正确认识。也就是相当于运用一种方式来传递最真实的信息，即使是投诉别人或者回复这样的信件。

Compare:

Please inform us the earliest shipment we can have as soon as possible.

(Incorrect place of modifiers)

❑ *Please inform us as soon as possible the earliest shipment we can have.*

(Correct place of modifiers)

Working as fast as possible, the goods are ready to be shipped.

(Incorrect use of noun and pronoun)

❑ *Working as fast as possible, we have got the goods ready to be shipped.*

(Correct use of noun and pronoun)

6.Conciseness 简洁

Conciseness means saying things in the fewest possible words without losing completeness or courtesy. A concise business letter should be precise and to the point, say things briefly but completely. To achieve conciseness of your letter writing, try to keep your sentences short, and avoid wordy expression and redundancy, or repetition, and eliminate excessive details.

简洁指在不影响完整和礼貌的情况下，使用最简洁的话语表达书信的内容。一封简明的商务信函应句句切中关键，用词简洁但完整。为了达到商务信函写作的简洁，书写时要删除多余的细节，尽量使用短小精悍的句子，避免啰唆、冗余或重复的表达。

Compare the following sentences:

We have begun to export our products to countries abroad. (Wordy)

我们开始向国外的国家出口我们的产品。（冗长）

❑   *We have begun to export our products.* (Concise)

  我们开始出口外贸的产品。（简洁）

Will you ship us any time during the month of May, or even June if you are rushed, for June would suit us just as well. (Unnecessary repetition)

您 5 月份可以任何时间发货，如您事务繁忙 6 月发货也可以，因为 6 月也正好适合我们。（不必要的重复）

❑   *Please ship us by the end of November.* (Rewriting)

  请务必在 11 月底之前发货。（改写后）

The concrete methods of making a letter concise are (使商务信函简洁的具体办法):

（1）Use a word to replace a phrase. 以单词代替词组

Enclosed herewith	enclosed
At this time	now
Due to the fact that	because
A draft in the amount of $1,000	a draft for $ 1,000

（2）Use a phrase to replace a sentence. 以词组代替句子

We are expecting you will reply us very soon.

❑   Hope to hear from you soon.

（3）Use words to replace clauses. 以词组代替从句

We require full-automatic washing machine that is of the new type.

❑   We require new-type full automatic washing machine.

（4）Avoid padded expressions. 避免不必要的表达

Please be advised that we have received your invoice.

❑   We have just received your invoice.

7.Clarity 清晰

Business misunderstandings result more often from unclear messages. Therefore, the writer must try to express his meaning clearly to make sure the message conveys exactly what he wishes to say. To achieve this he should try to:

商务活动中的许多误会很多时候都是由于不清楚的信息造成的。因此，作者必须清楚地表达自己的想法，以确保传达的信息就是自己想要说的的内容。为了达到这一点，必须做到：

（1）Avoid vague and ambiguous expressions. 避免含混不清与模棱两可的表达

As to the steamers sailing from Hong Kong to San Francisco, we have bimonthly direct services.

The word "bimonthly" has two meanings: twice a month, or once two months. The reader will feel puzzled about the meaning. Thus the sentence can be rewritten as follows:

"bimonthly" 有 "一月两次" 或 "两月一次" 两种意思。读者会觉得些许困惑。因此有以下几种改法。

❑   *We have two direct sailings every month from Hong Kong to San Francisco.*

❑   *We have semimonthly direct sailing from Hong Kong to San Francisco.*

❑   *We have a direct sailing from Hong Kong to San Francisco every two months.*

（2）Pay attention to the sentences structure. 注意句子结构

Compare the following sentences:

We sent you, by air, 4 samples of the goods, which you requested in your letter of May 10 by air.

❑   *We sent you 4 samples yesterday of the goods which you requested in your letter of May 10 by air.*

The goods differ not only in quality, but also in price.

❑   *The goods not only differ in quality, but also in price.*

Part III   Writing Techniques of business Letter Writing
商务信函写作技巧

There are many complicated steps in the whole process of business communication, such as establishing business relations, enquiries and replies, offers and counter-offers, complaints. In view of the characteristics of various business letters, specific writing techniques should be adopted to perfect the business letter writing. This part will try to analyze the writing techniques and etiquette which relate to the business letters in details with a sample letter.

在整个商务交流过程中，有许多纷繁复杂的步骤，如建立贸易关系、询价及回复、报盘与还盘、申诉。根据不同种类商务信函的特点，应采取针对性的写作技巧以完善商务信函写作。该部分将会结合例子详细分析信函的写作技巧及相关礼仪。

1.Establishing Business Relations 建立贸易关系

(1) In writing a letter for establishing business relation, you may often take the following steps

- ❑ State the source of information—how you have learned of this company.
- ❑ Briefly introduce your own company—the scope of your business, little "advertising" on your products or service.
- ❑ State your purpose in writing—what kind of business you want to do with them, e.g. to purchase their products, to sell your own products, to enter into a joint venture with them, establish/develop business relations, etc.
- ❑ Express the intention of cooperation and early reply.

在书写建立贸易关系的信函时，通常可以采纳以下几个步骤：一是说明信息来源，即通过什么方式或渠道了解到对方公司；二是简要介绍自己的公司，即公司的经营范围，借机给自己公司的产品或服务做一个简短的"广告"；三是表达写信的目的，期待与对方做一桩什么样的生意，例如购买他们的产品，或推销自己的产品，或与他们建立合资经营项目，或建立 / 发展贸易关系等；四是表达合作愿望，并期盼早日回复。

Sample Letter: Self-introduction by an exporter

Dear Sirs,

We have learned from our Commercial Counselor's office in London that you are interested in importing Chinese Cotton Piece Goods. As this item falls within the scope of our business activities, we shall be pleased to enter into direct business relations with you at an early date.

In order to give you a general idea of the products now available for export, we send you a copy of our latest catalogue and a pricelist. Quotations and sample books will be airmailed to you upon receipt of your specific enquiry.

We look forward to your early reply.

Yours sincerely,

Zhou Dai Chuan

Zhou Dai Chuan

敬启者：

我方从驻伦敦商务参赞处得知贵方有意进口中国棉制品。该产品属于我们的经营范围，我们非常乐意早日与贵公司建立直接的贸易关系。

为了让您对我方出口的产品有一个大致的了解，我们寄送了一份最新产品目录和价格表。一旦收到贵公司具体询盘，我们会将报价以及样本航空邮寄给您。

盼回复。

×××敬上

(2) In replying to such letters, you should

❑ Mention the date in which you have received the letter.

❑ Express thanks to your reader for the proposal.

❑ Provide information requested.

❑ Indicate clearly whether you accept the proposal or not.

❑ Give a reason if you decline it, and end your letter with a positive note for further business.

回复这类信件时，首先提及你收到该信件的日期并感谢对方函中的提议；其次提供对方要求了解的信息；再则清楚地表明是否接受对方的提议。如果要拒绝对方要求，请说明理由。信的结尾则以积极的口吻来描绘双方未来的合作。

The first impression matters very much. Be positive to follow the standard format and try best to avoid making mistakes. Be sure to answer in full without the least delay after you receive any letter of this nature. Only in this way you can create goodwill and leave a good impression on the reader.

第一印象很重要。应按照标准格式，并尽量避免犯错。在收到这种类型的信件后应及时完整的回复。只有这样，你才能够建立信誉，并给读者留下良好的印象。

Sample Letter: A reply to the above importer

Dear Sirs,

Thank you for your letter of the 16th of this month. We shall be very glad to establish business relations with your company.

In compliance with your request, we are sending you, under separate cover, our latest catalogue and price list covering our export range. We have also sent you some samples for your reference.

Payment should be made by an irrevocable and confirmed letter of credit.

If you find business possible, please fax or e-mail us for offers.

Yours sincerely,
Zhou Dai chuan

敬启者：

感谢您本月 16 日的来信。我们非常高兴能够与贵公司建立贸易关系。

按贵方要求，我们另邮了出口产品的最新目录和价格表。我们还向您发送了一些样品，供您参考。

付款应使用不可撤销的保兑信用证。

如贵方愿意洽谈，请通过传真或邮件来索盘。

×××敬上

2.Enquiries and Replies 询价及回复

(1) How to write an enquiry letter

❑ Be specific and state clearly what you want, the goods needed, a catalogue, a price list, a sample, a quotation, etc, so that the seller can offer what you need.

❑ Keep the enquiry concise and to the point.

❑ If it is the first enquiry, start your letter by informing how you have obtained their name and address. Meanwhile, you can give a brief introduction of your own business. Some details about what you would like to get from the exporter would be mentioned in the end.

❑ The tactic often used in order to invite better terms is to give the seller some hope of substantial orders or continued business by saying "Should your prices be competitive, we shall place an order..." or "If your quotation is favorable, we'll place regular order with you."

如何书写询价信函：信函内容要明确，并清楚地表明您想要什么、需要的商品、目录、价格表、样品、报价单等。这样销售方可提供您所需要的。询价信函需简明扼要。如果这是第一次询价，应以告知对方如何获得他们的名字和地址作为信函开头。同时，您也可以对您公司做一个简要的介绍。信函结尾应提及你想从出口方获得的一些详细信息。为了能够得到更优厚的条件，通常要使用一些"策略"，即给销售方　种将会有大量订单或继续进行合作的希望。有这样几种说法："如果您的价格具有竞争性，我们将会订购……"或"如果您的报价优惠，我们将会长期订货。"

Sample Letter: General enquiry and reply

Dear Mr. Wang,

We have seen your advertisement at http://www. Made-in-China.com and are particularly interested in your bamboo and straw articles. We would like to have details of your various types, including sizes, materials and prices.

We are large dealers in arts and crafts, having over 15 years experience in this particular line of business. Provided quality and prices are satisfactory, there are prospects of good sales in our market .

When replying, please state terms of payment and discounts you would allow on purchases of quantities of over 100 dozen of individual items.

We look forward to your early reply.

Sincerely yours,
Henry

敬启者：

我们在 http:// www. Made-in-China.com 网站上看到贵公司的广告，对您公司销售的草编竹制品尤为感兴趣。我们希望了解不同类型的详细信息，包括大小、原料和价格。

我们是本地区工艺品的主要经销商，在这一行业经营长达 15 年之久。如果产品质量和价格令人满意，该产品在我方市场将会很畅销。

请您回复此函时告知支付方式及订购各品种数量超过 100 打所能给予的折扣。

盼回复。

×××敬上

(2) How to reply an enquiry

As we know, enquiries mean potential business. Therefore, replies to enquiries must be prompt, courteous, and helpful. Make sure that the reply covers all the information asked for and all the points you want to make. In writing a reply to an enquiry, you may:

❑ Express thanks to the inquirer for his or her interest in your products.

❑ Answer the questions asked and provide other relevant and necessary information.

❑ State briefly to first enquirer the strengths and advantages of your products.

❑ If you are unable to supply the products required, give a reason or explanation in addition to expressing regret. Always end your letter positively by offering other products as substitutes so as to create a good impression, which hopefully may result in more business.

众所周知，询价意味着潜在的商业机会。因此，回复询价信函时，一定要及时、礼貌、乐于助人。确保函中回复所询问的信息和想要陈述的内容。对于询价函的回复，首先感谢询价者对产品感兴趣。其次回答询价中所提出的问题。提供其他相关必要的信息。针对询价主要强调自身产品的长处和优势。倘若无法向对方提供所需产品，除了表示遗憾之外，还应说明缘由。信函的结尾通常会提供其他产品作为替代品来满足需求，给对方留下好印象，以期带来更多的商机。

Sample Letter: Reply to importer's enquiry

Dear Mr. Henry

We are very glad to receive your enquiry of February 3 and thank you for your interest in our products.

We are sending you our quotation sheet and a copy of our latest catalogue giving the details you asked for, and hope that some of our products will be suitable for your market.

On regular purchases of over 100 dozen of individual items, we would give a discount of 3%. As to payment, we usually accept payment by sight L/C. We assure our clients of delivery within 20 days after receipt of L/C.

In addition to bamboo and straw articles, we also deal in carvings, porcelains, wooden products and a wide range of Christmas gift items, details of which you will find in the catalogue. If you need any further information, please let us know.

We look forward to welcoming you as our customer.

Yours sincerely,

Mr. Wang

Sales Manager

敬启者：

很高兴收到贵公司 2 月 3 日的来信，感谢贵方对我方产品的关注。

我们将报价单和一份最新产品目录发送给您，提供了您要求的详细信息，希望我们的一些产品能够适合你们的市场。

如果定期采购各品种超过 100 打以上，我们将给予 3% 的折扣。关于付款，我们一般接受即期信用证的付款方式。我们向客户保证在收到信用证后 20 天内交货。

除了草编制品以外，我们也经营雕刻品、瓷器、木制品以及各种各样的圣诞礼品，详细信息可以在目录中查询。如果贵方需要更多的信息，请告知我方。

恭候您的光临。

×××敬上

3.Offers and Counter-offers 报盘与还盘

(1) A letter of offer or quotation

❑ A letter of offer or quotation is usually composed of the following three parts:

❑ An expression of thanks for the enquiry, if any;

❑ Details of the goods, prices, trade terms, discounts or commissions, terms of payment, the time of delivery, the time period in which the offer is valid;

❑ A wish of the offer will be accepted.

报盘或报价信函通常由以下三个部分组成：对询盘表示感谢；产品、价格、贸易条款、折扣或佣金、付款方式、交货期、报盘有效期限的详细信息；表达对报盘被接受的期待。

Sample Letter: A firm offer for plush bear

Dear Mrs. Celia Clemens,

Re: Plush Bear Item No. 1003P

We thank you for your Email of March 4, 2008, enquiring for the captioned goods.

As requested, we offer firm, subject to your reply reaching here by March18, as follows:

Plush Bear Item No. 1003P as per sample, each in a plastic bag and then in a box, 25 boxes to a carton with white and brown equally assorted.

Unit Price: USD 10.59 per dozen, CIF Singapore.

Payment: by Irrevocable Letter of Credit.

Quantity: Minimum order 500 dozen, maximum present capacity 1,000 dozen a month.

Delivery: within 30 days after receipt of the relative L/C.

We hope the above will be acceptable to you and await your early order.

Yours faithfully,

Paul Zhou

敬启者：

感谢贵方 2008 年 3 月 4 日来函询问我方标题货物。

按贵方要求，现报实盘如下，以贵方 3 月 18 日前回复至我方为有效。

编号 1003P 毛绒熊按样成交，每个毛绒熊用塑料袋包装，并装入盒中，25 盒装一箱，白色和棕色均匀搭配。

单价：CIF 新加坡价每打 10.59 美元。

付款方式：不可撤销信用证。

数量：最小订货量为 500 打，目前最大容量为每月 1000 打。

配送：在收到相关信用证的 30 天内

我们希望以上信息会使你满意，并望能早日收到订单。

××× 敬上

(2) A letter of counter-offer

A letter of counter-offer is to be written, which should include:

❑　An expression of thanks for the offer;

❑　Reason for inability to accept the offer;

❑   A counter-offer (your own idea including terms and conditions acceptable, etc.);

❑   A wish of the counter-offer will be accepted (urging the reader to accept early);

❑   A wish of other business opportunities in future if necessary.

书写还盘信函时，应包含：对报盘表示感谢；不能接受报盘的缘由；还盘（自己的想法，包括可以接受的条款和条件等）；希望该还盘能被接受（说服读者尽早接受）；如必要，表达对未来其他的商业合作契机寄予希望。

Sample Letter: A counter-offer for plush bear

Dear Mr. Zhou,
Re: Plush Bear Item No. 1003P

We've received your E-mail offer of 5th March for Plush Bear Item No. 1003P with thanks.

All the terms contained in the offer are acceptable except the price. While appreciating the quality of your commodity, we find your price on the high side. Now in Europe, many suppliers, mainly from Asia, have come into the market with a much lower price than yours. The chief sellers, worrying about their market share, are again lowering their prices. Such being the case, to accept your quotation would mean little profit to us.

However, we would like to place a trial order with you if you could make an 8% reduction in your price. Should this transaction prove to be successful, we'd certainly place more substantial orders on a regular basis.

We hope you will reconsider this matter and send us a new offer.

Yours sincerely,
Mrs. Celia Clemens

敬启者：
贵公司 3 月 5 日来函收悉，感谢贵公司对编号 1003P 毛绒熊的报盘。

除了价格以外，报盘里所有的条款都可以接受。虽然我方对贵方的商品质量很满意，但认为价格偏高。现如今，欧洲的很多供货商主要来自亚洲，并以低于你方价格进入市场。总销售商担心他们的市场份额，又一次降低他们的价格。在这种情况下，如接受贵方的报价，对我们来说也就意味着微薄的利润。

然而，如果贵方价格能降低 8%，我们非常乐意向贵方试购。如果此次交易成功，我们定会长期大量地订购。

我们希望贵方能重新考虑并向我方提供新的报价。

×××敬上

(3) A letter of re-counter offer

A letter of re-counter offer should cover the following particulars:

- ❑ An expression of thanks for a counter offer;
- ❑ Stating what shall be amended;
- ❑ A wish of a favorable reply.

再还盘信函应包含以下细节：对还盘信函表示感谢；说明哪些部分要修改；恭候佳音。

Sample Letter: Exporter's reply to a counter-offer

Dear Mrs. Celia Clemens,

Re: Plush Bear Item No. 1003P

Thank you for your fax of March 18. We are indeed sorry that you found our price too high.

Actually the prices we quoted you are narrowly calculated and are very realistic. As I am sure you know, we operate in a highly competitive market in which we have been forced to cut our prices to the minimum. If it were not for the regular orders we received from a number of our customers, we could not have quoted such low prices. We believe a fair comparison of quality between our products and those from other sources will convince you of the reasonableness of our quotation.

However, in view of our future cooperation, we would exceptionally give you a 3% quantity discount if you order exceeds 8,000 dozen.

We hope you will accept our proposal and look forward to your trial order.

Yours sincerely,
Paul Zhou

敬启者：

感谢贵方3月18日来函。对于贵方认为价格太高，我们深表歉意。

实际上，我方的报价是经过精打细算的，它非常合乎现在的行情。我确信您知道，为应对市场的激烈竞争，我们的价格被迫降至最低。如果不是因为有许多客户发来固定订单，我方就不可能报出这么低的价格。相信通过公正地比较我方及其他供应商的产品会使贵方确信我方报价的合理性。即使如此，基于未来的合作，倘若贵方订单数量超过 8000 打，我方将破例给予贵方 3% 的折扣。

希望能接受我方提议。期盼收到贵方试订单。

×××敬上

4.Complaints and Settlements 抱怨和理赔

(1) Rules of complaint

The letter of complaints or settlements is intended to obtain better service, hoping that the problem can be settled properly and quickly. It is usually made by the importers who suffered losses against the exporters, such as wrong goods delivered; shipment overdue; shipment damaged, or short; goods in inferior quality; goods badly packed. These are valid reasons for complaining.

A letter of complaints should be written as follows:

❑ Begin by regretting the need to complain.

❑ Mention the details of the goods complained about, including the name of the article, the contract number, the name of the ship, the date of delivery, etc.

❑ State the reasons for being dissatisfied and ask for an explanation.

❑ Refer to the inconvenience caused.

❑ Suggest how the matter should be settled.

抱怨或索赔信函的目的是为了获取更好的服务，对已出现的问题求得尽快并妥善的解决。它通常是买方由于对收到的货物不满而书写的，如：货物虽抵达，但与订单所载不同；货物未按时到达；货物有损毁现象或数量短缺；货物质量低劣；货物包装拙劣等。这些均是抱怨、索赔的正当理由。

抱怨信函应这样书写：开头首先应对前来抱怨表示遗憾，同时提及抱怨的产品的具体细节，包括商品名称、合同号、船名、交货期等。陈述抱怨的理由，并请求对方给出解释。最后提及由于问题造成的不便之处，并提出解决的建议。

Sample Letter: Complaint about inferior quality

Dear Sirs,

We duly received the documents and took delivery of the dress materials supplied to our Order No. LNG-521. We are much obliged to you for the promote execution of this order.

After careful examination, however, we are both surprised and disappointed to find that the quality of these materials is certainly much below that of the samples you sent us.

We are enclosing a cutting sample from the goods we received. You will admit that these materials do not come up to the sample on which we passed the order.

As the materials are quite unsuited to the needs of our customers, we hold the goods at your disposal.

Please look into the matter and let us know what you can do about it as soon as possible.

Yours faithfully,
Mark Twain

敬启者：

我方已按时收到了装运单据，并提取了合同号为 LNG-521 的衣料。我们十分感谢订单的及时执行。

但经过仔细的检查，我们既惊讶又失望地发现这些衣料的质量确实大大低于您发给我们的样品。

兹随函寄上我们从收到货物中剪取的一份抽样。您将会确认这些衣料比不上订货的样品。

这些衣料非常不合我们客户的需求，我方代为保存该货，等候处理。

请着手调查此事，并尽早告知我们您将采取什么措施。

×××敬上

(2) Rules of settlement

The following are the rules for writing the letter of settlements:

❑ Take the complaint seriously.

❑ Explain what has happened and why it has happened.

❑ Ask for necessary cooperation from the customer.

❑ Do not shirk responsibility. If you are wrong, you should admit your mistake and apologize sincerely. You can promise that you will try every effort to prevent the error from happening again, but the trouble is caused by other people, you may promise to contact them and help to resolve the problems.

❑ End with a friendly, positive attitude.

下面是书写理赔信函的原则：重视对方的抱怨。解释发生了什么，为什么会发生。向客户请求必要的合作。不要推卸责任。如果是你的错，你必须承认错误并真诚地致以歉意。你可以保证你将会付出一切努力防止该类事情再次发生。但是，如果这个错误是由他人造成的，你可以承诺将会与他们联系，并协助解决这个问题。最后以友好、积极的态度结束信函。

Sample Letter: Settlement of inferior quality

Dear Sirs,

We very much regret to learn from your letter of March 21 that you are not satisfied with the dress materials supplied to your Order No. LNG-521.

Tracing our records, we find that there has been some mistake in our selection of the materials meant for you.

We are very sorry for this carelessness on our part. To settle the problem, we would like either to replace the inferior materials as soon as possible or to give you a special allowance of 30% for the invoice amount.

We apologize once more for any inconvenience our mistake may have caused you. We assure you that the same mistake won't happen again.

I hope this matter will not affect your good impression of us and look forward to your decision as to which of the above two adjustments is preferable to you.

Yours faithfully,
John Wendy

敬启者：

从贵方 3 月 21 日来函获悉贵方对合同号为 LNG-521 的衣料不满意，我们甚感遗憾。

追查我们的记录发现，在我们为贵方选择衣料时出现了差错。

我方为这次疏忽深表歉意。为了解决这个问题，我方愿意尽快替换残次品，或给予贵方发票金额 30% 的特例折扣。

对该错误给您造成的诸多不便，再次表示歉意。我方向贵方保证不会再发生此类错误。

我方希望此事不会影响贵方对本公司的良好印象。贵方可以在上面提出的两种解决方案中选择对贵方更有利的，恭候贵方的决定。

×××敬上

Situational practice for etiquettes 礼仪口语实景

Make up or search for more situational conversations that may occur in conducting business trade and put them into practice.

(At the Guangzhou Trade Fair, A is a Spanish buyer, inquiring about prices at a bed-cover stand.)

A: Good morning. My name is Henry Jones. We are one of the major companies in selling bed-covers in Barcelona, Spain. I'm very interested in your bed-cover. I have seen your exhibits and catalogues. They are attractive. Here is a list of requirements. I'd like to have your lowest quotations, CIF Barcelona, Spain.

B: Thank you for your inquiry, Mr. Jones. Will you please tell me the quantity you require so as to enable us to sort out offers?

A: OK, I will do that. Could you give me an indication of the price?

B: Here are our latest FOB price sheets. All the prices in the sheets are subject to our final confirmation.

A: For how long does your quotation price remain open?

B: It's open for three days. When can you decide the size of your order?

A: That will depend on your price. If your price is reasonable and I can get the commission I want, we can place an order immediately.

B: In principle, we don't allow any commission. But if your order is large, we will take it into consideration. From the price sheets, you will find our prices are very competitive. And heavy inquiries witness the quality of our products. You know, the prices of materials have gone up sharply. But the prices of our products haven't changed much.

A: I'm very pleased to hear that. How long will it take you to deliver the goods?

B: Usually we deliver the goods within 3 months after receipt of the covering letters of credit.

A: Good. I can't make the decision by myself. I will call my head office in Spain and consider the price carefully. If they think the prices are favorable, we can place order right away. I will come back to you tomorrow. All right?

B: Right. See you tomorrow.

Terminology related 相关礼仪术语

Proper Etiquette for Writing a Business Meeting Sign 商务会议标牌写作礼仪

At a time when most customs and behaviors of polite society, especially in matters of business, seem to be from a bygone era, there are guidelines that should be adhered to in the creation of a sign for a business meeting. They are not written in any business-etiquette books, but certain guidelines will ensure that meeting attendees get the information needed to find the meeting without undue hassle and without having to resort to asking someone for help.

What is the Meeting?

Many larger meetings are held at huge convention centers or in hotel meeting rooms. And meetings might be conducted simultaneously. When a meeting attendee enters the lobby of the building, there often is more than one sign in the lobby directing people to meetings. So, for starters, your sign should clearly display the name and logo of your company. This quickly informs attendees that they are in the right place. If the meeting has a particular title, announce it in a big, bold typeface. If there are break-out sessions, list those as well.

Where Is the Meeting?

Make sure your sign gives clear directions to your meeting, including floor number and room number (or name). If the location is particularly complex, provide other information, such as "Elevator Bank B." A large directional arrow will point attendees in the right direction.

What Time Is the Meeting?

Surprisingly, providing the meeting's time is the least important part of the business sign. If the person is there, he already has a general time for the meeting. But remember to include the start and end times on the meeting sign below the title and location.

文明社会的大多数规范和行为（尤其是商业领域），都源自于远古时代。同样，在制作商务会议的标牌时也是有规律可循的。以下这些规律在商务礼仪书也许找不到，但是与会者却能轻松找到所需的信息，而且不必借助他人。

什么会议?

很多大型会议都选在大型会议中心或宾馆会议室举行。这里可以允许多个会议同时举行。当与会者步入大厅时，常常会看到多个指引不同会议的标牌。因此，新手在制作标牌时，应清晰地展示公司名称和公司商标，以快捷地指引与会者抵达正确的会议现场。如果会议有特定的名称，应用大黑体标明。在休会期间，同样要摆出标牌以作指引。

会议在哪里召开?

所制作的标牌要清晰地指明会议场所所在，列出楼层、房间号（或名称）。如果位置比较复杂，应提供其他信息，如电梯B等。同时大的方向箭头也可将与会者指引到会议现场。

会议何时召开?

令人意外的是，会议时间是标牌上最不重要的信息。因为如果与会者已经抵达，就会获悉会议的大致时间。但是标牌上会议名称和位置下方还应写明会议开始和结束的时间。

Useful expressions for etiquettes 礼仪用语集锦

The followings are appropriate expressions you may use when writing business letters:

● In writing a letter for establishing business relations
建立商务关系信函中的用语

- ❑ We have learned your name and address from...
从……我方得知您的姓名和通信地址。

- ❑ ...has advised us to get in touch with you concerning...
……推荐我们就和您联系。

- ❑ ...has referred us to you for establishing business relations with your corporation
……推荐我方和贵公司建立商业关系。

- ❑ Through the courtesy of the..., we come to know your name and address.
经……礼荐，我方得知您的姓名和通信地址。

- ❑ We note with pleasure from...that you are interested in establishing business relations with us on supply of...
我方欣喜地得知贵公司就……供货愿意和我方建立商业关系。

● In replying to a letter for establishing business relations 对建立商业关系信函的回复

- ❑ If you want to know more about our products, please feel free to let us know.
如贵方想进一步了解我方产品，欢迎随时来信联系。

- ❑ If you need more details, please inform us as soon as possible.
如贵方需要了解更多详情，请尽快来函。

- ❑ Should you want to get more information, please don't hesitate to let us know.
如贵方需要了解更多详情，请尽快来函联系。

- ❑ If you are interested in our products, we will quote you our best price.
如贵方有意购买我方产品，我方会提供最优惠的报价。

● In writing an enquiry letter 询价信用语

- ❑ The goods are more popular with our customer.
这种产品更为我方客户青睐。

- ❑ The goods are selling fast (or enjoy fast sale).
这种产品很畅销。

- ❑ The goods are universally acknowledged.
这种产品得到广泛的认可。

- ❑ The goods are unanimously acclaimed by our customers.
我方客户普遍认可这种产品。

- ❑ The goods have been well received.
  这种产品很受欢迎。

- ❑ The goods have earned a good reputation.
  这种产品享有良好的声誉。

- ❑ The goods have commanded a good market.
  这种产品已占领了市场。

- ❑ The goods have received favorable reception.
  这种产品很受欢迎。

- ❑ The goods met with excellent reactions.
  这种产品反响很好。

- ❑ The goods have enjoyed great popularity in world market.
  这种产品在国际市场上很受欢迎。

● In writing a letter for complaint 投诉信用语

- ❑ We are very sorry to /It is with regret that we have to inform you that the goods under Contract No. 132 have been damaged...
  我方很遗憾地告知贵方合同 132 号产品受损……

- ❑ Thank you for your letter dated...advising us of the shipment of our order...On checking the goods received, we found that...
  感谢日期为……的来信告知我方货物已装运。在核查收到的货物时，我方发现……

- ❑ We have duly received the goods of your shipment of...But unfortunately...
  我方已按时收到你方……发运的货物。但遗憾的是……

- ❑ On examination, we find that the goods do not agree with the original sample.
  在检查货品时，我方发现货品和原样本不符。

- ❑ A thorough examination showed that broken bags were due to improper packing for which the suppliers are responsible.
  经过彻底检查，破损的包装袋是因为不当包装造成的。供应商对此负有责任。

- ❑ It would be necessary for you to give this matter best attention if you wish to...
  如果贵方希望……贵方有必要对此予以足够的关注。

- ❑ We trust that you will make every effort to prevent our taking a step which would not be as welcome to us as to you.
  我方相信贵方会尽一切努力避免我方采取令双方不愉快的举措。

- ❑ We have duly received the goods of your shipment of...But unfortunately we find...
  我方已按时收到你方……发运的货物。但遗憾的是我方发现……

- ❑ Unfortunately you have not sent all the goods we ordered; the following are missing.
  遗憾的是贵方并未发送我方订购的所有货物。遗漏了以下货物。
- ❑ Kindly adjust this complaint and make us a reimbursement as soon as possible.
  请妥善处理此次投诉，尽快向我方作出赔偿。
- ❑ Please look into the matter as one of the urgencies and let us have your reply as early as possible.
  请紧急调查此事并尽早给我方答复。

● In writing a letter for settlement 处理事件的信函用语

- ❑ We have received your complaints of..., for which we apologize.
  我方已收到贵方就……的投诉，对此我方深表歉意。
- ❑ We apologize once again for...
  我方再次对……表示歉意。
- ❑ We are making a number of modifications to our organization which will ensure that such a delay will not occur again.
  我方在企业内部进行了很大调整，以确保此类延误不再发生。
- ❑ I'd like to offer you my personal assurance of better service in the future.
  我愿以个人的名义保证后期会提供更好的服务。
- ❑ I hope this matter will not affect your good impression of us.
  我方希望此事不会影响贵方对我方的良好印象。
- ❑ Please accept our many apologies for the trouble caused to you by our error.
  由于我方的失误对贵方造成了麻烦，请接受我方的歉意。
- ❑ I promise no shortage of goods should happen again.
  我方承诺货物短缺不会再发生。
- ❑ We hope this won't affect the good relationship between us.
  我方希望此事不会影响双方的良好关系。

Exercises（课后练习）

I. Questions and answers: answer the following questions according to the information you have got in the previous reading.

1. How many parts are included in a business letter? What are they?
2. Can you illustrate the differences between the indented style and full block style?
3. What are the principles of business letters? What must we do to ensure courtesy in a business letter?

4. Which kinds of business letters will be needed in the whole process of business communication?

5. What are the writing techniques in sending the complaint letter?

II. Expressions: match the terms in column A with the Chinese equivalents in column B.

A	B
letterhead	附件
enclosure	理赔
postscript	报价
indented style	还盘
semi-block style	信头
counter-offers	缩格式
quotation	附言
settlement	改良齐头式

III. Translation: translate the following statements into Chinese to learn about Email etiquette.

1. Writing style: Follow the rules of grammar and punctuation when composing your email. Avoid slang, acronyms and short forms like "u" instead of "you".

2. Composition: Given the flood of email we get daily, it's best to keep your emails short and to-the-point. If you have to make a number of points, use bullets to cover all your points briefly.

   If you are replying to a thread of email, consider deleting the older text in the body of your email, or summarizing it in a few lines.

   It's a good idea to add a signature at the end of your email, which includes your phone number and other contact details. This would be particularly useful for emails sent to clients or recruiters, or other people outside your organization.

3. Subject line: The lack of a subject line or a vague subject like "Hello" or "I have a question"can be annoying to busy people. They also make it harder for the receiver to search for your email in their inbox.

   Be specific in your subject line and mention if the matter is urgent. Instead of saying "I have a question", say "My holiday plans; not urgent".

   At the same time, don't make the subject line too long or detailed.

Also, don't start discussing a new topic under the same subject line. This also makes it difficult to identify mails about specific queries. It's best to send separate emails for separate topics.

4. Get the name right: Email recipients can get angry if the body of your email has the wrong spelling of their name or, even worse, if you address the person as "Mr." when it should really be "Ms." always double-check spellings and titles before sending your email. If you are not sure whether the recipient is male or female either use the person's first name or the full name.

5. Caution on "Reply All": This is a tricky button on our email box because if used without care, it can be a source of much embarrassment. One of the most common problems is that your message has gone to people who should not be reading it. Use Reply to all infrequently and after careful thought.

6. Before hitting "Send": Emails can be easily forwarded and thus be read by more people than you think. So re-read your emails carefully before sending it, to make sure that it is not offensive and that it doesn't say anything that could get you into trouble.

7. Time frame: How quickly you need to reply to an email typically depends on the nature of the email. In general, you should reply immediately. If you know you don't have an immediate answer to a particular query, reply to acknowledge the email and give the person a time frame of when you think you'll be able to respond.

8. Calling after Email: It might be tempting to call up the person you just emailed, but desist. It can be annoying for the recipient.

Give the person some hours or even a day to think and respond, no matter how eager you may be for the reply. If it's urgent, mention that in the subject. If anything is an important matter, call the person first alerting them to the email.

9. Attachments: In general, avoid sending large files as attachments since they clog up the recipient's inbox. If you are sending pictures, resize them to a smaller resolution. If you absolutely have to send a large file, call the recipient to check first.

10. When not to send email: Don't send emails for every little thing and especially not for something that can be tackled easily over the phone or in person.

IV.Cloze: choose the suitable statements from the box and complete the passage.

> A.Keep Them Formal and Factual
>
> B.Be Customer Friendly
>
> C.Relegate Technical Details To Attachments
>
> D.Carefully Plan Your Letter
>
> E.Limit Them To One Page

Here are a few tips I have picked up while writing literally hundreds of business letters over the past 20+ years. This is a slightly modified version of the tips included in my eBook, "Instant Business Letter Kit".

_____1_____. By definition, business letters should be short and to the point, preferably one page in length. Studies have found that busy business people do not like to read beyond the first page, and will actually delay reading longer letters.

_____2_____. Often, it is necessary to include detailed technical information as part of a business letter package. In such cases, use the main letter as a cover letter that lists and briefly explains the attached (or enclosed) documents.

_____3_____. Generally speaking, the tone and content of business letters should be formal and factual. Feelings and emotions do not have a place in business letters.

_____4_____. Before writing the letter, take a few minutes to list all of the specific points you need to cover. Sometimes it may even mean a call to the recipient or his/her company to confirm a specific point. Remember, the purpose of the letter is to tie up all of the details on the subject at hand, so that more letters won't have to be written back and forth.

_____5_____. When writing directly to customers, always focus on their needs and their perspective. Put yourself in their position and imagine what it would be like receiving your letter. Everyone can do this, since we are all customers of some other business in some part of our lives.

Case study:

Case 1

Your department has recently moved to a new building. You are not satisfied with the way the removal company dealt with the move of your furniture and equipment and have decided to write a letter of complaint to the removal company about it.

Write the letter to the removal company, including the following information:

❑ details of the move and what was moved;

- ❑   what was unsatisfactory;
- ❑   what you had expected from the company;
- ❑   what you expect to happen now of work.

Case 2

You are dissatisfied with the poor service that has recently been provided by the company responsible for delivering your products to your customers.

Write the letter to the company:

- ❑   informing them of the fall in the standard of their service;
- ❑   explaining why you are dissatisfied;
- ❑   describing the bad effect the service has had on your business;
- ❑   detailing what action you intend to take if the service does not improve.

 Extension（拓展阅读）

Do More With Less!

For over a decade, the message at work has been "Do more with less!" As writers, we have this challenge too. And we can be much more efficient if we use less wordiness. By cutting down on extra words, we cut down on both writing and reading time.

The paragraph below contains 70 words. Can you cut it down to 35 words or less?

This document is for the purpose of giving the reader a detailed explanation of the inventory process. It describes the activities we currently do in the majority of instances on a daily and weekly basis. In order to provide an introduction to the process for employees who work on a temporary basis, we also have prepared an overview, which describes the highlights of the inventory process in just two pages.

Here is a 30-word revision:

This document explains the inventory process in detail. It describes our usual daily and weekly activities. We also have prepared a two-page overview to introduce the process to temporary employees.

Which paragraph above is clearer—the 70-word version or the 30-word revision?

To lighten up your sentences, watch for heavy phrases like these:

for the purpose of = for

the majority of = most

in order to = to

provide an introduction = introduce

on a daily basis = daily

on a regular basis = routinely

Do you think you can do more with less? Try this experiment:

When you finish writing a paragraph or a page, imagine it needs to be one-third shorter because of space constraints. Then see how many words you can cut. You'll probably be surprised about the excess baggage your sentences are carrying. And your readers will thank you.

After-reading tasks （读后任务）

When you finish reading the text above, get into the groups and discuss with your group members about the following tasks and fulfill them.

Task 1

Compare the following two versions of business mails:

The original mail

Dear Sir：

Thank you for your message of October 5, telling us the availability date of the above title. Unfortunately our local customer asked us to reduce the quantity of this order from 50 to 25 copies.

Could you, therefore, back order 25 copies instead of 50 and send them as soon as they become available via Air Express?

Yours sincerely,

...

The refined mail

Dear Sir:

Thank you for your message of October 5.

Unfortunately our customer has requested that we reduce (the quantity of) this order from 50 to 25 copies.

Therefore, would you please send by air freight only 25 copies as soon as the books become available?

Yours sincerely,

...

After reading the mails above, discuss with your group members about the differences you have found in the mails and find out why the author has made such modifications. Finally, cooperate with your group members to set up the principles that a business writer should follow.

Task 2

Generally speaking, courtesy is the basic element that every business letter writer pays much attention to, but how to show the courtesy is a question. See the underlined part in the first mail and discuss with your group members whether they are appropriate.

The original mail

Dear Tang:

Further to your call today, we are writing to advise you of our special rates for groups on Tour 016B to Italy.

We are able to offer a 12% discount on the basic price for groups of more than 30. Unfortunately, we are unable to offer discounts on any of the supplementary charges.

Hoping this information will help you.

Best regards,

Diana Green

And then study the refined mail to see what modifications the author has made and find out with your group members why he has done so.

Dear Tang:

Thank you for your call today about our Tour 016 to Italy.

We are pleased to inform you that we can offer a special 12% discount on the basic price for groups of more than 30.

Unfortunately, we cannot give discounts on any of the supplementary charges.

Please call again if you need further information.

Best regards,

Diana Green

Task 3

After having finis hed the supplementary reading, discuss with your group members in what way etiquettes can be reflected in business writing, being a business writer. What aspects should be taken into consideration to ensure the good manners in business interactions?

Self-Study（自学反馈）

If possible, summarize what you have learned in this unit with the help of the following table.

Focus of this unit:

Guidelines for etiquette:

1.

2.

3.

...

Summary:

Application:

1.

2.

3.

...

Feedback:

Chapter Eight
Etiquette in International Business Negotiation
国际商务谈判礼仪

Objectives (学习目标)

After you have studied this chapter, you should be able to:

- ❑ Have a command of the etiquette in international business negotiation
- ❑ Handle some problem situations in international business negotiation
- ❑ Cultivate the cross-cultural awareness when communicating in international business negotiation

Lead-in (导读)

If you work in a field in which you have to negotiate often, it's very important that you know the etiquette associated with negotiating, such as how to speak to a potential client and how to behave when the negotiation process is prolonged. These courtesies will help you to avoid awkward situations and make a the positive first impression.

It is surely not enough to be acquainted with the local etiquettes. Negotiators who may come from another nation are different from each other in manners. Even though negotiators are well prepared, it is not so easy to reach a satisfactory agreement between negotiators across cultures. Negotiation can be easily broken down due to a lack of mutual understanding of etiquettes. Therefore, professionals in international business world will be never too careful with the study of etiquettes across cultures.

如果你所在的专业领域经常需要谈判，那么了解与谈判相关的礼仪就尤为重要。要学会如何与潜在客户交谈；要懂得在谈判变得旷日持久时，如何行为处事。这些礼节有助于避免尴尬局面，留下积极的第一印象。

在谈判时，只熟悉本国礼节肯定是不够的。谈判双方可能来自不同国家，彼此在礼仪规范上会有很大差异。即使谈判双方认真准备，也可能很难让来自不同文化背景的谈判方达成协议。很可能因为对对方礼仪规范的误解而导致谈判失败。因此，国际商务人士对待跨文化礼仪要格外谨慎。

Test yourself（自我测试）

To start with, take a test to see to what degree you have mastered the etiquette in international business negotiation. Please use Yes or No to make responses to the following statements.

1. The most common form of greeting in the corporate world is the handshake. However, if you are in the Middle East, a nod of acknowledgment may be best when greeting someone of the opposite sex.　　Yes ☐ No ☐

2. In some countries such as Finland and Germany, small talk is not part of business culture, and meetings start precisely on time.　　Yes ☐ No ☐

3. After negotiations, a German or Finnish professional may host a dinner or a trip to the sauna for casual conversation.　　Yes ☐ No ☐

4. While some companies depend more on a favorable relationship when making a final decision in a negotiation, it is always proper etiquette for you to have facts and figures ready to present to each meeting participant.　　Yes ☐ No ☐

5. In Australia, it is appropriate to use "hard selling" or persuasion to get a businessperson to side with you in the negotiation process.　　Yes ☐ No ☐

6. In countries like the U.S. the use of "hard selling" or persuasion is inappropriate and could result in the end of a potentially positive business relationship.　　Yes ☐ No ☐

7. In the Middle East and parts of Africa, bargaining is common and expected—both sides make offers on an item or service until a satisfactory price is reached.　　Yes ☐ No ☐

8. Following up with the negotiation proceedings in the appropriate way, such as sending a short email, will show that you are genuinely interested but don't want to seem too pushy.　　Yes ☐ No ☐

9. Learn the culture of the people you will be negotiating with. This is a sign of respect and an indication of how you will behave during the business process.`　　Yes ☐ No ☐

10. Make the best use of the time before and after the negotiations. Engage in small talk with the professionals before the negotiations begin, and have short conversations after negotiations have ended for the day.　　Yes ☐ No ☐

Part I Negotiators as Hosts
作为东道主的谈判者

In this chapter, we divide negotiators into two groups: the hosts and the guests. Hosts refer to those negotiators holding meetings in their own country or city while guests are those who come to negotiate with the host party in their country or city for a business purpose.

本章将谈判者分为两种群体：东道主和宾客。东道主是指在自己的国家或城市举办会议的谈判者，宾客是指那些出于商业目的到主办方国家或城市与东道主进行磋商的谈判者。

1.Welcoming the Guest Party 迎接宾客方

The host negotiator should prepare well for every aspect of the meeting, such as welcoming the guests, choosing the meeting site or arranging the meeting agenda. Make everything perfect so that your guests will feel comfortable and thus both parties will find it easier to build a good relationship with mutual understanding and trust.

东道主的谈判代表应做好会议各个方面万全的准备，如迎接宾客，选择会议场地，以及安排会议议事日程。使一切有条不紊，方便宾客，这样双方更容易建立起相互理解与信任的友好关系。

（1）Setting up a reception group 建立接待组

This group is responsible for arranging everything necessary for the guests. Group members should include employees from the logistic department, the communication department, the transportation department etc. If it is an international negotiation, do not forget to include an interpreter in the group. Staffing the reception team in an effective way will not only facilitate good arrangements and preparations for each section of the negotiation but also help deal with anything unexpected that might crop up in various situations.

该组负责为宾客安排一切必要的事宜。接待组成员应包含后勤部门、通信部门、交通部门等的员工。如果这是一个国际性的谈判，请不要忘了在该组中加入一名口译译员。有效地安排该接待团队的人员配置，不仅可以促进谈判各个部分更好的安排和准备，还可以帮助处理各种情形的突发状况。

（2）Collecting information about the guests 收集宾客的信息

Before making the arrangements, the host should gather information about his guests. How many of them? How many males and females? What are their positions in their company? Only after collecting all information can the host plan specific details.

在做准备前，东道主应收集宾客的信息。人数是多少？男性和女性分别是多少？他们各自在公司的职位是什么？只有在收集所有信息后，东道主才能计划具体细节。

（3）Making a reception plan 做一个接待计划

A reception plan and agenda should be drafted based upon the collected information. Fax the plan and agenda to the guests to ask for their opinions and agreement. If possible, make some changes in accordance with their suggestions. If more than one language is involved, translate the plan into the language the counter party understands. Once the counter party accepts the meeting agenda, get it printed. Leave a copy of the agenda in the hotel rooms or give it to the leader of the guests.

根据收集到的信息，应该起草一个接待计划和议程。将计划和议程传真给宾客，询问他们的意见并期许得到认可。如果有什么意见的话，根据他们的建议做出修改。如果涉及一种以上的语言，将计划译成对方能理解的语言。一旦对方接受了本次议程，将其打印出来。在宾馆的房间内留一份议程，或者交予宾客中的领导者。

2.Meeting Guests and Seeing Guests off 迎接和欢送宾客

When people first meet, they will have an initial impression of each other. And whether this first impression is good or not will influence the negotiation. A good first impression might help both sides to build a good relationship and a poor impression might be an obstacle to reaching an agreement. You might find the following suggestions useful.

当人们第一次会面时，双方将有一个初步印象。并且不管这第一印象是好还是坏都将影响此次的谈判。良好的第一印象会有助于双方建立友好的合作关系，相反，差劲的第一印象可能会是此次达成协议的障碍。你会发现以下的建议非常有用。

（1）Confirming the time again 再次确认时间

Confirm the time and place. Arrive at the airport or railroad station earlier than your guests are expected to show your respect. Never make your guests wait for you. When your guests are leaving, pick them up in their hotel and take them to the airport or railroad station. Or you might go directly to airport or railroad station to say goodbye to them.

确认时间和地点。要先于你的客人到达机场或火车站，以显示你对他们的尊重。当宾客离开时，可到宾馆接他们并送至机场、火车站。或者直接去机场或火车站与他们道别。永远不要让你的宾客等你。

（2）Introducing yourself or being introduced 介绍双方

When both sides meet, you could introduce yourself or be introduced by others. Tell others your name, title and your position in the company. You should say your name clearly and distinctly, making sure the other party can hear it accurately. Also, make sure you get the other party's name right. If you are not sure, repeat it or ask them to repeat it to be sure you have the correct name of them.

当双方会面时，你可以介绍你自己或由其他人介绍。告诉对方你的姓名，头衔以及在公司的职位。你应清楚明了地说出你的名字，确保对方能准确无误地听到。另外，确保你也得到了对方正确的名字。如果你不确定，重复或请求他们重复以确保你得到了他们正确的名字。

（3）Taking cars 乘车

The most important guest should be seated at the right side of the host when taking cars. The seat on the right, beside the car window is the honored one. Guests should be invited to get into the car from the right side while the host enters from the left. If the guest takes the seat of the host, just let it be. If it is a big car, no strict rules have to be followed. In countries like Great Britain where drivers sit on the right side and drive along the left side, the rules are just the opposite.

当上车时，最重要的客人应坐在主办人的右侧。右边靠窗户的座位是贵宾座。应将客人从右边迎入车内，而主办人则从左边进入车内。如果客人坐在了主办人的位置，就维持现状。如果是一辆大型车，没有严格的规则需要遵循。像英国这样的国家，司机坐在右边并沿左车道行驶，规则正好相反。

3.Choosing the Negotiation Room and Arranging the Seats

The environment and the seating arrangement in the negotiation room should demonstrate respect to the guests. The seating arrangement is an especially sensitive task that requires careful advance attention.

谈判室内的环境以及座位的安排应显示出对宾客的尊重。座位安排是一个尤其敏感的差事，需要预先仔细地斟酌。

（1）Choosing the proper negotiation room 选择合适的谈判室

The company's meeting room can be used as the negotiation room. If possible, prepare two to three rooms. One room will be used for negotiation, and the other two for both sides' private discussions. An additional room could be set aside for people to take coffee or refreshment.

公司的会议室可用作谈判室。如果条件允许，可以准备 2 ～ 3 个房间。一个用作谈判，另外两间用作双方的私下讨论的场所。可以预留一个额外的房间作为与会者品用咖啡或茶点的休息室。

（2）Arranging the seats in appropriate order 座次安排

① Rectangular or oval tables 矩形或椭圆形桌

Rectangular or oval tables are always used in bilateral negotiations. In most occasions, the negotiation parties will sit face to face. If the table is positioned horizontally facing the door, the seats facing the door are the ones for the honored guests while the opposite seats are for the hosts. If the narrower end of the table faces the door, the seats on the right are for guests while those on the left are for hosts. Interpreters will be seated at the right side of the speakers. It is advisable to prepare name cards to avoid mistakes.

在双边谈判中总是使用矩形或椭圆形桌子。在大多数情况下，谈判双方将面对面而坐。如果桌子对着门水平放置，那么对着门的座位是宾客的，而对面的座位是东道主的。如果是尾部较窄的桌子对着门，右边的座位留给宾客，左边的座位留给东道主。口译译员将坐在讲话者的右侧。准备姓名卡以避免犯错是一个明智的做法。

② Round table 圆形桌

Round tables are used mainly in multilateral negotiations. Internationally, we term this a "round table meeting". Participants will sit around the table for the meeting. This arrangement minimizes the status differences among people and helps to build a friendly atmosphere.

圆桌会议主要用于多边贸易谈判。在国际上，我们将其称作"圆桌会议"。与会者将围桌而坐，进行会议。这种安排可尽量缩小人与人之间的地位差异，有助于建立友好的气氛。

③ U-shaped seat arrangements U 形桌

Small discussions can be held with people sitting on sofas, without a table. Hosts would be seated on the right and guests on the left. In this case, interpreters will sit behind the speakers. Such U-shaped seat arrangements will bring people closer and help them feel free, but this arrangement is not quite suitable for formal meetings.

小型的讨论可以安排坐在沙发进行，不需要桌子。主人坐右边，客人坐左边。在这种情况下，口译译员将坐在说话者的后面。这种 U 形座位安排会使人们更加亲近，感觉自在。但这种安排并不适合正式的会议。

4.Serving Partners Through Dinner Parties 宴请宾客

Dinner parties are always essential during negotiating process, because these contribute to create a more relaxed and less tense atmosphere where both sides can behave less aggressive. In such an atmosphere, people will be more willing to make concessions or offer more attractive

conditions. Many different kinds of dinner parties can be arranged, depending on the negotiators' purposes and budgets. Usually we divide them into formal and informal ones.

宴会在整个谈判进程中是必不可少的。因为这样有助于营造一个更为轻松并自在的环境，谈判双方表现得不那么好争斗。在这种气氛下，人们将会更乐于做出让步或提供更具吸引力的条件。根据谈判者的目的和预算，可以举办许多不同种类的宴会。通常我们将其分为正式的和非正式的。

（1）Different kinds of dinner parties 各种不同的宴会

The followings are some common dinner held by host negotiators:

以下是一些常见的由东道主的谈判代表举办的宴会：

① Formal dinner party 正式宴会

In a formal dinner party, participants must dress formally. "Formally" here refers to shirt and tie for a men, and evening dress for ladies. Never run the risk of wearing casual dress or you will be kicked out of the negotiation. In addition, you should pay close attention to the seating. Usually, seats will be arranged according to the ranks or titles of the guests. The most highly respected guest will be seated next to the host. In such formal parties, dishes always include soup and several main courses, cold dishes, desserts and fruit. Never pour a drink yourself; always allow someone else to do it for you.

在正式宴会中，参加者必须穿着正式。"正式"在这里指的是男士着衬衫、戴领带，女士着晚礼服。不要冒险去穿便装，否则你会被逐出谈判。另外，应注意座位安排。座位通常根据客人的职级或职衔来安排的。最受尊敬的客人的座位将紧邻于主人的位置。在这种正式宴会中，菜式通常包含汤和一些主食、冷盘、甜点和水果。切勿自己倒饮料，等待有人为你服务。

② Informal dinner party 非正式宴会

These dinner parties provide the best chances for people to build good relationships. There are no very strict rules or etiquette you have to follow. Choose to sit anywhere you wish, wear whatever you like and help yourself freely. Of course do not go to extremes. No matter how relaxed you are in this kind of informal parties, it is still important to follow basic business etiquette. Besides that, always keep in mind that in this circumstance alcoholic beverage is not welcome.

非正式宴会为人们建立友好关系提供了最好的机会。没有什么很严格的标准或礼节需遵守。选择你想坐的任何地方，穿任何你想穿的，自己尽情享受。当然也不能太过了。在这种非正式宴会中，不管你有多放松，遵循基本的商务礼仪仍然重要。除此之外，请铭记于心，在这种情况下，含酒精的饮料是不受欢迎的。

③ Working lunch 工作午餐

This option is also an informal form of dinner during the process of negotiation. The host may have ready-made food, usually fast food, delivered to the negotiating site, which allows the two parties to continue their discussion while they are sitting around the negotiation table and having lunch. Generally, it is the host who orders and pays for the meal.

这种形式也是在谈判进程中非正式的宴会。东道主可能有现成的食物，通常是快餐，送到谈判场地。这使得双方一边围坐在谈判桌前享受午餐，一边仍继续讨论。一般来说，由主办方订餐并买单。

（2）Organizing the dinner party 组织宴会

Sometimes good organization of a dinner party facilities the ability to reach an agreement quickly or motivates the other side to make some concessions. So never take the arrangement of dinner parties lightly. Spend some time and you will be rewarded sooner or later. The following are some suggested steps you might follow.

成功的宴请有时有助于促成尽快达成协议，或使对方做出让步。因此不要轻视宴会的安排组织。花一些时间，迟早会获得回报。你可以遵循以下步骤。

① What 什么

Make sure that you know the objectives for holding this party and then decide whether it should be a formal one or informal one.

确保你知道举办此次宴会的目的，并决定是否应该是正式的或非正式的。

② Who 谁

Decide who you are going to invite and all together how many persons should be included. Take into consideration the status, nationalities, national habits and customs of the guest party members.

决定你要邀请谁，一共有多少人应被列入名单。考虑宾客成员的地位、国籍、民族习惯和风俗。

③ When 什么时间

Choose the right time. It would be better if you could ask for the guests' suggestions. Never make the mistakes of inviting people to party during their country's legal holidays.

选择合适的时机。最好征求客人建议。切勿在客人国家的法定节假日时邀请他们前来赴宴。

④ Where 哪里

It is really a delicate matter to choose the appropriate venue for a party. Of course, never host your guests in the hotel where they are staying. Then your choices will depend on how much budget you have, what goals you want to reach and who you are going to invite. Always remember when scheduling the meal, never ask the guests where they would like to eat. Instead, pick two restaurants, pick two different hours, and offer your guest those options.

为宴会选择一个适当的地点确实是一个棘手的问题。当然，不要在宾客入住的酒店宴请他们。然后，你的决定取决你的预算、你的安排以及你想邀请谁。当安排宴会行程时，切记不要问他们想去哪里吃。相反，挑两间餐厅，选择两个不同时段，给你的宾客提供这些选项。

⑤ Where to sit 在哪里坐

In international practice, the closer to the host, the higher the status is. Usually the person on the right side of the host is the most important one in this dinner party and the person to the left is less important. Offer your guest his or her choice, but in no case should your guest be facing a mirror or the bathroom or kitchen doors.

在国际习惯中，越靠近主人，地位越高。通常在主人右侧的来宾是宴会中最重要的人，左边的来宾次之。在特殊情况下，可让来宾选择，但绝不要让来宾面对镜子、盥洗室或厨房门。

⑥ When to arrive 什么时候到达

Once your guests arrive, you should appear as if you have just arrived. Do not order a drink until your guests have all arrived.

一旦宾客到达时，你应该出现，表现出好像刚到似的。在所有的宾客全部抵达后再点饮料。

⑦ When to pay 什么时候付款

Arrive at the restaurant early enough to pay the bill ahead of time.

提前到达餐厅，好预先支付账单。

5.Signing the Contract 签订合同

When both sides have reached an agreement, they will hold a ceremony to sign the contract. This verifies that the agreement has the power of law.

The most important issue in signing ceremony is to make an appropriate seating arrangement. Generally speaking, there are three arrangement layouts. Negotiators may choose any one of them depending on the specific negotiation situations.

当双方已经达成协议，他们将举行签约仪式，证实该协议具有法律效力。

在签字仪式上，最重要的问题是要适当地安排座位。一般来说，有三种安排布局。谈判者可以根据具体的谈判情况而选择其一。

（1）Side-by-side arrangement 肩并肩的安排

This arrangement is the most common style for signing ceremonies. The table is placed horizontal to the door. All the participants will be seated behind the table, with the guests on the right and hosts on the left. The signatories will sit in the middle.

这样的安排是签约仪式最常见的风格。桌子被放置在与门的水平位置。所有与会者都将坐在桌子后面，客人在右边，主人在左边。签字人将坐在中间。

（2）Face-to-face arrangement 面对面的安排

This arrangement is almost the same as the first one. The only difference is that the two sides will sit face to face instead of side by side.

这种安排几乎与第一种一样。唯一的区别是，双方将面对面而坐，而不是并排。

（3）Free-style arrangement 自由式安排

The free-style arrangement is usually used in multilateral signing ceremonies. The table is also horizontal to the door, but there are no fixed seats for participants. Each one will go to the signing table when it is his or her turn and then return to his or her original seat.

自由风格的安排通常用于多边签字仪式。桌子也被放置在与门的水平位置，但是参与者没有固定座位。每个人当轮到他们的时候都可以去签约桌，然后再返回他或她原来的座位。

6.Signing Ceremony 签字仪式

There are some specific steps in the signing ceremony:

签字仪式有具体的步骤：

（1）Announcing the opening 宣布开幕

At this moment all the participants enter the signing hall and take their seats.

在这一刻，所有的参与者进入签约仪式厅，并入席。

（2）Signing the document 签署文件

The signing rule is: each party signs its own copy of contract first and then the copy of the other party. In accordance with the etiquette of signing, one's signature should be the first on one's own copy and the second on the copy of the other party. This method is called "signing by turn". This is to make sure that both parties are obviously equal in rights and responsibilities.

签名的规则是：每一方先签署其自己的合同副本，然后签署对方的副本。根据签署的礼仪，一个人的签名应是其副本的第一份，对方副本的第二份。这种方法被称为"转签署"。这是为了确保双方在权利和责任上是明显平等的。

（3）Exchanging copies 交换合同

While exchanging the copies, the negotiators shall shake hands with other party to express congratulations on the successful cooperation. Sometimes they might exchange the pens they have just used, to be kept as a memento. All the people then warmly applaud to express their happiness.

在交换副本的同时，谈判者可与对方握手从而对成功合作表示祝贺。有时，他们可能会交换他们刚刚使用的钢笔，将保留以作纪念。然后所有的人都热烈鼓掌，以表达他们的喜悦之情。

（4）The congratulatory toast 祝酒共贺

At the end of ceremony, people will toast with a cup of champagne to celebrate. This is a common practice around the world.

在仪式结束后，人们将敬一杯香槟庆祝。这是一个世界各地较普遍的做法。

Part II　Negotiators as Guests
作为宾客的谈判者

1.Do as Romans do 入乡随俗

Since you are in other's country, remember this old saying "when in Rome, do as the Romans do". This is the golden rule you should always follow. Accept the arrangements made by your host, and observe what others do and how they do. Doing this can help you avoid making some silly mistakes that might jeopardize the success of the negotiation.

既然你在对方的国家，记住这样一句老话"入乡随俗"。这是你应始终遵循的黄金法则。接受东道主的安排，并观察别人做什么，他们是怎么做的。这样做可以帮助你避免犯下一些危及谈判成功的愚蠢的错误。

2.Asking for Changes 请求变更

It is always nice to "Do as Romans do". But if this would involve you in some special taboos of your own culture or if there are time constraints, do not hesitate to voice your concerns. On most occasions, your host will be happy to assist or accommodate you.

"入乡随俗"始终是很好的，但如果涉及他国文化的一些特殊禁忌，或者有时间限制，坦承您的顾虑。在大多数情况下，主人将会很乐意协助或满足您的。

3.Dining Etiquette 用餐礼仪

Always practice respectable table manners when engaging in a business dinner. Table manners usually play an important role in making a good impression on negotiators. They are visible signs of manners and therefore are essential to negotiation success. You can find more specific details in chapter 5.

在参加商务宴会时，应始终遵循尊敬有礼的餐桌礼仪。餐桌礼仪在给谈判者留下良好印象中起着举足轻重的作用。它们是举止的外在表现，因此对谈判的成功至关重要。你可以在第五章中学习到更具体的细节。

Part III Taboos of Business Negotiation of Different Cultures
各国的商务谈判禁忌

People from different countries have different values, different attitudes and different experience. They have different strengths and different weakness from one another. In fact, good manners in negotiation vary from country to country. Getting to grips with the counterparts' acceptable manners helps to avoid conflict. Here, let us have a review of etiquette in a few countries.

来自不同国家的人有不同的价值观，不同的态度和不同的经历。他们各有不同的长处和弱点。事实上，谈判的礼貌举止因国家而异。掌握对方国家的礼貌举止帮助我们避免一些冲突。在这里，让我们了解一些国家的礼仪禁忌。

1.America 美国

- ❑ Meet them head on instead of skirting around problems.
- ❑ Do not criticize their country's politics or economics.
- ❑ Avoid discussions of war, politics and religions.
- ❑ Do not talk around things without coming to any decision.

切中问题要害，不要打擦边球。不要批评他们国家的政治或经济。避免讨论战争、政治和宗教。不要谈那些无关结果的事情。

2.France 法国

❑ Avoid drinking hard liquor before meals or smoking cigars between courses.

❑ The French are sensitive to personal privacy, so do not ask them about their family and their private life. Even more important is that you should not ask how their company performs.

避免饭前喝烈性酒或两道菜间抽雪茄。

法国人对个人隐私尤为敏感，所以不要问他们的家庭和他们的私人生活。更重要的是，不要问他们公司的执行方式。

3.Britain 英国

❑ Call them "the Britons" instead of "the English".

❑ Britons like humorous people, but negotiators from abroad should remember that humor rarely translate well.

❑ Britons don't like "yes" men or "yes" ladies.

称呼他们为 "the Britons"，而不是 "the English"。英国人喜欢幽默的人，但来自国外的谈判者应该记住，幽默很难翻译准确。英国人不喜欢什么都说 "是" 的男士或女士。

4.Japan 日本

❑ Take special care in handling business cards that given to you.

❑ The greeting is the bow.

❑ If you are invited to social event, punctuality is not expected. It is the custom to be "fashionably late".

❑ Concern with "Face" is essential.

小心对待对方给你的名片。问候方式是鞠躬。如果你被邀请参加社交活动，不需要特别准时。"时髦地迟到" 是该国文化习俗所接受的。"面子" 是非常重要的。

5.India 印度

❑ This is a hierarchical culture, so greet the eldest or most senior person first.

❑ Don't forget that Hindus (80% of the population) do not eat beef and that neither Muslims (12%) nor Hindus eat pork.

❑ Yellow, green and red are lucky colors, so try to use them to wrap gifts.

这是一个分等级的社会，因此，先问候前辈或职位最高的人。

要记住：占人口 80％的印度教徒不吃牛肉，占人口 12％的穆斯林和印度教徒都不吃猪肉。

黄色、绿色和红色是吉祥色，所以要尽量使用它们来包装礼物。

Situational practice for etiquettes 礼仪口语实景

Make up or search for more situational conversations that may occur during the business negotiation and put them into practice.

Model 1

A: We recently have developed some new products. I think you will be interested in it.

B: Do you have a catalogue?

A: Of course. Here you are.

B: Thank you. Yes, they are very attractive. How about the market?

A: We've made a market research. These products have great potential. This is the market analysis report. You can have a look.

B: Thank you, but how about the price?

A: This is the price list.

B: Oh, they're too expensive. I'm afraid our company can't accept the price. If you can reduce the price by 5%, we will consider your offer.

A: They're not expensive at all from long-term perspective. You will benefit greatly from the deal.

B: Well, I have to clear that with manager first.

Model 2

A: We've heard of your company for a long time, and have confidence in your business and financial status. But the problem is we are not very satisfied with the design and style of your products.

B: I know that our silk products displayed at Guangzhou Autumn Fair last year were not to your satisfaction. But since then, we have got some new designs. I hope you will be interested in them.

A: Perhaps you are right, Mr. Smith. But I'm not selling goods that remain on the shelf. I'm selling the goods at a larger profit. You're interested in that, aren't you?

B: Of course. All businessmen are interested in making money. That's our main purpose of doing business.

A: Well, Mr. Liu, I was much impressed by your show room. I've already seen some items we'd like to order, although I'd still like to study them a bit further.

B: I'm very glad to hear that, Mr. Smith. By the way, if your order is a large one, we'll be ready to give you a special discount.

A: OK, Mr. Liu, I'm very glad we are likely to conclude this first transaction with you soon. We've settled all the problems about price, insurance, packing and shipment. I hope our friendly negotiation will also lead to an agreement on the terms of payment.

B: I hope so too, Mr. Smith. I am sure through our mutual effort, we can conclude this transaction to the satisfaction of both parties.

Model 3

A: Now that we've satisfactorily dealt with the question of payment terms, I'm desirous to know if it's possible to effect shipment during March?

B: I'm sorry we can't effect shipment in March.

A: When is the earliest we can expect shipment?

B: By the middle of April, I think.

A: That would be too late. These goods are urgently required by our customers for the selling seasons in May. Besides, our Customs formalities will take quite a long time. You must deliver the goods before April, or else we won't be able to catch the shopping season.

B: It's all very well for you to say that. But the problem is that our factories have of a lot of back orders on hand. I'm afraid it's very difficult to improve any further on the time.

A: Can't you find some way for an earlier delivery? If we place our goods on the market at a time when all other importers have sold theirs at profitable prices, we shall lose out.

B: How's this then? We'll make an effort to advance the shipment to early April.

A: All right. I take you at your word. May I suggest you put it down in the contract? Other terms and conditions remain the same as in previous dealings.

B: OK. We'll do everything to advance shipment. Thank for your great effort.

Terminology related 相关礼仪术语

Negotiation Style 谈判风格

Negotiation style is about the attitude with which you approach your negotiations. Your beliefs, personality, skills, agenda, even sex, are all factors that will influence the negotiation style you choose to use. And you may choose to use different negotiation styles to serve your different needs in different situations. There are three major styles in negotiations: collaborative (win-win), competitive (win-lose), and a combination of both.

谈判风格是你对待和进行谈判的态度和方式。你的信仰、性格、技能、议事日程，甚至性别都足以影响你决定选择的谈判风格。在不同的情况下，你会选择不同的谈判风格来满足不同的需要。谈判中有三种主要的谈判风格：合作式（赢—赢）、竞争式（赢—输）以及二者的结合。

Useful expressions for etiquettes 礼仪用语集锦

The followings are appropriate expressions you may use during the business negotiations:

- ❑ Your price is much higher than what we were expecting to pay.
  贵方价格超过我方预期。

- ❑ Your price is not so attractive as that offered by other suppliers.
  和其他供应商相比，贵方价格缺乏吸引力。

- ❑ Why, your price has soared. It's almost 25% higher than last year's.
  贵方价格上涨幅度太大。几乎高于去年价格的 25%。

- ❑ In view of our good cooperation in the past, we accept your counter-offer.
  鉴于以往的合作，我方接受贵方的还盘。

- ❑ If your order is large enough, we're prepared to reduce the price by 5%.
  如贵方订单量大，我方拟将价格降低 5%。

- ❑ For a good start to our business relationships, we'll give you a 5% reduction this time.
  为给我们的商贸关系一个好的开端，我方本次交易将给予 5% 的折扣。

- ❑ This is really our rock-bottom price. We can't make any further reduction.
  这确实是我方底价，我方无法再减价了。

- ❑ This is really our floor price. If you can't accept it, I'm afraid we have to call the deal off.
  这确实是我方底价。如贵方无法接受，我方恐怕只能取消本次交易。

- ❑ Our price can meet any competition in the markets.
  我方价格在市场上是极具竞争力的。

❑ Our price is already 10% lower than that available from other makers.
我方报价已比市场上低了 10%。

Exercises（课后练习）

I.Questions and answers: answer the following questions according to the information you have got in the previous reading.

1.What is the effect of an initial impression on reaching an agreement in a negotiation? What can the host do to leave a good first impression on the guest?

2.What are the different ways of arranging the seats?

3.How does the host prepare for serving partners through dinner parties?

4.What are the aspects that should be taken into consideration in signing the contract?

5.How should the guest response in the process of a negotiation?

II.Expressions: match the terms in column A with the Chinese equivalents in column B.

A	B
greetings	决定（谈判）策略
small talk	问候
presentation	达成共识
deciding on strategy	签署合同
waiting for a decision	寒暄
reaching an agreement	等待（对方）决定
signing the contract	报告

III.Translation: translate the following statements into Chinese to ensure to learn about Business Negotiation Etiquette.

1.Before the negotiations officially begin, it is essential that you present yourself as friendly and polite to give the impression of trustworthiness. Learn the culture of the people you will be negotiating with. This is a sign of respect and an indication of how you will behave during the business process.

2.It is also common for some professionals to engage in small talk before the negotiations begin and to have short conversations after negotiations have ended for the day. This gives everyone time to become more comfortable with one another and is the gateway to building a lasting business relationship.

3.If you will be presenting information that is meant to sway a client in a certain direction in a business deal, be sure that your presentation is concise, fact-based and easy to follow. Being thoroughly prepared for the presentation and ready to answer any questions is likely to make new clients more at ease when it comes to doing business with you.

4.When you are deciding which negotiation strategy to use, considering the negotiation etiquette of the professionals you are working with is imperative. In some cases, it is best to simply state the facts regarding your stance in the negotiation, to be honest about your intentions and to respectfully listen to all the opinions presented at the meeting.

5.Once all the information has been presented and it's time to come to a decision, using proper etiquette to respect this part of the process will help to secure the business deal. In many companies, the final negotiation decision is made from the top down, meaning that executives will likely have additional meetings to determine the negotiation outcome. Being patient and accommodating during this time shows that you respect the process and are not simply focused on getting "your way".

IV.Cloze: choose the suitable statements from the box and complete the passage.

A.listen raptly, think creatively and ultimately persuade others

B.exert leverage to persuade others

C.think in terms of making an exchange

D.negotiate your way out of each of these situations

E.work with the other person to hash out a more substantive, mutually beneficial agreement

Your employees come to you with problems ... Your bosses propose that you attain certain goals ... Your clients complain to you and make demands ... You can_____1_____. That means you must move beyond the predictable response: nodding your head and giving stock answers. Instead, you want to _____2_____—identifying what others want from you and what you can offer in return.

You may not refer to it as negotiating, but you are constantly bargaining with others. You might be pitching your proposal, recruiting an employee, purchasing a software package, leasing space or seeking capital to expand your business. All these challenges test your ability to _____3_____. If you're too timid to negotiate, you'll lose countless chances to advance your cause or attain your objectives. Whether you're considering doing a quick favor for someone or making a major sacrifice, you face a decision: either give a yes-no answer without conditions

or _____4_____.

There's nothing wrong with giving a straight answer when you're fielding a request. But the most effective communicators prefer to _____5_____. Rather than always providing snap answers when asked for something, these shrewd individuals capitalize on opportunities to extract a quid pro quo—an equal exchange where both parties willingly give and take.

V. Case study: in business negotiation, careful consideration should be taken to make the decision on strategy. When you are deciding which negotiation strategy to use, it is imperative to consider the negotiation etiquette of the professionals you are working with. Discuss in groups to find out the best negotiating plans for the partners from the following countries.

　　1. U.S.
　　2. Australia
　　3. Middle East and parts of Africa
　　4. China

 Extension（拓展阅读）

International Business Negotiation Etiquette

Becoming knowledgeable in every country's "silent language" of etiquette is essential for developing good business relationships overseas. One of the first things you need to do is mind your meeting manners, advises Ann Marie Sabath.

If you will be conducting business in an Asian or Pacific Rim country or region, you need to learn in which countries or regions it is better to make small talk before starting a meeting and in which countries or regions it is better to keep chatter to a minimum and get down to business. You need to learn such particulars as when phrases such as "I understand" or "we will see" will actually mean "no". Here are some pointers:

Australia

Get to the point. Although small talk is part of the relationship-building process in many cultures, one important tip to keep in mind while conducting business with Australians is that words are taken at face value. For that reason, be direct. Say what you have to say and expect your words to be taken literally. In return, you will be expected to interpret what Aussies say to you in the same direct manner.

China

The best advice for successfully getting through a Chinese business meeting is to "go with the flow". The Chinese business culture may appear regimented, dictatorial, and rather slow moving to Westerners. Be sure to allow your Chinese hosts to set the tone by allowing them to initiate greetings, seating suggestions, and negotiations. The Chinese have a strict hierarchical system and place emphasis on rank. Thus, it would be wise to select one person, usually a senior team member, to be your spokesperson for the group. The Chinese will do the same, and they may be irritated if others attempt to speak out. Be aware that certain phrases may mean "no". They include "it is inconvenient", "I am not sure" and "maybe".

Hong Kong, China

The larger the Hong Kong firm, the farther in advance meetings should be scheduled. Prior to your arrival, send a list of all delegates attending, in ranking order with titles next to each name. Most likely, the Hong Kong team will be seated and awaiting your arrival. Enter the room in hierarchical order and sit across from the Hong Kong person who holds the same position of equal status to your own. Social conversation will start all meetings and should continue until your Hong Kong Chinese leader moves the talk to business. You will notice that one person, usually a high-ranking officer, will act as the group's spokesperson. Your team should do the same. Negotiations will be a slow, tedious process. Because a group consensus is the norm in decision-making, you will probably not get a "reading" at the first meeting. The Hong Kong team will want to discuss the proposal in private.

Taiwan, China

Avoid discussing money early in a business relationship. While the Taiwanese recognize the importance of profit, this society encourages concern for the good of the whole and, thus, does not give precedence to money issues. Agreements are only as good as the piece of paper they are written on. It is very common for negotiations to continue after an agreement has been signed.

Indonesia

When establishing business relationships with Indonesians, you should be patient and diligent. Indonesian businesspeople are slow and deliberate when it comes to making decisions. If you attempt to rush them through the negotiation process, you risk being regarded unfavorably. Always remember that a more low-keyed, thoughtful appeal will assist you in maintaining harmony with the individuals across the table from you. If the Indonesians with whom you are meeting make few comments, don't view their silence as a negative response. Frequently, part of the business practice in this country is to remain aloof until a group meeting can be held to gather a consensus. In addition, remember that these people are naturally soft-spoken, so be aware of your tone of voice and avoid being loud or harsh-sounding. Like the country's society, Indonesian

business is hierarchical and decision-making lies with senior management. Be sure you are meeting with top officers, especially when a deal reaches the final stages.

Japan

A customary Japanese meeting begins with small talk to establish rapport. Take the cue from your Japanese customers to know when it is time to begin discussing business. It is important that you clarify what you are going to present by putting it in writing beforehand, so that everyone will have this information in front of them. Be sure to take notes when business is discussed by others. "Yes" phrases that may mean "no" include "we will think about it", "we will see" and "perhaps". It may take three visits and a few years for a business relationship to officially get off the ground. By being aware of this before going to Japan, foreigners will have a much more realistic attitude about what to expect.

Malaysia

In Malaysia, believing in the other person is vital to a strong business relationship. One way to get to know each other is through small talk, which is an important part of establishing rapport. Use this conversation as a way to get to know the other person, and also to allow this individual to become acquainted with you. Negotiations will be lengthy and you should have every detail of your proposal worked out before presenting it. Building long-term relationships with individuals from Malaysia is a long-term process. Therefore, expect to travel to Malaysia a few times before the decision-making process is solidified. Even once you have reached a decision with your Malaysian associates, they may try to renegotiate. Written contracts aren't regarded as set in stone.

Philippines

The beginning of the meeting should be reserved for establishing rapport—for instance, by engaging in small talk or by enjoying a meal together prior to the start of the meeting. You may also work on rapport before the meeting takes place by getting together for a sports outing or the like. When another person is talking, be sure to listen intently without interrupting. Breaking in while someone else is talking is considered offensive. There is a Filipino term called pakikisama, which emphasizes the importance of fellowship and making group decisions. This is an important concept to be aware of as you conduct negotiations.

Singapore

While many Westerners would not think twice about staying seated when their managers enter a room, this is not the case in Singapore. Stand when someone higher in rank than you or one generation older than you enters a room. Wait for them to begin eating before you do. When sitting in a chair, keep your feet flat on the floor, rather than crossing your legs in front of elders or hierarchical superiors. Avoid challenging, correcting or disagreeing with an elder person or superior in a public setting. Besides causing them to lose face, you will lose the respect of others. This rule should also be followed when you are with your boss and are in a meeting with Singaporeans. A Singaporean may actually mean "yes" when he or she says "perhaps", agrees to your proposition and then offers to be of assistance, and says yes then asks you a related question about what he or she has agreed to do. Some phrases that may sound like "yes" but may mean "no" to a Singaporean include "It may not work out", "My schedule may not permit me..." and "Yes, but..."

South Korea

It is part of the South Korean meeting ritual to begin by offering guests a beverage. Accept a drink when it's offered to you, even if you only choose to sip rather than drink it. If a South Korean is bothered or confused by something that has been said, he or she will likely not express this concern verbally, but instead will expect you to know it from his or her body language or facial expression. When planning meetings, be sure to build in several breaks for smoking. Smoking is very common in South Korea, so this courtesy will be much appreciated.

Thailand

Keep in mind that the Thais are a bit less formal than others when conducting business. However, obvious breeches of Thai etiquette will be considered rude and will hurt your efforts. Asking if there are any questions or opinions from your Thai associates should be done in an indirect manner. Blunt questioning is considered bad form. The Thai team will want to meet several times with you and your team, as well as with you alone, before making any final decisions.

Vietnam

Business meetings with the Vietnamese are relaxed, lengthy affairs. Be sure to schedule ample time. Also, prepare to be invited to a meal following your meeting. The most senior member of the Vietnamese team will enter the room last and sit at the head of the table. However, don't be surprised if this person doesn't run the meeting himself and has appointed a junior member to lead the discussion. Having your business literature translated into Vietnamese will be appreciated and will move the meeting along more swiftly.

After-reading tasks（读后任务）

When you finish reading the text above, get into the groups and discuss with your group members about the following tasks and fulfill them.

Task 1

Read the text above, a great deal of knowledge of etiquette of negotiation in eastern and western countries will be obtained. In order to keep in mind, taking notes and make classification may be recommended. Thus, put the information of etiquette from the text you have learned into the table and keep it for later reference.

Countries	Small talk	Relationship	Decision-making	More
China (including Taiwan, Hong Kong)				
Japan				
Indonesia				
South Korea				
Singapore				
Malaysia				
Vietnam				
Australia				
Thailand				
Philippines				

Task 2

What you have read about the etiquette of negotiation in the text above probably has aroused your interest in the further details of more countries. So you may work with your group members to surf the internet to find out more principles you can follow when dealing with cross-cultural negotiation or more fun in such etiquettes of different cultural background, which you may have never imagined.

Task 3

Effective classroom learning should motivate the readers to achieve more outside the classroom. More development should be done after class. You must have learned a lot when you finish the learning of this unit. Besides the list of reference books your teacher has given to you, try to find more practical or interesting books concerning the etiquette in negotiation through search in the library or online. Share your findings with your group members and also with your teacher and suggest more reading activities then...

✐ Self-study（自学反馈）

If possible, summarize what you have learned in this unit with the help of the following table.

Focus of this unit:
Guidelines for etiquette: 1. 2. 3. ...
Summary:
Application: 1. 2. 3. ...
Feedback:

Chapter Nine
Business Travel Etiquette
商务旅行礼仪

Objectives（学习目标）

After you have studied this chapter, you should be able to:

- ❑ Have a command of the basic etiquettes of business travel
- ❑ Handle some problem situations you may come across in business travel
- ❑ Cultivate the cross-cultural awareness when travelling in different countries

Lead-in（导读）

This is an age of globalization and nations all round the world have come very close as it is imperative for all of them to work together for fast progress. Dream jobs are generally considered to involve travel of some kind. This could involve a daily commute by train, regular trips up and down the motorway or long-haul flights to a sunnier destination. Failure to maintain high business standards at all times could impact on your career in a negative manner. Therefore, whatever the location and reason, for a business trip maybe you will want to create a good, professional impression on everyone you meet on the way. It is important to know that foreigners expect newcomers to adapt to their culture and mannerisms when visiting their country. Always bear in mind that a little preparatory research in the business etiquette of a foreign country can go a long way for a meeting that can seal the fate of your company.

当今是一个全球化的时代，世界各国之间的距离拉近了，这就要求各国必须合作起来应对时代的快速发展。有些工作需要涉及商务旅行。这些商务旅行既包括日常的通勤交通、定期的高速公路驾驶，还包括长途飞行，才能到达理想的目的地。如果不能在旅行期间始终保持专业的水准，有可能会因为忽略礼仪而对交易产生负面影响。因此，无论身处何地，由于何种原因，都要在商务旅行中，给遇见的人留下良好的职业印象。当地人都希望来访的人能适应他们的文化和礼仪规范，了解这一点至关重要。一定要对到访的国家的商务礼仪做好前期研究，这一点会在商务洽谈中发挥长足的作用，甚至会影响公司商务谈判的成败。

Test yourself（自我测试）

To start with, take a test to see to what degree you have mastered the basic etiquettes of business travel. Please use Yes or No to make responses to the following statements.

1. A junior executive defers to a senior executive. He is the one to sit on the jump seat in the taxi or limousine, or in the middle seat of the car or plane. Yes ☐ No ☐

2. Keep luggage light. Don't expect anyone else to carry it for you. Yes ☐ No ☐

3. If you are not likely to run the risk of being sleepy and not at your best, you may book a dinner meeting. Yes ☐ No ☐

4. If you use someone's office during your stay in another city, leave a gift as thanks. Yes ☐ No ☐

5. In hot weather you may remove your jacket at will and you don't have to follow your host's cues. Yes ☐ No ☐

6. For women, conservative is again the key word. No backless, sleeveless, or strapless dresses for business. Yes ☐ No ☐

7. It would be unusual for a woman to travel to the Middle East countries on business. If you should be heading that way, remember that arms must be covered and necklines buttoned to the top. Yes ☐ No ☐

8. Business is expected to be conducted from 9:00 a.m. to 5:00 p.m. in many countries. Yes ☐ No ☐

9. Be patient with gift giving in Singapore as a recipient may "graciously refuse three times" before accepting your gift. Yes ☐ No ☐

10. For specific pointers on particular countries, call or write to that country's embassy. Yes ☐ No ☐

Part I Basic Etiquette of Business Travel
商务旅行基本礼仪

With the development of international business, a growing number of business cooperation across the nations has appeared. When the businessmen travel to another country for the business, they will catch in the throes of making travel plans, packing, and preparing for whatever business awaiting them. Etiquette is probably the last thing in their minds. We are fairly good at extending etiquette to people who have direct impact on our lives, but we sometimes fall short when it comes to the travel etiquette.

We Chinese are always proud of our civilization which has a history going back to 5,000 years ago. Nevertheless, today, we have to make great efforts to polish China's international image as a "civilized" nation, which is being undermined by the vulgar, impolite and undisciplined behavior of some citizens travelling abroad. Therefore, be a courteous traveler. Do not annoy locals and make a better world for all of us.

随着国际贸易的发展，跨国合作也越来越多。而当商务人员以商务为目的到他国旅行时，他们会用心制订旅行计划，收拾行李，为未来的业务做准备。然而，礼节却可能常常被忽略。我们对与自己息息相关的人礼数周全，却往往忽视了商务旅行中的礼仪。

我们一向颇为自豪的是中华的文明史可以追溯到 5000 年以前，可是作为礼仪之邦，如今这一形象正被部分国人在境外表现出来的粗鲁、无礼和不自律的行为所损害，我们一定要努力改善中国的国际形象。因此，我们要做文明游客，不要冒犯当地居民，共同创造一个更美好的世界。

1.On the Way 在途中

Trains, planes, and automobiles: Each of these modes of transportation presents its own set of concerns for the business traveler.

火车、飞机和汽车，每一种交通方式都向商业旅行者展现它独特的文化。

（1）Take a flight 搭乘航班

If there is one place on earth where an ordinary citizen must always follow directions, it is an airport. Airports have stricter rules regarding security.

如果有一个地方是所有公民都要听从指令的，那就是机场。机场在安全措施方面有着比其他交通方式更严格的规定。

① Get on the plane 登机

Leave enough minutes for check-in and be attentive to the boarding announcement. Holding the whole plane waiting for you is not noble or superior at all.

You'd better not overload your luggage, otherwise when check-in formalities,also need to remove overweight goods, in order to meet the prescribed standards for weight, or have to pay an extra charge, it will no doubt cost your time, energy and money. If it says you can only carry one luggage on, that doesn't mean two or three.

For security check, remove all metal items beforehand and put them in your carry-on bag. To keep on pulling things out like a magician risks to irritate the person in the next turn. All belongings against carry-on luggage stipulation shall be put into checked luggage.

乘客应预留足够的时间办理登记手续并注意聆听登机广播。让所有乘客等你一个人，决不会显出你的尊贵或优越。

行李最好不要超重，不然在办理登机托运手续时，还得将超重物品取出，以达到规定的重量标准，或者要额外付运费，这无疑费时、费力又费钱。如果规定可以随身携带一件行李，那就不要带两件或三件。

安检时，请将所有金属物品提前拿出并放入随身的行李包中。像变魔术似的不停地掏东西可能会惹恼下一位等候的乘客。所有不准随身携带的物品应该装入托运的行李箱内。

② Get off the plane 下机

Do tell the flight attendant if you need to deplane quickly. He or she may be able to move you to a seat closer to the front.

Show respect to the attendants. If you have questions, pose them when you are being served. Never ring the call bell unless it's an emergency. Be patient when you make a request, say "Please" and "Thank you" and thank them when you deplane.

Mobile phones shall be turned off. Upon landing, please don't yell into your phone for phone conversations are meant to be private, neither shall you communicate every detail of your life by mobile phone. A simple message like "The plane has landed, see you in a while." will work perfectly.

如果你需要抓紧时间下飞机，请告诉飞机上的乘务员，他或她可能会给你换一个靠近下机口的座位。

尊重空乘人员。如果有问题，尽量在接受服务时提出，除非遇到紧急情况，否则不要随便按呼叫按钮。当你提出要求的时候应该有耐心，要说"请"和"谢谢"，当你下飞机时应该感谢他们。

手机应关掉。飞机降落后也请不要高声打电话——通话内容本应属于个人隐私；也不要事无巨细都在电话里一吐为快。简单一句"飞机抵达，一会儿见"足矣。

（2）On a train 在火车上

Business people who travel between major cities in the same general part of the country have the luxury of choosing rail over air. Be Compared to take a flight, one becomes even more key: the use of electronic devices. Unlike airline passengers, railroad travelers are able to use their personal mobile phones to conduct business, ring up friends. A simple rule of thumb for mobile phone use: if using the phone will disturb the people around you in any way, don't use it.

对于那些经常在一个国家同一地区的主要城市间旅行的商人，其优越性在于可选择乘火车，而不是乘飞机。相比乘飞机，其中最关键的区别是：电器装置的使用。与飞机上的乘客不同，火车上的旅行者可以用他们的手机处理业务，与朋友聊天。使用手机时，一个简单但重要的规则是：如果使用手机会影响你周围的人，那就停止使用吧。

2.At Your Destination 到达目的地后

（1）Go to the Hotel 去宾馆

No matter how weary you feel, be gracious as you check in at your hotel. If you have to make any special requests, a polite demeanor will get you further than a brusque one. Pay attention to be a polite tenant, you should take the following tips.

不管你有多累，订房间的时候也应该保持着你的礼貌形象。如果你需要提一些特别的要求，礼貌比唐突会让你显得更有风度。要努力做一个有礼貌的客人，就要学习以下几点：

① In the room 在客房里

Put trash in trash cans. Don't mess up rooms. Have personal items off beds and in concentrated areas (so maids can make beds).

Be environment friendly. Don't waste water or other energy even you have paid for it. Pile dirty towels in one place in the bathroom, such as the tub or under the sink so that the maids can find them to wash.

Report anything that is broken or does not work to the front desk as soon as you see it. Remember that you will be held responsibility for any damages to the room or its facilifies.

将垃圾放入垃圾箱内，保持屋内整洁。不要将个人物品放在床上，而应集中摆放（便于服务员整理床铺）。

注意环保，不要因为付过钱就浪费水或其他能源。将用过的毛巾集中放在浴室里的某个地方——浴缸或盥洗盆内，以便服务员收集清洗。

如果发现物品损坏或设施失灵，及时向前台报告，不然酒店可能要你对屋内设施的损坏负责。

② At the public area 在公共区域

Noise should stay within rooms. Do not intrude on other guests especially after 10:00 p.m. (Remember guests can be below, beside, or above your room). Hallways, restaurants and stairwells are public areas. Be aware of your voices, their volume and what you are talking about.

Keep luggage out of public passage. You will be told when to put your luggage on the bus. Leave it in the room until it is time to load it.

不要让噪音传出客房，晚上 10 点以后更不要打扰其他客人（记住其他客人就住在你的楼上、楼下或隔壁）。大堂、餐厅和楼梯间都是公共区域，注意说话的音量和谈话的内容。

行李不要阻塞公共通道。行李何时放上旅行车会有人通知，届时再将行李拿出房间也不迟。

（2）To be prepared for the next day meeting 准备明天的会议

Call your host to let him or her know you've arrived. Confirm the time of your meeting: "I'll be there at eight o'clock sharp tomorrow morning. Look forward to seeing you then."

If you are scheduled to give a presentation, plan on after arriving at the destination. Take any visual aids with you, including equipment for presenting them, or some materials which will be utilized in the meeting.

打电话给你的接待者，让他们知道你已经到达。确认你开会的时间："我会在明早上八点准时到达那儿，到时见。"

如果你被安排做演讲，在到达后就应该做好准备。带上用于展示的设备和所需用的材料等。

3.To Be Safe 确保安全

Try to hold an awareness of safety, especially for the business women. Don't be lulled into thinking that your briefcase, laptop, and no-nonsense attire protect you against unwanted attention. Balance a desire to be friendly and to learn about your surroundings with a healthy dose of common sense, especially if you are travelling alone. Doing the following will increase your sense of security.

要有安全意识，尤其是女性。不要光想着你的公文包、手提电脑、穿着会不会使你引人注意成为焦点。调整一下心情，自然而友好地对待周围的人和事，特别是当你一个人旅行的时候。照下面的去做将增强你的安全意识。

（1）At your hotel 在酒店

Electronic keys have reduced the incidence of hotel room break-ins dramatically since their introduction, but you can also take extra precautions. Don't allow anyone into your room unless he or she is expected and you're absolutely positive you know who it is. Even though the chambermaid who comes in the evening make beds for you will have a key, she could always knock first and announce who she is when you answer the door. Other hotel personnel should be announced by the front desk before showing up at your room. Never open your door without first checking through the peephole to confirm that it is either a service you ordered or someone you know.

Use discretion when getting into an elevator with a sole male occupant. If you become uneasy once inside, push the button for the next floor and get out. Many hotels will also see to it that you are escorted to your room.

虽然自从电子钥匙产生以来，酒店里房间被非法闯入的几率大为降低了，但是还是要特别小心。不要让任何人进入房间，除非是你邀请的和你认识的人。即使晚上来铺床的女服务员有钥匙，她也应该事先敲门并回答她是谁之后才可以让她进来。酒店其他工作人员进你房间之前应由前台预先通知。你应该在猫眼里确认来人是否是你叫的服务员或你认识的人，否则千万别开门。

和一个男性单独在电梯里时一定要保持清醒，如果你感到不自在，按一下按钮，在下一层就下电梯。很多酒店会有这样的安排让服务员负责护送你回房间。

（2）Out and about 外出

If you've driven to your destination and find yourself driving at night, park in a visible, lighted place. Look around before getting out of the car. Get your car keys ready when returning to the car, and then glance under the car and in the backseat before getting in. If someone appears to be following you as you're walking to your car, walk past it to find help. Likewise, if you're walking on the street and sense you're being followed, do an about-face, cross the street, or duck into a store.

如果是在晚上你开车出去，要把车停在一个显眼的、光线好的地方。然后在下车前先观察一下周围。当你回到车旁要事先准备好钥匙，上车前瞟一眼车底和后座。如果你朝车的方向走去有人跟踪你，别去开车，应去求助。同样的，如果你在街上感觉被人跟踪，立即向后转，过马路，或闪进商店去。

Part II　Foreign Customs and Holiday Etiquette 外国习俗与节日礼仪

The slogan "Be prepared" takes on new meaning whenever you travel to another country with the aim of doing business. When you land on foreign soil, pass through customs, and step out into an unfamiliar world, always remember this: You are representing your country as much as your company. How you behave will either reinforce or counteract your hosts' conception of your country—and this, in turn, will affect the outcome of your business negotiations. So, you should know the basic facts about the country you're visiting at least.

当你到另一个国家做生意时，"出发之前做好准备"的口号就被赋予了新的意义。当你去国外时，置身于不同的习俗中，进入一个完全陌生的世界。你将代表所在的公司和国家，在那里的行为举止将直接影响接待方对你和国家的看法或扬或抑，当然最终也会影响到你参与商务谈判的结果。

1.A Cocktail Party 鸡尾酒会

A cocktail party is a largely informal social gathering generally featuring mixed drinks, light refreshments and an intimate guest list. An informal cocktail party may be an alternative to a formal dinner party. An invitation to an informal cocktail party should mention any special food arrangements, especially if the party is scheduled during regular dinner hours.

While a typical cocktail party often does live up to its expectation of flowing alcohol in an adult setting, it is not necessarily regarded as an exercise in public intoxication. Guests should demonstrate some restraint and drink responsibly out of respect for the party's host. Most mixed drinks are designed to be sipped over a period of time, as well as savored for their unique flavors. An informal private cocktail party may not have the same safety controls in place as a public bar or nightclub, so guests may have to monitor their own alcohol consumption and ability to drive home safely.

A well-planned cocktail party is often an exciting thing. Guests may share a common bond, such as work or school, or they may only know the host or a handful of other guests. Meeting new people can be much easier under the relaxed atmosphere of a cocktail party. A good cocktail party host should provide a selection of soft drinks and non-alcoholic versions of popular cocktails to designated drivers and those who choose not to drink alcohol for personal or religious reasons.

鸡尾酒会是一个非正式的社交聚会，调配的酒饮、点心各式各样，宾客云集。一个非正式的鸡尾酒会可替代一个正式的晚宴。邀请参加一个非正式的鸡尾酒会时，应提及特别的饮食安排，尤其是如果鸡尾酒会安排在一般的晚餐时间时，应特别注意。

通常鸡尾酒会会满足人们对美酒的渴望，但不要因此而在社交场合大醉。客人应加以克制，并出于对主人的尊重而小酌一点。大多数混合型酒的设计就是为了啜饮，以品尝其独特的风味。非正式的私人鸡尾酒会不像酒吧或夜总会有安全控制，所以客人需要控制自己的酒量以保证可以安全开车回家。

精心策划的鸡尾酒会往往令人兴奋。客人可以分享工作或学习时的共同经历，也许他们可能只认识主人或少数其他客人。在鸡尾酒会上如此轻松的气氛下，可以更容易地结识新朋友。一个好的鸡尾酒会的主办人会提供一些软饮料和不含酒精的鸡尾酒供司机或那些因为个人或宗教原因不能喝酒的人选择。

2.Buffet 自助餐

A buffet, sometimes is also called cold dish dinner. The food arrangement could consist of one long serving line with both cold and hot items, and a collection of smaller stations dedicated to a particular part of the meal, such as cold salads, meats, vegetables or desserts. A buffet may be completely self-served, with appropriate serving tools such as slotted spoons or tongs, or there may be workers assigned to carve meats or prepare made-to-order dishes such as egg omelets.

Buffet-style dining has become very popular. But to behave a good manner when facing the lure of the buffet, you should arm yourself in advance with these anti-binging strategies.

Being meticulous about table manners may lead to eating more elegant. The abstemious people were also more likely to use chopsticks, so if these are available, forget the knife and fork. Unless you're a skilled chopstick manipulator, these utensils will probably force you to eat more slowly.

Remember that your eating habits are just a small part of the overall impression you will make. In conclusion, don't eat too much in the buffet.

自助餐，有时亦称冷餐会。食物安排包括冷食和热食，摆成一条供客人选用；和一个方台，摆有一些餐会特殊的部分，如冷沙拉、肉类、蔬菜或甜点。自助餐可以是全自助的，配有适当的服务工具，如开槽汤匙或钳子，或有服务员分配肉类，或已准备好的煎蛋。

自助餐式的用餐方式已变得越来越受欢迎。但是当面对诱人的满桌食物时要举止得体，要预先了解不致忘形于美食的策略。

注重餐桌礼仪可以使你就餐更优雅。就餐时，有节制的人会更倾向于使用筷子，通常来讲，用筷子可能会迫使你吃得慢些，除非你使用筷子非常地熟练。因此，如果有筷子可供使用，放弃刀子和叉子。

记住你整体印象中的一小部分就是你的饮食习惯。总的来说，不要在自助餐上吃太多。

3.Christmas Day 圣诞节

The name Christmas is short for "Christ's Mass". Christmas is a Christian holiday that celebrates the birth of Jesus Christ. In the 4th century the Roman Catholic Church chose December 25 as the day for the Feast of the Nativity, and Christmas, the feast of the nativity of Jesus, is on 25th December every year.

For most people who celebrate Christmas, the holiday season is an occasion for gatherings of family and friends, feasting, and giving gifts. The celebration of Christmas became increasingly important to many kinds of businesses. One of the most important Christmas traditions is receiving gifts from Santa Claus. Today, Santa Claus brings presents to children in many countries, including the United States, Canada, Great Britain and Australia. In Great Britain Santa Claus is also called Father Christmas.

A traditional Christmas dinner in America includes stuffed turkey, mashed potatoes, cranberry sauce, and a variety of other dishes. Roast turkey is the most popular main course not only in the United States, but also in Canada, Australia, and New Zealand. Some families have ham or roast goose instead of turkey. Favorite desserts include mince pie or pumpkin pie, plum pudding and fruitcake. In Britain, Christmas dinner is eaten at noon, and the dinner usually includes roast turkey or goose, Christmas pudding with mince pies, and accompanied by wine.

"圣诞节"这个名称是"基督弥撒"的缩写。圣诞节是个基督教节日，庆祝耶稣基督诞生。公元 4 世纪，罗马天主教会将耶稣的诞辰定在 12 月 25 日。圣诞节便是于 12 月 25 日纪念耶稣的诞生。

对于大多数过圣诞节的人来说，这个节日是家庭、朋友聚会的日子，享用美酒佳肴的日子，互赠礼物的日子。圣诞节的庆祝活动对许多工商企业也变得日益重要了。圣诞节的重要传统之一是接受圣诞老人赠送的礼物。许多小孩子相信自己在圣诞节收到的礼物来自圣诞老人。现在，许多国家，包括美国、加拿大、英国和澳大利亚，都有圣诞老人把节日礼物送给孩子们。在英国，圣诞老人也叫" Father Christmas "。

在美国，圣诞节宴席上的传统食物有填馅的火鸡、土豆泥、越橘酱等。烤火鸡不但在美国，在加拿大、澳大利亚和新西兰也是圣诞宴席上最普遍的主菜。也有的人家不吃火鸡，而吃火腿或烤鹅。人们最喜欢的饭后甜点包括甜馅饼或南瓜馅饼、李子布丁和水果蛋糕。在英国，圣诞宴在中午举行，传统食品有烤火鸡或烤鹅、圣诞布丁、甜馅饼和葡萄酒。

4.Easter 复活节

Easter is the Christian commemoration of the resurrection of Jesus as a religious holiday. Over the spring equinox, after the first full moon on the first Sunday comes Easter. In the early years, there have been controversy over the date of Easter, causing momentary confusion. Until 325 AD, the priests of the Church decided to celebrate the unification of the Easter.

There are a lot of traditional Easter celebrations. Easter egg is the most typical symbol. In ancient times, eggs are often seen as more children and grandchildren and a symbol of resurrection, because they breed new life. Later, Christians also give new meaning to the egg that it is a symbol of the tomb of Jesus and the life of the future is born from it. Easter eggs are often dyed red to represent the crucifixion of Jesus when the blood flows, and also a symbol of happiness after the resurrection. There is an ancient custom that street children roll the cooked eggs down the hillside: who broke the last egg, will win all the eggs. White House play this game every year, rolling eggs on the lawn only.

Rabbit is a symbol of Easter. Now every Easter, in the United States all candy shops sell the Easter Bunny and eggs made with chocolate. The children eat these eggs with relish. Also they can be a good gift to the relatives and friends.

复活节是基督教纪念耶稣复活的一个宗教节日。每年春分过后，第一次月圆后的第一个星期日就是复活节。早年对复活节的日期曾经有过争议，引起一时混乱，直到公元325年，教士会议才决定整个教会统一在这一天庆祝复活节。

复活节有不少传统的庆祝活动，复活节彩蛋是最典型的象征。古时人们常把蛋视为多子多孙和复活的象征，因为它孕育着新的生命。后来基督教徒又赋予蛋以新的含义，认为它是耶稣墓的象征，未来的生命就是从其中挣脱而出世。复活节人们常把蛋染成红色，代表耶稣受难时流的鲜血，同时也象征复活后的快乐。还有一种古老的习俗，街头的孩子们把煮熟的彩蛋从山坡上滚下：谁的蛋最后破，谁就获得胜利，全部彩蛋都归获胜者所有。美国白宫每年也玩这种游戏，不同的是把蛋放在草坪上滚动。

兔子也是复活节的象征。现在每逢复活节，美国大小糖果店总要出售用巧克力制成的复活节小兔和彩蛋。孩子们吃起来津津有味。将小兔和彩蛋送给亲戚朋友，也不失为上佳礼品。

🔊 Situational practice for etiquettes 礼仪口语实景

Make up or search for more situational conversations that may occur during the business trip and put them into practice.

Model 1   Booking a flight

A: I want to make a reservation to Frankfort for next Monday.

B: Just a minute. I'll check the schedule.

A: I prefer a morning flight.

B: The only flight available is Eastern Airlines Flight 256, which leaves at 10:15 a.m.

A: What's the economy class fare?

B: It's $595 one way.

A: Is it a direct flight?

B: Yes, it's non-stop.

A: What time does it arrive in Frankfurt?

B: It arrives at 7:30 p.m.

Model 2　Going through customs after landing

A: May I see your passport and your customs and health declaration forms, please?

B: Yes, here you are.

A: Thank you.

B: What's your occupation?

A: I'm Director of the International Trading Co.

B: So you're here on business.

A: Yes. I've been invited by the United Electronics Ltd.

B: How long do you plan to stay in this country?

A: Four days.

B: Is this all your baggage?

A: Yes, it's all here.

B: Do you have anything to declare?

A: I suppose not, except a bottle of whiskey. That's duty-free, isn't it?

B: Okay. Here's your passport and your customs declaration. I'll keep your health declaration.

A: Is that all for customs formalities?

B: Yes. You're through now. Have a pleasant stay.

 Terminology Related　相关礼仪术语

China's tourism law concerning etiquette 中国有关礼仪的旅游法规

It's hard being a Chinese tourist. Reviled for bad behavior one day and ripped off by everyone from taxi drivers to pickpockets the next, China's newly minted traveling classes are having a tough year.

In typical fashion, the Chinese government appears intent on regulating away some of that pain. On October 1st China's tourism industry came under a new set of rules, most intended to curb corruption in domestic travel and ease the burden on guides, groups and tourists traveling within the country. The law includes at least one clause that seems to have been inspired by a series of incidents that have revealed the apparently bad manners of Chinese tourists, on the mainland and overseas.

The number of Chinese traveling at leisure, both domestically and abroad, has grown tremendously in recent years, boosted by rising incomes, a less restrictive passport regime and softer limits on spending. The new tourism law aims to help the tourists themselves, mainly by preventing practices like the forced-march shopping excursions that are often led by ill-paid tour guides. The law also provides helpful advice to the many millions of mainland Chinese who do their pleasure-seeking abroad.

Section 13 advises Chinese tourists to behave themselves wherever they go in the world. The article is a nod to high-profile embarrassments like the one that a teenager caused by carving his mark—"Ding Jinhao was here"—into an ancient wall in the Egyptian ruins at Luxor earlier this year. Chinese tourists have drawn scorn after posting online snapshots of their own hunting and devouring endangered sea clams in the Paracel islands, and others have produced fake marriage papers at resorts in the Maldives, in order to take advantage of free dinners. (Closer to home, the new law might have given pause to the group of Chinese tourists on Hainan island who inadvertently killed a stranded dolphin by using it as a prop in group portraits.) Spitting, shouting and sloppy bathroom etiquette has made the Chinese look like the world's rudest new tourists, from London to Taipei and beyond.

身为中国游客可真不容易：一会儿因举止不当受尽辱骂，一会儿又遭到出租司机宰客、扒手抢劫。对中国新兴旅游人群而言，今年过得真心不容易。

一如既往，中国政府打算通过调控来解决问题。今年十一，一套新的中国旅游政策出台，其中多数内容旨在整治国内旅游业中的腐败现象，并减轻国内导游、旅游团及游客的负担。政策中不少条例的制定，是针对于以往中国游客的恶劣言行在海内外旅游市场引发的不良事件。

近几年，随着收入的增长，以及出境限定和消费限制的放宽，中国的国内外休闲旅游人数急剧上升。旅游新政策还规定，禁止导游为了增加收入，强迫游客购物等行为。此外，新政策也为在境外旅游的中国游客提出了有关条例。

其中第 13 条规定：中国游客出国旅游应注意言行举止。此条法律条文也是对某些事件的高调回应——例如，今年年初，一名中国少年在埃及古迹上刻上了"丁锦昊到此一游"字样；有游客在帕拉塞尔群岛捕捞并食用珍稀海鲜，并把其照片晒到网上；在马尔代夫，有某游客为了吃顿免费餐，甚至伪造结婚证；在中国海南，为了拍张集体照，有人竟然屠杀了一只无辜的海豚。到处都能发现随地吐痰、大声喧哗不讲礼貌的中国人——中国人似乎已被评为世界上"最粗俗无礼"的游客了。

Useful Expressions for etiquettes 礼仪用语集锦

The followings are appropriate terminology you may use during the business trip:

1. May I have a window seat?

能帮我订一张靠窗的座位吗?

Sorry, there aren't any left. Would you like an aisle seat?

抱歉,靠窗的座位已卖完了。您来一张靠走廊的座位好吗?

2. I'm in a hurry. Could you get me on an earlier flight?

我赶时间,请帮我订一张早点的航班好吗?

We could put you on stand-by.

给您张站票吧。

3. Would you mind changing places with me? So I can sit next to my friend?

您方便和我换个座位吗? 这样我能和朋友坐在一起。

No, not at all.

好的,没问题。

4. A piece of my baggage is missing. Could you help me to find it? It was booked on Flight 123.

我遗失了一件行李。您能帮我找找吗? 行李登记的是 123 航班。

Please give me your ticket and baggage check. I'll check with the plane and see what I can do.

请把机票和行李单给我。我和该航班联系一下看看。

5. Your attention, please. This is the final call for Eastern Airlines Flight 217 non-stop to Tokyo boarding now at Gate Ten. Please have your boarding pass ready.

请注意,这是最后一次通知。东方航空直飞东京的 217 的航班现在在 10 号门登机。请准备好登机牌。

6. Japan Air Lines regrets to announce that Flight JAL 745 to San Francisco, scheduled to depart at ten a.m. has now been delayed. Further details will be announced shortly.

日本航空公司遗憾地通知各位,原定于上午 10 点飞往旧金山的 745 次航班现在推迟登机。具体事宜稍后通告。

7. Will you please cash this traveler's check?

请将这张旅行支票兑付现金。

Certainly. We'd be glad to cash it for you.

好的,很乐意为您服务。

8. What denomination?

换成什么面值的?

It doesn't make any difference. Maybe fifties and some smaller bills.

无所谓，50 或更小的面值都可以。

9. Could you give these pounds in U.S. dollars?

请将这些英镑换成美元好吗？

Certainly.

当然可以。

10.What's the exchange rate for U.S. dollars today?

今天的美元兑换率是多少？

Today's rate for cash purchase is US $1.60 to the pound.

今天美元兑英镑的比率是 1.6 美元兑 1 英镑。

 Exercises（课后练习）

I.Questions and answers: answer the following questions according to the information you have got in the previous reading.

1.Which aspects should be taken into consideration to ensure a good image during air travel?

2.Is there anything that needs to be concerned with regard to the train travel etiquette?

3.What tips can a traveler follow to make a polite tenant?

4.What should be paid attention to in a cocktail party?

5.What customs do we have to know about the foreign holidays and events?

II.Expressions: match the gift-giving customs in column A with the countries in column B.

A	B
	Poland
gift expected	Russia
	Brazil
gift on a sequent visit	Spain
	Japan
	England
gift not expected	Australia
	Singapore
	United States

III.Translation: Translate the following statements into Chinese to learn about country-specific business etiquette.

1.China

Always address a person using his or her family name. For example, use Mr. Wong rather than Alfred Wong. For business purposes, it is tradition to call a Chinese person by his surname along with his title, such as "Director Wong" or "Chairman Lee".

If possible, receive a business card with both hands.

Take a quick look at the card before putting it your front shirt pocket; never in your back pocket, as this is seen as a sign of disrespect.

Begin meetings with small talk.

Don't try to become too friendly too fast. The Chinese culture frowns upon quick informality.

Don't be overbearing in your introductory manners. A simple nod or a slight bow, and in some cases a soft handshake, are proper greeting tools.

2.France

Avoid calling your associates' personal numbers for business related issues. If it cannot be avoided, do so before 9:00 p.m.

For corporate letters or e-mail, use a very formal and business-like approach.

Don't use first names during a business meeting.

Don't show up late for meetings.

Don't bring up business at the start of a dinner/meeting.

3.Belgium

Greet someone with three kisses on the cheek, alternating from one cheek to the other.

Don't point your index finger at somebody.

Don't place your hands in your pockets while talking to someone.

Don't yawn, sneeze, blow your nose, or scratch yourself in the presence of others.

4.Italy

When greeting each other, you may kiss each other's cheeks and offer a long handshake.

Don't refuse repeats on your plate if they offer seconds.

5.Germany

Knock before opening a closed door.

Don't shake someone's hand while your other hand is in your pocket.

IV.Cloze: choose the suitable statements from the box and complete the passage.

> A.Colleague Confidentiality
> B.Comfort Zone
> C.Business Gifts
> D.Business Success Entertaining
> E.Customs and Cultures

_____1_____

Foreign business travel offers the opportunity to explore different cultures and customs and to create productive business relationships. It also provides many potential stumbling blocks, so a little bit of research is recommended before travelling to even a frequently visited destination. Understanding what is expected of you, in a variety of professional situations, will also stand you in good stead and help you overcome any difficulties.

Exchanging business cards is considered a mark of respect in most countries and provides an ideal ice-breaker, although you must remember to accept the card graciously and to handle it respectfully.

_____2_____

When travelling for business, maintaining a smart, polished appearance may not be necessary for the whole duration of your trip. Checking dress code for specific events, conferences and meetings you may be attending is recommended. Ensure you wear suitable attire in darker colors that reflect the nature of the business you work in, but also pack a number of smart, casual items of clothing that you can wear during personal relaxation time.

_____3_____

If you are travelling with a work colleague or boss there may be an opportunity to share thoughts and feelings of a more personal nature than you are used to sharing in the workplace during office hours. Although the mood may be less formal it is worth remembering that your working relationship will continue in the same manner once you return from the business trip. Therefore keeping your discussions and the content of your conversations, confidential is of utmost importance.

_____4_____

Sending a follow-up thank you note to the individual or organization that looked after you on your business trip is a gesture that will be remembered in a favorable way for a long time. It will also help you to maintain a friendly working relationship and good communication.

Giving small gifts, such as a pen or commemorative item, may be appropriate at the end of a business deal or as a thank you for services provided by colleagues. Inviting your host out to dinner and/or the theatre also shows appreciation.

_____5_____

In order to maintain the best professional impression you will have to follow business entertaining etiquette which may occur in less formal surroundings. Business lunches can provide a productive opportunity to exchange information, ideas and to secure a deal, and you must take the lead from your host. Lengthy lunches, breakfast meetings or informal after-hours drinks each offer an opportunity to follow business etiquette rules that can potentially enhance your career and professional reputation.

V.Case study: in today's global business environment, most businessmen travel regularly, both to domestic and to international destinations. When planning for business travel or preparing for the actual business commitments and engagements while on business trips, it is necessary to make a checklist of the items that are going to be taken with. Discuss in the groups what should be included on the checklist. For example:

1.Detailed schedule of meetings, engagement, appointments

2.Trip holders

3.Passport and/or visas

4.Cash or travelers' checks

5.Credit cards

6.Up-to-date calling (business) cards

7.Tickets

8.Expense account forms

9.Up-to-date address book with telephone numbers

 Extension（拓展阅读）

Etiquette for Business Travel

This is an age of globalization and nations all round the world have come very close as it is imperative for all of them to work together for fast progress. Multinational corporations have their offices in almost all countries and to carry on operations smoothly, they need some employees to relocate for some time and work at their foreign offices. Those jobs, which involve traveling for company work abroad, are considered to be quite prestigious in society. Top-notch companies pay for air tickets, luxury accommodation and all needs of their employees when they are in a foreign land. At the same time, it is the duty of employees to maintain the business travel etiquette so that they create a good impression about themselves and their company when they are meeting with their clients. So, refer to the business travel etiquette tips given below to make your journey a happy and successful one.

Pack Your Essentials Properly

Before your departure, the main business travel etiquette would be to make sure that you are taking along all essential items which you will be needing there. It should not happen that you leave important documents and fall into trouble later on. Along with the documents and office related things, packing the best clothes you have-both formal as well casual is also important. Other essentials such as your laptop, mobile phones, etc., should also be apart from your packing list for travel. Packing for a trip will be easy if you can prepare a list of the essential things.

Follow Airport Guidelines

So, you are going abroad on a business trip with some of your colleagues and are quite excited about the same. The first suggestion on business travel etiquette is to reach the airport on time and co-operate with the airport authorities by completing all the formalities properly. When you meet your colleagues at the airport, greet them with a warm hello followed by a handshake. Getting help from travel agents while traveling by air is a good idea. You should possess important travel documents such as passport, visa, identity and age proof, nationality proof, etc. Once you enter your plane, follow all instructions and air travel tips given by the cabin crew and staff and do not argue with them. Air travel restrictions are common for all and so abide by them to avoid falling into difficulties. Be polite and humble as this can alone get you a gentleman's tag.

Look Good and Presentable

Among the various business travel tips, being presentable and looking decent is an important one. So, whenever you are on a business trip, look into the mirror and make sure that you are wearing ironed, clean and good clothes. Wear the necktie and suit properly to look like a sincere professional. Have good posture while walking and sitting and a smile on your face. Maintain eye contact with people while talking and talk sensibly as these are the signs of a person having good body language. This is also one of the most commonly suggested international travel tips.

Conduct

Throughout your travel, your conduct should be extremely good. Do not make gestures and actions which can be irritating for other people or your own colleagues. If you are traveling with your boss, do not get too casual; give him the respect which he receives in the office. There would not be any ban on cracking jokes, laughing or having fun, but you should know exactly when to indulge in some good fun. Carefully listen to what the other person is speaking and then give your own opinion. You cannot just start entertaining everyone in an ongoing meeting or serious discussion!

Party Behavior

Party behavior is also a part of the business travel etiquette. Often these days, parties are arranged in hotels or restaurants for employees for some recreation. However, since it is an office party, you need to follow some behavioral norms. Avoid over drinking and making any kind of obscene gestures which can annoy the people around. Always be in your senses and be extra polite when it comes to interacting with female colleagues.

Dining Etiquette

In the course of your business travel, you are always under observation. So, even while dining with your colleagues, you must follow important etiquette. Never go late for the dinner and keep others waiting for you. If this happens, apologize immediately for your late arrival. Start your dinner along with all others and not before them. Avoid talking over the phone while eating or talking too loudly which can be disturbing for others. If you have to attend an urgent call from someone, then excuse yourself and come back immediately after attending the call.

By following these business travel etiquette, your journey would be a very memorable one. If you are planning for a business trip in a hurry, then these last-minute air travel tips will help you a lot.

(http://www.buzzle.com/articles/business-travel-etiquette.html)

After-reading tasks（读后任务）

When you finish reading the text above, get into the groups and discuss with your group members about the following tasks and fulfill them.

Task 1

It may not be easy to maintain the image during a tiring business trip, but it may ensure a successful business experience. Have you ever got or heard such experience of a business trip which may be a success or a failure? Share it with the group members and discuss about what you have found in the examples. Refer to the tips in the text above and summarize the proper way of how to behave in a business trip.

Task 2

Watch the movie *Up in Air* and get into the life of a businessman who seems to live in air. You may be interested in the theme of the movie, which may motivate the audiences to think further, what we would like to focus on is the professional image that the hero has showed in the movie. So find such model examples from the movies or career life and describe the career image or habits that they have been cultivating to facilitate their success. After that, write a report to summarize what you have learned from them. Share your report in class finally.

Task 3

People who are good at traveling can be very knowledgeable. Handling the trifles in the trip can be very frustrating, such as booking the tickets, booking the hotel rooms, scheduling the succession trips, adjusting to any change of plan and things like these. So find the more tips to get prepared for the situations mentioned above to ensure that you can pack anytime and begin a business trip on your own. When you are ready, one of the group members sets the destination of the business trip for the rest of the group. All of you should write down how you will get over a series of booking and purchases with the help of internet. When your work is done, each of you will report in the group and to see who has got the most effective and profitable arrangements.

Self-study（自学反馈）

If possible, summarize what you have learned in this unit with the help of the following table.

Focus of this unit:
Guidelines for etiquette: 1. 2. 3. …
Summary:
Application: 1. 2. 3. …
Feedback:

Chapter Ten
An Introduction to Multi-Cultural Business Etiquette
各国商务文化礼仪

Objectives（学习目标）

After you have studied this chapter, you should be able to

- ❑   Have a command of the etiquettes and taboo of some major countries
- ❑   Handle some problem situations in cross-cultural business setting
- ❑   Cultivate the cross-cultural awareness when doing business globally

Lead-in（导读）

Etiquette, which is an important part of the country's culture and the nation's spirit, is a major attachment of group's image. At the same time, it can also be regarded as the important software to obtain international fame. In today's world, with global companies as well as countries populated and influenced by different religions and cultures, it's important to develop good business relationships by taking the time to learn more about the culture of the countries you're doing business with. This will give you insight into the ways of communication that will be more appreciated by both parties of participants. This chapter aims to introduce the etiquette guidelines to follow in different culture and religions.

礼仪作为社会文化和民族精神的重要组成部分，是国家形象的主要表现。同时，礼仪也被看作是获得国际声誉的重要软件。在当今世界，跨国公司广为开设，而各国有着不同的宗教和文化背景，各国人民的形象也不尽相同，因此很有必要花时间了解有贸易往来的国家的文化，以建立良好的商业关系。了解对方的商务礼仪有助于找到交易双方都乐于接受的交流方式。本章旨在介绍不同文化和宗教背景下应遵循的礼仪规范。

Test yourself（自我测试）

To start with, take a test to see to what degree you have mastered the etiquette and taboo of various countries. Please use Yes or No to make responses to the following statements.

1. Punctuality is highly valued in the southern regions such as Spain or Portugal, while standards are looser for Scandinavians, Germans, Britons, and other northern people.

Yes ☐ No ☐

2. The "OK" sign, formed by making a circle of the thumb and index finger is used to show approval. Yes ☐ No ☐

3. In France, meetings are to discuss issues, not to make decisions. Yes ☐ No ☐

4. Business cards are infrequently distributed in the US and are not usually exchanged unless you wish to contact the person at a later date. Yes ☐ No ☐

5. No smoking during Ramadan. Foreigners at this time can't smoke in front of the locals; otherwise it would cause great resentment. Yes ☐ No ☐

6. When conducting business in the US, it is vital to establish a good, solid relationship with your counterparts in order to secure successful future negotiations. Yes ☐ No ☐

7. If you are invited to an Arabs or Latin-American home, do not praise or admire the articles in the host's house excessively; otherwise it would cause great embarrassment. Yes ☐ No ☐

8. Americans have a tendency to dislike long periods of silence during negotiations and in conversations in general. Yes ☐ No ☐

9. The Japanese are non-confrontational. They have a difficult time saying "no", so you must be vigilant at observing their non-verbal communication. It is best to phrase questions so that they can answer yes. Yes ☐ No ☐

10. To slap someone on the back is a gesture often used to show camaraderie, appreciation or praise in American culture and as such should be taken as a compliment. Yes ☐ No ☐

Part I The Business Etiquette and Protocol of Some Major Countries
主要国家的商务礼仪及行为规范

1.Europe 欧洲

As you move from the north of Europe to the south, the most obvious differences in manners concern time and space. Scandinavians, Germans, Britons, and other northern people place a very high value on punctuality, while standards are looser in the southern regions. In Spain or Portugal a visitor might be kept waiting thirty minutes before being greeted with the utmost courtesy. Southern Europeans also have a more intimate personal comfort zone, preferring to stand about two feet apart when they converse. For northerners, the acceptable distance is about four feet, and anything closer is seen as an invasion of privacy.

The standard greeting throughout Europe is the handshake, for both men and women. It is usually polite for a woman to extend her hand first. Most continentals shake hands before and after each meeting, while in Great Britain a single introductory shake is sufficient. Throughout Europe, formality in address is the rule: Never call another person by his or her first name until clearly invited to do so, and be careful to use any professional titles such as "Doctor," "Professor," or "Advocate,".

In general, all business and social appointments should be scheduled at least two weeks in advance. In northern countries, being exactly on time is essential; meetings start promptly, move quickly to the matter at hand, and tend to follow a tightly scripted agenda. In southern countries such as Spain and Greece, while you should plan to be on time, your host may not be. Meetings are more likely to start late, interruptions are not unexpected, and there is no attempt to hurry the outcome. In these regions, patience and courtesy are the keys to successful business negotiations.

In Eastern Europe, with its relatively undeveloped infrastructure, the etiquette tends to resolve around logistical challenges. Be sure to set up meetings far in advance; it may take months to finalize visas and other travel arrangements. Once you arrive, multiple meetings will likely be required to wrap up business dealings. This is especially true in Russia, where extreme caution in making decisions is the norm and being too ready to compromise is regarded as a sign of weakness.

从北欧到南欧，感觉最明显的差异可能就是时间和距离的不同。斯堪的纳维亚人、德国人、英国人等把守时看得很重，而南欧国家的人守时观念则不是那么严格。在西班牙或葡萄牙，客人可能要等 30 分钟左右才能得到主人的款待。私下交流时，南欧国家的人喜欢近距离亲密接触，当他们交谈时，彼此站的距离相隔两英尺左右。而对于北欧人来说，双方之间可以接受的距离大约是 4 英尺，小于这个距离就被看作侵犯对方的隐私。

整个欧洲普遍的问候方式是握手，男性和女性都一样。通常，女性应先伸出手。欧洲大多数人会在会议开始和结束时握手，而在英国，只在介绍时握手就够了。欧洲特别注重称呼的礼节：除非对方允许，否则不能直呼其名，使用任何职业头衔，如博士、教授、律师时应特别谨慎。

一般来说，所有的商务会谈都应该提前两周安排好。在北欧国家，一般要求准时赴会，而且会议进展很快，直切主题，严格地按拟定日程进行。而在南欧诸如西班牙和希腊等国家，虽然要求客人准时到达会场，但是主人却可能会迟到。因此，会议一般会晚些时候开始，而且随时会被打断，并不急着得出结果，达成决议。在这些地区，耐心和礼貌是商务谈判成功的关键。

在东欧，因为基础设施相对落后，礼仪试图化解后勤保障中的矛盾。若要安排会议则必须提前通知。因为办签证和其他旅行事项可能要花几个月的时间。一旦到达东欧国家，涉及商务交易方面的多边会议就会席卷而来，在地跨欧亚两大洲的俄罗斯尤其如此，而商务抉择时尤为谨慎已成为其惯例，在他们看来商务谈判过于妥协让步，则被视为软弱。

（1）Britain 英国

There is still some protocol to follow when introducing people in a business or more formal social situation. This is often a class distinction, with the "upper class" holding on to the long-standing traditions: introduce a younger person to an older person. Introduce a person of lower status to a person of higher status. When two people are of similar age and rank, introduce the one you know better to the other person.

Punctuality is important in business situations. Scots are extremely punctual.

在商务或更正式的社交场合介绍某人时，仍有一些外交礼仪需要遵守。这就是通常所说的等级区分，上层社会坚持着一个传统：将年轻的一方介绍给年长的一方；将地位较低的一方介绍给地位较高的一方。而当两个人的年龄和社会阶层相仿时，则将你较熟悉的一方介绍给另一方。

守时在商务场合里非常重要。苏格兰人是非常准时的。

（2）Germany 德国

If you are invited to a German's house: Arrive on time as punctuality indicates proper planning. Never arrive early. Never arrive more than 15 minutes later than invited without telephoning to explain you have been detained. Send a handwritten thank-you note the following day to thank your hostess for her hospitality.

German do not have an open-door policy. People often work with their office door closed. Knock and wait to be invited in before entering. German communication is formal. As a group, Germans are suspicious of hyperbole. They will be direct to the point of bluntness.

Meetings adhere to agendas strictly, including starting and ending time. Maintain direct eye contact while speaking. At the end of a meeting, some Germans signal their approval by rapping their knuckles on the tabletop.

There is a strict protocol to follow when entering a room: The eldest or highest ranking person enters the room first. Men enter before women, if their age and status are roughly equivalent.

如果被邀请去德国人家里的话，务必准时到达，因为准时意味着的有合理的计划。切勿提前到达，也不要在没有打电话解释你被耽搁的情况下迟到15分钟以上。赴约翌日，要发送一张手写的感谢信，以感谢女主人的热情好客。

德国人没有开着门的习惯。他们工作时，通常会关着办公室的门。进门前应先敲门并等待对方回应。德国人的沟通非常正式。在德国人的意识中，对别人夸张的说法表示怀疑，他们通常会直言不讳。

他们开会严格遵守会议议程，包括开始和结束时间。发言时会用眼睛直视交流。会议结束前，德国人会通过在桌面叩指关节来表达赞成。

德国人进入房间时遵守一条严格的礼仪规则：最年长者或职位最高者先进入房间。如果年龄和地位大致相同，男士先于女士。

（3）France 法国

In France, Friends may greet each other by lightly kissing on the cheeks, once on the left cheek and once on the right cheek.

If you are invited to a French house for dinner, you must pay attention to following tips:

① *the Arrive on time.*

② *Be kindly.* If you are invited to a dinner party especially in Paris, please send a bunch of flowers in the morning of the occasion so that they may be displayed that evening.

③ *Dress well.* The French are fashion conscious and their version of casual is not as relaxed as in many western countries.

French business behavior emphasizes courtesy and a degree of formality. Mutual trust and respect is required to get things done. Trust is earned through proper behavior. Creating a wide network of close personal business alliances is very important.

In business, the French often appear extremely direct because they are not afraid of asking probing questions. Do not try to schedule meetings during July or August, as this is a common vacation period. If you expect to be delayed, telephone immediately and offer an explanation. Meetings are to discuss issues, not to make decisions. Avoid exaggerated claims, as the French do not appreciate hyperbole.

在法国，朋友之间通过轻吻面颊来打招呼，左右脸颊各一次。

如果你被邀请去法国人家里吃饭，要注意以下几点。

① 准时到达。

② 友好。如果被邀请去一个大型晚宴，尤其是在巴黎，要在晚宴当天上午送上鲜花，这样可以在晚宴上摆设出来。

③ 穿戴整齐。法国人很注重时尚，他们眼中的休闲装也不像其他西方国家那么随意。

法国的商业行为强调礼貌和一定程度的正式。把事情做好需要相互信任、相互尊敬。通过恰当的行为可以赢得信任。建立广泛的私人商业社交网络是非常重要的。

在商务活动中，法国人表现得尤为直接，他们不怕对方提出一些尖锐的问题。不要在7～8月安排会议，因为这是法定的公共假期。如果希望推迟会议，应立即电话联系，并做出解释。会议是用来讨论问题，而不是做决定的。法国人不喜欢夸张，应避免使用夸大的言辞。

2.North America 北美洲

The hand shake is the common greeting. Handshakes are firm, brief and confident. Maintain eye contact during the greeting. In formal circumstances, you may want to use titles and surnames as a courtesy until you are invited to move to a first name basis.

The continent of North America includes the United States, as well as Canada and Mexico, and customs in these three countries are quite similar. Building a trustworthy relationship with professionals in Mexico is the best way to begin negotiations. It is best not to be overly persuasive, and to avoid any sort of conflict during points of disagreement because this makes a bad impression. It is always recommended to engage in a few minutes of small talk with Mexican business people after the regotiations have ended.

Generally speaking, in the United States the working week consists of Monday to Friday, 9 am.-5 pm. However, due to the strong work ethic, it is common practice for the majority of Americans to work long hours and overtime. It is also customary to take as few as ten days holiday per year.

In the North America, business people value punctuality, and it is appropriate to arrive a few minutes before the meeting begins. There is not much time for small talk, although pleasantries will be exchanged, because the people there like to get to the business of the meeting quickly.

In Mexico, an amount of time is spent in small talk before the meeting, and it is not uncommon for Mexican professionals to arrive late for about 30 minutes after the international professionals have made it to the meeting site.

During business meetings in Canada, it is common for individuals in the French areas to use gestures and touch one another's arms when speaking. In the English regions of the country, body language is much more reserved in a professional setting.

It is not required to give a gift at the first business meeting in North America; however, it is acceptable to give an initial gift in the United States or Mexico—a small token, such as a present with a company logo, is appropriate. Gifts are often given at the end of negotiations in Canada—a quality bottle of wine or liquor is an acceptable gift.

If invited to the home of a professional in Mexico or the United States, it is customary to bring flowers or chocolates to the host; Canadians don't often invite colleagues to their homes.

握手是常见的问候方式。握手要坚定、简短和自信。在问候时，保持眼神的交流。在正式的场合中，礼貌起见，应用头衔和姓氏称呼对方，除非对方允许你直呼其名。

北美大陆包括美国、加拿大以及墨西哥，这三个国家的习俗非常的相似。在墨西哥与内行人士建立一个值得信赖的关系是开拓合作最好的方式。不要过于游说别人，在意见不合时避免争执，因为这样会留下不好的印象。在谈判结束后，建议与墨西哥商人小谈几分钟。

一般来说，在美国每周的工作时间为周一至周五，上午9点至下午5点。然而由于具有很强的工作观念，大多数美国人工作时间长，习惯加班。每年只有10天以内的休假是很普遍的。

北美洲的企业家重视守时。在会议开始前几分钟到场是得体的做法。尽管会客套几句，但并没有太多时间进行寒暄，因为北美的人们期望尽快进入会议议题。

在墨西哥，在会前会花很多时间进行寒暄，墨西哥的行内人士晚到30分钟的情况并不少见。

在加拿大的商务会议中，在讲法语的地方，使用手势并在讲话时碰触对方的手臂是很常见的。在该国家讲英语的地方，进行专业会议时，肢体语言相对少见。

在北美洲，初次会谈不需要馈赠礼物。不过在美国和墨西哥，初次赠予象征性的小礼物是可以接受的，例如，可赠送带有公司徽标的礼物。在加拿大，通常是在谈判结束时才赠送礼物。一瓶优质葡萄酒或烈性酒是不错的礼物。

如果应邀去墨西哥或美国商界人士家做客，送主人鲜花或巧克力是合乎习俗的。而加拿大人通常不邀请同事去他们家。

United States 美国

Americans socialize in their homes and "backyards", also in restaurants and other public places. It's not at all unusual for social events to be as casual as a backyard barbecue or a picnic in the park.

Arrive on time if invited for dinner; no more than 10 minutes later than invited to a small gathering. If it is a large party, it is acceptable to arrive up to 30 minutes later than invited.

Americans are direct. They value logic and linear thinking and expect people to speak clearly and in a straightforward manner. To them if you don't "tell how it is" you simply waste time, and time is money. If you are from a culture that is more subtle in communication style, try not to be insulted by the indirectness. Try to get to your point more quickly and don't be afraid to be more direct and honest than you are used to. Americans will use the telephone to conduct business that would require a face-to-face meeting in most other countries. They do not insist upon seeing or getting to know the people with whom they do business.

美国人会在家里、后院、餐馆或其他公共场所组织社交活动。美国人常把社交活动安排得像后院烧烤或公园野餐一样随意。

如果应邀参加晚餐，应准时到达；参加小型聚会迟到不应超过 10 分钟；如果是一个大型宴会，迟到 30 分钟是可以接受的。

美国人非常直接。他们注重逻辑性和线性思维，欣赏清晰坦率的表达方式。对于他们来说，如果你不告诉他们到底要怎样的话，那就完全是在浪费时间，而时间就是金钱。如果在你的国家更倾向于含蓄的表达，那就尽量不要因为表达方式的差异而造成误会。在美国要尝试尽快进入主题，敢于打破习惯，更加直接和坦诚。美国人可以在电话中做生意，而并不一定非要见到或了解与其做生意的人。其他很多国家的人，做生意则可能会采取面对面的会谈方式。

3.South America 南美洲

Proper business etiquette varies by region, and sometimes within the regions themselves. In South America, many countries share similar business etiquette. To be ready for business transactions in South America, there are some key rules you need to be aware of to prevent misunderstandings or delays.

不同的地区有着不同的商务礼仪，有时一个地区也会有不同的礼仪要求。在南美洲，很多国家都有相似的商务礼仪。如果你准备在南美洲进行商业贸易，应了解一些重要的礼仪原则，以避免产生误解或延误。

（1）Greetings 问候

When greeting business counterparts in South America, there are several common characteristics. In most countries, you should wait for your host to introduce you to others. First greet the person who is the eldest or who has the highest position. A handshake and eye contact is usually the appropriate greeting. Use formal names and honorifics until your counterpart begins to use a more informal name with you.

在南美洲问候商业伙伴时，有几个共同的原则。在大多数国家，要等主人把你介绍给别人，接着先去问候最年长或职位最高的人。问候时应握手并有眼神交流。使用得体的称呼和敬语，直到你的商业伙伴开始用非正式方式称呼你。

（2）Business Cards 商务名片

It is common for business cards to be exchanged during the first meeting. In most cases, you should have two sides to your business card: English and Spanish. In Brazil, you should have English and Portuguese on the card. It is recommended that you present the business card with the native speaker's language facing up. In Venezuela, you should include your education and professional status on the business card.

第一次商务会面时，一般要交换名片。大多数情况下，商务名片上两面都应有文字：英语和西班牙语。在巴西，名片上应该印有英语和葡萄牙语。递出名片时，建议将有对方母语的一面朝上。在委内瑞拉，商务名片上应该包括教育背景和专业身份。

（3）Punctuality 守时

In almost all of South America, punctuality is only expected of you. Regardless of their punctuality, you are expected to arrive on time. Your South American counterparts will usually be late to meetings, although they will see themselves as being on time. Venezuela is an exception to this rule. Most Venezuelan business professionals arrive on time to meetings.

几乎在整个南美洲，守时只是对你而言的。不论当地人守时与否，你都应该守时。南美洲的商业伙伴通常开会都会迟到，并认为自己是按时到的。委内瑞拉是个例外。大多数委内瑞拉的商务人士都会按时抵达会场，参加会议。

（4）Meetings 会见

According to Kwintessential, almost every business meeting in South America begins with small talk. Most will also end with small talk. Business doesn't begin until after your counterparts have learned more about you and have become more comfortable. Because punctuality is less important to South Americans, your business transactions will take time and debate, regardless of deadlines. You will have to be tactful in attempting to get your transaction completed in the time allotted.

南美洲几乎所有的商务会议都是从闲聊开始的，大多数会议也会以闲聊告终。只有当你的商业伙伴了解你并感到放松了，才会开始谈生意。因为南美人并不那么注重时间观念，所以商业交易通常会旷日持久，而不顾及时间的长短。可见，想让生意按预定的时间谈成，是需要相当的技巧的。

（5）Holidays 假期

Holidays across the continent include: New Year's Day (Jan. 1), Labor Day (May 1), Columbus Day (Oct. 12) and New Year's Eve (Dec. 31). Every country also has a variety of other holidays throughout the year to celebrate Independence Day, Patron Saint Day and other events. The two weeks around Christmas and Easter are also times not to schedule business transactions, as many South Americans are on holiday.

南美洲共同的假期包括新年（1月1日）、劳动节（5月1日）、哥伦布日（10月12日）和新年前夜（12月31日）。每个国家也有各自的假期庆祝独立日、守护神节和其他节日。不要把圣诞节和复活节前后的两周纳入商业计划表，因为这时很多南美人还在度假。

（6）Attire 着装

Business dress code is similar to the United States. Your accessories need to be of good quality, as South Americans tend to notice accessories and treat you according to how you appear. According to the experts, residents of the east coast dress more informally than those on the west coast.

南美洲商务着装规范类似于美国。服装配饰一定要质量好，因为南美人会特别注意配饰，根据你的形象来款待你。根据专家研究发现，东部海岸的居民比西部海岸居民着装更随意。

(http://www.ehow.com/about_6702510_business-etiquette-south-america.html)

Brazil 巴西

With increased globalization in the business arena, the world truly continues to get smaller. Many U.S. business people are spending more time meeting with international clients, so it is important to understand the culture and etiquette of the nationality with which one is dealing to have an effective business transaction and ultimately a good long-term relationship. With its young population, plentiful natural resources and agriculture, and strong industry, Brazil has potential as a major player in the world market. Working successfully with Brazilians is your first step toward harnessing that potential. The following instructions are of great use.

Though your business will likely be done in English, learn some Portuguese phrases. Your Brazilian associates will appreciate your making the effort. By all means, don't forget that the national language in Brazil is Portuguese, not Spanish.

Dress conservatively and professionally in muted colors for men and women. Light colors are acceptable for summer (December to February). Clean, well-manicured nails are important for women.

Be on time, but do not be surprised if your Brazilian hosts take a more relaxed approach to schedules. In the big cities of Rio and St Paul, you may find that being punctual holds more importance than in other regions.

Begin the meeting in a leisurely manner, taking some time to make small talk with your Brazilian associates. Jumping right into the meeting is seen as rude, and like other South Americans, Brazilians find it important to know the individuals with whom they are doing business. Building personal relationships is important. In fact, you will probably find that it takes several trips to the country to really get your business going there.

Use attractive visuals in your presentation, and make sure you have any materials you intend to distribute translated into Portuguese and English. Be tolerant of interruptions, which often simply show that there is interest in the discussion, and keep your manner non-confrontational at all times.

Be prepared to wait for final decisions. As noted earlier, it may take a while to build the business relationship. Also, in this hierarchical business structure, final word must ultimately come from the highest-ranking executive.

随着全球化推进，世界的范围也在缩小。例如，很多美国商人花大量的时间和国外客户打交道，来了解交易对方的文化和礼仪，以有效地达成交易，建立起良好的长期商务关系。巴西年轻劳动力多，自然资源丰富并且工业发达，有望成为国际市场的主要组成部分。成功地和巴西人合作是利用其资料的第一步。具体方法如下。

尽管很多生意都是用英语谈成的，但学些葡萄牙语也会很有用。你的巴西同行会欣赏你在语言上下的工夫。一定不要忘记巴西的国语是葡萄牙语，而不是西班牙语。

男女着装应保守正式，色彩不要张扬。夏季（12月至2月）可穿浅色。女性指甲应保持整洁，经常修剪。

要守时。但如果巴西东道主不太严格遵守日程表的安排也不要感到意外。在里约热内卢和圣保罗等大城市，你会发现守时比其他地区更严格。

用轻松的方式开始会议，多花时间和巴西同行闲聊。在巴西直接进入会议主题被认为是不礼貌的行为。像其他南美人一样，巴西人认为了解自己的生意伙伴很重要。建立私人关系也很重要。实际上，你会发现你要多次造访巴西这个国家，才可能真正做成与当地人的生意。

在商务演示中应使用有吸引力的视觉材料。如有资料需派发，要确定资料已被译成英语和葡萄牙语。在演示中，要容忍被打断。中途打断通常意味着对方对目前讨论的这一点感兴趣。始终不要出现反感的情绪。

不要急着作出决定。如前所言，建立商业关系会需要一段时间。而且，在这种层级商业结构中，最后的决策会由最高职位的管理者来作出。

4.Oceania 大洋洲

The South Pacific region of the world contains both diverse countries and cultures. Within this area are a large number of relatively small island groups. Other countries include New Zealand, and Australia. Many of the inhabitants of this region emigrated from other areas of the world, and have subsequently shared residence with the local native populations. Therefore，it is not easy to be acquainted with the local cultures. Here let us take Australia as an example to give a glimpse of local etiquettes in this area.

南太平洋地区国家众多，习俗多样。这个地区有许多相对较小的岛国。较大的国家包括新西兰和澳大利亚。当地很多居民是来自世界各地的移民，与当地原居民共处。因此，当地文化复杂，了解起来并不容易。我们以澳大利亚为例来了解该地区的文化礼仪。

Australia 澳大利亚

Australian rules of social etiquette are a little different from most countries around the world. The rules do not relate to how a fork should be held, or who should be served first at a dinner table. Instead, most of Australia's rules relate to expressing equality. Basically, as long as you appreciate that Australians want to be treated as equal irrespective of their social, racial or financial background, anything is acceptable.

Displays of wealth may be seen as signs of superiority and frowned upon accordingly. Likewise, the acceptance of generosity may be seen as a sign of inferiority. Likewise, it may be frowned upon.

The relaxed attitude of Australians has been known to cause problems. Because Australians are difficult to offend, they are not sensitive to causing offence in others. To outsiders, Australians often appear very blunt and rude. They tend to call a spade when perhaps more tact is required.

Furthermore, because Australians see people as equal, they frequently offend international visitors who feel a more respectful attitude is warranted. Australians may refer to some foreigners as "mate" instead of using more respectful titles such as Sir, Madam, Mrs, Mr, Ms, lord, and Your highness.

澳大利亚的社会礼仪和世界上大多数国家略有不同。该国大部分礼仪注重的不是如何拿餐叉，或餐桌上应该先为谁服务，而是如何体现平等的原则。基本上，只要给予澳大利亚人平等的对待，忽略社会、种族、经济背景等，那一切都可以被接受。

炫富被认为是在表现优越感，经常会招致反感。同样，接受施舍被认为是自卑的表现，也同样令人反感。

澳大利亚人无拘无束的态度同样容易产生问题。因为澳大利亚人很难感到被冒犯，所以很容易冒犯别人，却意识不到。在外人看来，澳大利亚人是率直无理的。因此，有时候需要一些技巧来应对他们的直来直去。

而且，由于澳大利亚人平等待人，而有些客人认为自己理应受到特别尊重，因此他们经常会感到被冒犯。澳大利亚人可能会称呼外宾"伙计"，而不用先生、女士、某某先生、某某夫人、某某女士、大人、阁下等尊称。

① Splitting the bill at a restaurant 餐厅付账各付各的

In most Asian countries, if a group of friends go out for dinner, the wealthiest member of a dining party may offer to pay for the entire meal. Furthermore, if a man and woman go to dinner, irrespective of whether they are friends or lovers, the man will usually pay. This is not the case in Australia. If a group of friends go to a restaurant, the bill will be split amongst all the diners. It is unlikely that one individual will feel an obligation to pay for others. Nor do any of the other members of the dining party want to be paid for. In business, these rules are bent a little as a bill may be picked up as a way of fostering "good relations."

在大多数亚洲国家，如果一群朋友出外就餐，会由其中最富有的一位埋单。如果一男一女一起用餐，无论他们是恋人还是朋友，通常由男士埋单。在澳大利亚不是这样。如果一群朋友去餐厅吃工作餐，餐费会由用餐者平摊，没有人觉得有义务为所有人埋单。也没有人愿意由他人埋单。在生意场合，上述规则却恰好相反，因为埋单会被当作一种促进"良好关系"的手段。

② Taking the piss 开玩笑

Around the world, most jokes are based on some variety of derogatory theme. In order to avoid offending the victim's feelings, most nationalities usually only say the joke when its victim is not present. In Australia, this can be a risky thing to do. Some Australians don't like people making jokes about groups that they are not part of. If they hear a joke about a different group, instead of laughing, they may get angry.

Targets of a piss-take are expected to reply in kind. An insulting joke in return often increases an Australian's appreciation for you.

It is also worth being careful about what things you take the piss about. There are no hard and fast rules. It is recommended that no piss be taken until you get to know your friend well and understand what makes them laugh or angry. Then you take the piss and so help them feel better about whatever is troubling them in his or her life.

在世界各地，大部分玩笑都是基于各种不敬的主题。为了顾及被开玩笑者的感受，通常都是当对方不在场时才开玩笑。可在澳大利亚，如果这样做就要小心了。因为有些澳大利亚人不喜欢开那些不在场的人的玩笑。如果他们听到有人这样开玩笑，不但不会笑，还可能会生气。

通常认为，被开玩笑的人应该以同样的方式回应，因此回报一个智慧型的笑话反而会赢得他人对你的赞赏。

同样值得注意的是拿什么开玩笑。这里没有金科玉律。建议先了解朋友的性格喜好，再开玩笑，让他们在烦恼时转换心情。

③ Tipping 给小费

Tipping is optional in Australia. In restaurants, a tip is only left if above average service has been delivered.

Taxi drivers are usually only tipped if they initiate a good conversation and don't rip off their customers. (When getting into a taxi, sitting in the front seat is the etiquette. The back seat feels too much like one is being chauffeured and it is difficult to have a conversation.)

Bar staff are not usually tipped unless a customer has thoughts of seducing them. Even if the staffs are not tipped, they will continue to serve you on your subsequent visits. No grudge is held against those who don't tip.

在澳大利亚不一定都要给小费。在餐馆，只有接受了超值的服务才会给小费。

出租车司机只有在发起了一场愉快的谈话，也没有"敲竹杠"的情况下，才会拿到小费。（坐出租车时，应坐前排。坐在后排感觉更像雇主，而且谈话也不方便。）

酒吧员工通常不必给小费，除非顾客有引诱他们的想法。即使没拿小费，酒吧员工也会尽心为你服务的，而不会对不给小费的顾客心怀不满。

④ Seek and express empathy, not sympathy 寻求和表达共鸣，而非同情

In America, people feel no shame when talking about the fact they are seeing a counselor or psychiatrist. Oddly, revealing one's emotional distress almost seems to be a status symbol. In Australia, an ethic of "no worries" reins. Irrespective of whether they have just lost two legs in a car accident or their business has just collapsed, Australians try to maintain a facade of cheerfulness. If you feel the need to talk about your problems, it is more polite to try to turn the problem into a funny story.

在美国，人们对找心理顾问或看心理医生毫不避讳。展现个人的情感挫折几乎成了一种有身份的象征。而在澳大利亚，"粉饰太平"的道德观盛行。无论是在事故中失去双腿还是生意破产，澳大利亚人都会竭力表现出兴奋的假象。如果想和澳大利亚谈谈你面临的问题，最好是把你所说的问题编成一个滑稽的故事。

5.Asia 亚洲

Asia is the most culturally diverse region on earth. The people of Asia share a common trait: a rigorous, deeply ingrained sense of courtesy, which includes respect for the elderly, personal humility and a readiness to subordinate one's self to the group, and meticulous avoidance of any controversy or confrontation. Nothing must disturb the harmonious flow of proper social intercourse, since such a disruption could well cause individuals to lose face (suffer public embarrassment)—a disgrace that Asians will go to extremes to avoid.

Requests are rarely answered with the word "No" Instead, you'll receive a polite evasion such as "Perhaps, but not yet." or "Very interesting, we'll consider it." For the same reason, decisions tend to be reached by consensus, which takes time. In general, no agreement is final until each issue is resolved to everyone's satisfaction. One of the supreme Asian virtues is patience.

亚洲是全世界文化最具多样性的地区。亚洲人有一个共同的特点：对礼节有一种严格的、根深蒂固的感情，包括尊敬老人，谦逊，时刻准备为集体作贡献，小心翼翼地避免任何争论或对峙。亚洲人会不遗余力地避免任何破坏正常和谐的社会交往的行为，因为这些行为会使个人丢脸（当众难堪），而被视为耻辱。

一般来说，对方提出的请求是很少被直接拒绝的。相反的，你会听到礼貌的借口，如"可能吧，但是不是现在"或者"很有意思，我们会考虑的"。同样的道理，作出一个决定也需要大多数人的认可，这需要不少时间。一般是直到每个细节使每一个人都满意了之后才会做出最后的决定。亚洲人最优秀的美德之一就是有耐心。

When you show up for a meeting, be on time; in most Asian countries, arriving even just a few minutes late to a business engagement is considered an insult. There are exceptions, but they apply only to your host; in Indonesia, for example, people of higher rank may be intentionally late to a meeting as a sign of status. Indians respect punctuality but don't always observe it themselves; keep flexible to allow for sudden rescheduling.

Greeting styles vary. In Indonesia, the handshake precedes a slight nod or bow, while Japanese businesspeople often shake hands with Westerners while bowing to one another. In Thailand, the traditional way of greeting is nestling (palms together at chest level with head inclined in a slight bow). Again, however, westerners are likely to be greeted with a handshake—and the same holds for South Korea and the Philippines. In India, a handshake is standard for everyone. In general, avoid touching your host after the initial greeting.

Professional titles are very important throughout Asia. Unless invited to do otherwise, address people by their titles (use the equivalent of "Mr." if they don't have any) and their family names. In Japan, and other Far Eastern countries, the family name comes first and the last name is after it.

参加会议时，请务必准时出席，在大多数亚洲国家，哪怕迟到几分钟也被看成是一种不尊重对方的表现。但是也有例外，就是只允许主人迟到，比如在印度尼西亚，地位高的人为了显示自己的身份可能故意迟到。印度人喜欢准时的人但他们自己往往不准时，当对方突然改变时间安排时，应能变通。

问候方式也是各不相同。在印度尼西亚，握手要比点头示意或鞠躬好，而日本商人常常与西方人握手，而和本国人互相鞠躬致意。在泰国，传统的打招呼的方式是合十礼（手掌并于胸部并前身微前倾）。不过同样的，他们会和西方人握手，在韩国和菲律宾也是同样的情况。在印度，对于每个人来说，握手都是合适的。一般来说，在初次见面后应避免与人身体接触。

亚洲各国都非常重视称呼。除非得到他人允许，否则应该称呼对方的头衔（如果没有的话，就称呼"先生"）和他们的姓。在中国、日本和其他远东国家，姓排在前面，名在后。

（1）China 中国

Along with the constant development of Chinese culture and the Western culture, Chinese etiquette and the Western etiquette are fusions. However, in real life, the etiquette's impact due to cultural differences between China and the West still exists.

China is a state of ceremonies. Back to five thousand years ago, etiquette used to be the core of traditional culture. Up to now, the etiquette has been really reformed. Thus it becomes rituals of modern civilization. Chinese etiquette in Chinese culture plays a "quasi-legal" role. Etiquette's origins can be traced back to the early time of human beings. It should be said that at the very beginning of the history of the Chinese nation, etiquette was generated along with the human activities and with a primitive religion. Etiquette is the system to deal with the three relationships among the people, God and the ghosts.

There were "five ceremonies" in ancient China. The etiquette of sacrifice was "Jili", the etiquette of marriage was "Xili", the etiquette of greeting was "Binli", the etiquette of army was "Junli" and the etiquette of funeral was "Xiongli". In folkways, people divided the etiquette into "Sheng", "Guan", "Hun", and "Sang" these four parts. In fact, the etiquette can be divided into two main parts, one is politics, and the other is life.

The understandings of Chinese etiquette can help you raise your self-cultivation and improve your interpersonal relationship. To the officers, to understand each other's customs will be conductive to the exchanges between the different countries. A person who understands others' rituals and folk customs can be seen as respecting for others and can be easier to make a good impression on the other side.

In China, the most important relationship in the family is that between parents and son. Arranged marriage is therefore a practical consideration. Parents' spirit must be placed in household shrines and graves tended regularly. For the most of Chinese, respect and obedience to parental wishes are expected of the children. Parents are responsible for their children's education and marriage.

It is very important for the Chinese to have good relationships with others. They often regard good social relations as a symbol of personal ability and influence. Chinese seldom express what they think directly and they prefer a roundabout way. Neither show their emotions and feelings in public. They greet people with a handshake rather than an embrace or a kiss when they are greeting or saying good-bye. Consequently, it is better not to behave too carefree in public, even though you are well-intentioned.

Chinese are very warm and hospitable. It is granted to understand the age, occupation, income, marital status, children and other issues with each other. The westerners will generally not like that. Chinese will ask the price of goods which is bought by others directly. In the eyes of Chinese people, the price is only for items or rank. It is said the quality of goods. Chinese prefer to ask "where are you going?" when they meet others. This is just a form of greetings in China. But if it happens in the United States, it might make the other feel embarrassed, for it belongs to other's privacy you should not interfere in.

随着中国文化和西方文化的不断发展，中国礼仪和西方礼仪得到了融合。但在现实生活中，中西方文化差异也使礼仪不尽相同。

中国是礼仪之邦。追溯到 5000 年前，礼仪曾是传统文化的核心。如今，礼仪已发展成为现代文明的仪式。中华礼仪在中国文化中起着"准法律"的作用。礼仪的起源可以追溯到人类的早期。在中国历史初期，礼仪随着人类活动和原始宗教出现。那时，礼仪是处理人、"鬼"与"神"三者关系的一种体系。

中国古代有五礼之说，祭祀礼仪为吉礼，结婚礼仪为喜礼，问候礼仪为宾礼，军旅礼仪为军礼，丧葬礼仪为凶礼。民俗界认为礼仪包括生、冠、婚、丧四种。实际上，礼仪可分为政治与生活两大类。

了解中华礼仪有助于修身和改善人际关系。对于官员来说，了解建交国家的礼仪有助于国家间的交流。个人如果理解他人遵循的礼仪和民俗会被认为是对他人的尊重，容易给对方留下好的第一印象。

在中国，家庭内部最重要的关系是父母和孩子的关系。"包办婚姻"是出于父母对子女关心的实际考虑。父母的灵位要在家中神龛安置，并要定期去扫墓。对于大部分中国人来说，要求尊重和顺从父母的意愿。父母要负责子女的教育和婚姻。

中国人很看重和他人的关系。他们会把良好的社会关系看作个人能力和影响的象征。中国人很少直接表达他们所想的，而是委婉地去表达。中国人也不会在公众场合表达情感。他们在问候或道别时，会握手，而不会拥抱或亲吻。因此，即使你是好意，也最好不要在公共场合过于随意。

中国人热情好客。与西方人不同，在中国打听对方的年龄、职业、收入、婚姻状况、子女和其他情况被认为是理所当然的。西方人却难以接受。中国人会直接问对方所买商品的价格。在中国人眼中，价格代表的是质地和档次，即商品的质量。中国人问候他人会说"你去哪儿？"而在美国，这样问会让人尴尬，因为这会涉及他人的隐私，是不应该问的。

① Greeting People 问候

Chinese people seldom express their ideas or opinions directly but prefer a roundabout way. They will look towards the ground when greeting someone. Neither show their emotions and feelings in public. They greet people with a handshake rather than an embrace or a kiss when they are greeting or saying good-bye. Handshaking is the most common form of greeting with foreigner.

The Chinese have a terrific sense of humor. They can laugh at themselves most readily if they have a comfortable relationship with the other person. You should be ready to laugh at yourself given the proper circumstances. Greetings are formal and the oldest person is always greeted first. When you are meeting new people, you should always act in a polite and professional manner, use basic manners and be polite. Make sure to provide proper introductions for people in the group who do not know each other, and refer to everyone by his proper name or formal title. Address the person by an honorific title and their surname. If they want to move to a first-name basis, they will advise you which name to use.

中国人很少直接表达自己的看法和意见，通常比较含蓄。他们问候别人时很少有眼神交流。他们不会在公共场合表露感情。他们问候时，会握手，而不拥抱或亲吻。握手是问候外宾是最常用的方式。

中国人极有幽默感。如果和对方相处自在，他们很乐于自嘲。在适当的场合你要做好沉默的准备。正式的问候，应先问候长辈。第一次见面时，行为举止应该礼貌得体，运用基本礼仪，彬彬有礼。为互不认识的人作介绍时要得体，提到每个人的时候应用合适的称呼或正式的头衔。称呼他人时应用敬称和对方的姓。如果中国人想与你更亲昵些，他们会建议你用何种方式称呼他。

When meeting the Chinese in a business setting, sometimes more formal etiquette is required. Tips for meeting the Chinese in a business setting as follow:

You should arrive at meetings on time or slightly early. The Chinese view punctuality as a virtue. Arriving late is an insult and could negatively affect your relationship.

Pay great attention to the agenda as each Chinese participant has his or her own agenda that they will attempt to introduce.

Meetings require patience. Mobile phones ring frequently and conversations tend to be boisterous. Never ask the Chinese to turn off their mobile phones as this causes you both to lose face.

Guests are generally escorted to their seats, which are in descending order of rank. Senior people generally sit opposite senior people from the other side.

Written material should be available in both English and Chinese, using simplified characters. Be very careful about what is written. Make absolutely certain that written translations are accurate and cannot be misinterpreted.

Visual aids are useful in large meetings and should only be done with black type on white background. Colors have special meanings and if you are not careful, your color choice could work against you.

在商业场合问候中国人，礼仪要更正式些。商务情景下如何问候中国人，提示如下：

应准时或稍早到会。中国人视守时为美德。迟到会被认为是对对方的轻慢，会消极地影响彼此的关系。

要注意会议日程，因为每个与会者都有自己想要介绍的议程。

会议需要耐心。手机会不断响起，而且交谈嘈杂。但不要要求中国人关掉手机，这样会让彼此都感到尴尬。

来宾会被引领到座位，座位次序按职位由高到低排列。位高者通常分坐两侧。

书面材料应使用英文和简体汉字。注意：材料内容确保翻译准确，不会被曲解。

大型会议会使用投影仪等设备。应用白底黑体字。在中国，色彩是有意义的。如果不谨慎选错颜色，可能会适得其反。

② Table Manner 餐桌礼仪

The Chinese prefer to entertain in the public places rather than in their homes, especially when entertaining foreigners. If you are invited to their house, consider it a great honor. If you must turn down such an honor, it is considered polite to explain the conflict in your schedule so that your actions are not taken as a slight.

Seating place sequence should be paid attention to, just look at following principles:

Right is the honor guest and the left is the opposite. It is just the opposite of the western culture. The reason is that the Chinese food is always served by a clockwise direction, so the guests on the right can be cared more.

Center seat is the most honorable: When three are dining together, the person in the center position is higher than the people in the seats on both sides.

The seat facing the door: According to etiquette practices, when having dinner, the better seats are those facing the main entrance.

Better seats facing the landscape in the exclusive restaurants: There usually is elegant and beautiful scenery or the performances indoor which is for diner viewing. So the best viewing angle for watching is the best seat.

Best seats are besides the platform: If there is a special platform in the banquet hall, the table which closes to the platform is the main dining table.

What we have to pay attention to is that in the formal banquet, the tables should be in the same direction.

If it is a party, the direction of the honor guest in each table should maintain the same direction with the host table.

中国人更愿意在外宴请，而不是在家请客，招待外宾时尤其如此。如果你被邀请到中国人家中做客，要视作极大的荣幸。如果你不得不拒绝邀请，一定要礼貌地解释说和你日程表的冲突，以免被视为无礼。

在中国，要格外注意座次，其原则如下：

右边为贵宾位，左边则相反。这和西方文化恰好相反。原因在于中国上菜的顺序为顺时针，所以右边的客人会得到更多照顾。

中间的座位最为尊贵：当三人就餐时，坐中间的人职位应高于旁边两人。

面向门的座位：根据礼仪规范，用餐时，面向主要入口的位置更佳。

在奢华的餐厅，通常有秀雅的景观或室内表演供就餐者观赏。所以，最好的座位有最好的观景角度。

舞台旁的座位：如果在宴会大厅有舞台，靠近舞台的桌子是主餐桌。

应注意在正式宴会上，桌子应按同一个方向摆放，如果是派对，每张餐桌上的主宾位应朝向主餐桌。

General advice:

Wait to be seated. Never sit at the head of a table unless you are instructed to do so.

Never take food, or eat before an older person at the table.

If you ever take out a napkin for yourself, be sure to pass napkins to everyone at the table.

If you hold your bowl, palm the bowl from the bottom. Your fingers or thumb should never touch the lip of the bowl. Holding the bowl is acceptable, but is more casual. In a business setting, do not hold your bowl while eating.

When you take dishes, place it on top of your rice. Never mix your dishes with your rice. Never take more than one item at a time.

Soups are usually eaten last. Wait until you have nearly finished eating and then plan for the soup to be the last thing you eat.

If you eat at a Muslim restaurant in China, never ask for any pork dishes or even mention the word pigs. It can, and most likely will upset the owners and other patrons. But try the beef soup, the spicy dried beef, or the stomach linings. Most of the Muslims in China are part of the Huizu ethnic minority. Their cuisine is off-the-charts good.

Sometimes a guest will bring a friend, unannounced. This isn't a big deal, because there is always enough food for a few extra people.

A dinner can last hours. You'll hear "man man chi" mang times, and that translates to "slowly, slowly, eat." Don't only eat the dishes you like.

Chinese people may leave a lot of food behind at the table. Most of the time this food is recycled and fed to pigs, so don't worry about waste.

The more you eat, the happier your host will be. If you eat a small amount, especially if someone made a home-cooked meal, you may insult your host.

Never let anyone still eating feel rushed to finish their meal.

It is okay to answer your phone at a table, absolutely no one will care.

In a home setting, if you want to wash the dishes, never take any dishes away from the table unless it is clear that everyone has finished eating. If you do this, it is a cue to your guests that you want them to leave.

Chinese people love to walk, or "san bu" after they finish off a dish, they say it helps with digestion.

餐桌礼仪小建议：

等待就座。如果未被指示，不要坐在桌首。

若有长者同桌，勿先取食或进餐。

如果取用餐巾纸，记得为桌上每位都递送餐巾纸。

如果拿碗，应该托住碗的底部，不要让手指或拇指碰触到碗缘。端着碗是可以的，但较为随意。在商业场合，用餐时最好不要端着碗。

当你夹菜时，要将夹来的菜放在米饭上面，不要将菜和饭拌在一起。每次夹菜都不要超过一种。

汤通常是最后喝的。当你快用完餐时，可考虑喝点汤。

如果你在中国的穆斯林餐馆用餐，不要点猪肉类的菜或提到猪，否则很有可能惹恼餐馆老板和其他顾客。但你可以尝尝牛肉汤、孜然牛肉和牛肚。大部分穆斯林都是回族。他们的厨艺很棒。

有时候客人不事先告知，就多带个朋友来。这完全没问题，因为食物分量足够再多几个人吃。

在中国，通常一餐饭会持续几个小时。而且你会不断听到"慢慢吃"的礼貌话。就餐时不要只吃自己喜欢的菜。

中国人可能会在餐桌上剩下很多菜。大多数情况下这些食物会被回收，作为猪饲料，所以不要担心浪费问题。

你吃得越多，主人越高兴。如果你吃得很少，尤其是主人亲手做的菜，那主人会不高兴的。

当客人用餐时，不要催促他赶快吃完。

在餐桌上接听电话，没人会在意。

在家请客时，如果你要洗碗，不要在客人还在用餐的时候就开始从桌上撤掉餐盘。你这样做，是在暗示客人赶快离开。

中国人喜欢在餐后聊天或"散步"，他们觉得这有利于消化。

③ The Bill 账单

If you have been invited to eat, you can make an attempt to get the check, but don't actually pay the bill as you may lose the other party's face. If someone calls you to go out, they are expected to pay. Nonetheless, fighting over the bill is always a good way to gain points.

Don't ever try to give the host 50% of the bill to "pay your half". In China, as stated just above, whoever is inviting someone out to eat is expected to pay for everyone. If you want to immediately return the favor, offer to take the person who has paid out to a bar, karaoke, or to drink tea.

Stand up and start pulling the host by the arm and try to yank him back to his seat. Arm waving and arm pulling is always good.

If they manage to pay the waiter first, grab their money out of the waiter's hand and give it back to them, then give the waiter your money instead.

The bigger the scene you cause the better. Don't worry if they seem disgruntled, they actually will be delighted with your enthusiasm.

如果被邀请出外就餐，可以试着去结账，但不要真的埋单，以免让对方尴尬。因为对方邀请你就餐，他是准备埋单的。毕竟，抢着埋单是赢得好印象的一种方式。

不要给主人账单金额的一半来"付你那一半"。在中国，如上所述，请客的一方是会为所有人埋单的。如果你想马上回请，可以提出请大家去酒吧、KTV 或喝茶。

起身拉主人胳膊，把他猛拉回座位；挥动胳膊和拉胳膊在中国都是被允许的。

如果对方抢着埋单，可以把钱从侍者手上夺过，塞回给对方，把你的钱递给侍者。

动静闹得越大越好。不要担心主人会生气，实际上他会为你的热情而高兴。

④ Home Visit 上门拜访

In China, when a person wants to visit someone, the first question in his mind is what clothes are most perfect or suitable. He will take a lot of time to choose the clothes they like and even ask others to get some suggestions. The host also is troubled by the same question. He wants to show his hospitality to the guest, so the suitable clothes will make him seem polite to others, and also make the guest think they are respected by the host.

在中国，当你准备上门拜访时，第一个问题就是如何着装最为得体。准备拜访的人要花大量的时间选择合适的服装，甚至要征询他人的意见。主人会被同样的问题困扰。因为他想向客人表达自己的好客之情，得体的着装会表达主人的礼遇，会使客人感觉得到尊重。

⑤ Making an Appointment 约见

In China, if you want to visit somebody, you should make an appointment to make sure the time, the place and the number of people. In general, the place is also determined by the host. In a formal occasion, you'd better not let your children go with you, maybe you can leave them at home. And also, the time you choose should be acceptable, and try your best to avoid the rest time or dinner time.

在中国，如果要拜访某人，应先约见，定好时间、地点、见面人数。一般来说，主人可决定地点。在正式的场合，最好不要带孩子，将其留在家中。见面应选择彼此方便的时间，尽量避免休息时间和就餐时间。

⑥ Welcoming the Guest 迎客

When the guest comes, the whole family will come out and make greeting to the guest. After the guest came home, hosts should find a seat to let the guest sit down, and then offer tea and cigarette. Drinking tea with guest is China's traditional custom, and the host also offers all kinds of fruits to the guest. At this time, the guest should say some words to refuse such as "I don't need it", "it troubles you too much".

当客人到来时，全家会出来迎接。进门后，礼让客人就座，倒茶递烟。和客人喝茶是中国人的传统习俗。主人还会奉上各式水果。这时，客人应该说些客气话，比如"我不需要""太麻烦您了"等。

⑦ Sending Gifts 送礼

Chinese always pay more attention to choose the gifts which have practical values, while the westerners tend to pay more attention to the memorial values. In the West, it is polite to open gifts as soon as they are given to express appreciation. However, in China, the situation is quite the reverse. Many people send gifts without wrapping them, and if they wrap them, they usually tell the receiver what is inside, and the receiver will thank the sender and put the gift aside without unwrapping them since they already know what is inside. Normally the Chinese feel that if you open the gift as soon as it is given, you might embarrass the person who gives the gift and you might be thought greedy. So, Chinese people tend to open the gifts after the visitors have left.

中国人送礼注重的是实用价值，而西方人送礼注重的是纪念价值。在西方，礼貌的做法是尽快拆开礼物并表达谢意。而在中国，情况正好相反。很多礼物都没有另外包装。如果包装了，通常会告诉接受礼物的人里面的内容。收礼的人会感谢送礼人并将礼品放在一旁，不会拆开礼品包装，因为他们已经知道里面的内容。中国人一般认为如果你收到礼物马上拆开，可能会让送礼人很尴尬，也会被认为很贪财。所以，中国人一般会在宾客离开后再拆开礼物。

Here are some useful hints on giving gifts to the Chinese:

In general, gifts are given at Chinese New Year, weddings, births and more recently, birthdays.

The Chinese like food and a nice food basket will make a great gift.

Do not give scissors, knives or other cutting utensils as they indicate the severing of the relationship.

Do not give clocks, handkerchiefs or straw sandals as they are associated with funerals and death.

Do not wrap gifts in white, blue or black paper.

Four is an unlucky number so do not give four of anything. Eight is the luckiest number, so giving eight of something brings luck to the recipient.

Always present gifts with two hands.

Gifts are not opened when received.

Gifts may be refused three times before they are accepted.

给中国人送礼要注意以下几点：

一般来说，会在新年、婚礼、新生儿出生和生日时送礼。

中国人喜好饮食，所以食盒可以是份不错的礼物。

不要赠送剪刀、刀具或其他切割用具，因为这些表示断绝关系。

不要赠送钟、手帕或草鞋，因为这些与葬礼和死亡相关。

不要用白色、蓝色或黑色的纸包装礼物。

四是个不吉利的数字，所以不要送数量为四的礼物。八是最吉利的数字，所以送礼物时数量宜为八。

要用双手奉上礼物。

收到礼物时，不要当时拆开。

礼物要拒绝三次后，才可收下。

⑧ Making a Farewell 道别

In China, when the guest says that he must go, he would take actions right now unless the host said "don't go" again and again. If the guest insists on going, the host can stand up after the guest stands up and persuade the guest to stay longer.

在中国，当客人表示要告辞，主人要再三挽留，以免客人马上离开。如果客人坚持告辞，主人应在客人起身后起身，并尽力留客人多待会。

(http://www.easytourchina.com/fact-v976-chinese-etiquette)

（2）Japan 日本

On the rare occasion you are invited to a Japanese house: Remove your shoes before entering and put on the slippers left at the doorway. Arrive on time or no more than 5 minutes late if invited for dinner. If you must go to the toilet, put on the toilet slippers and remove them when you are finished.

Punctuality is important. Arrive on time for meetings and expect that your Japanese colleagues will do the same. Since this is a group society, even if you think you will be meeting one person, be prepared for a group meeting. The most senior Japanese person will be seated furthest from the door, with the rest of the people in descending rank until the most junior person is seated closest to the door. Never refuse a request, no matter how difficult or non-profitable it may appear. The Japanese are looking for a long-term relationship.

The Japanese are non-confrontational. They have a difficult time saying "no", so you must be vigilant at observing their non-verbal communication. It is best to phrase questions so that they can answer yes. For example, do you disagree with this? Group decision-making and consensus are important.

Written contracts are required. The Japanese often remain silent for long periods of time. Japanese prefer broad agreements and mutual understanding so that when problems arise they can be handled flexibly.

Using a Japanese lawyer is seen as a gesture of goodwill. Note that Japanese lawyers are quite different from Western lawyers as they are much more functionary. Never lose your temper or raise your voice during negotiations. Some Japanese close their eyes when they want to listen intently.

日本人很少邀请别人到家里做客。去日本人家中做客，在进入门口之前脱掉你的鞋子，穿上预留的拖鞋。赴宴时，应准时或迟到5分钟之内。如果你要去洗手间，穿上摆放在那的拖鞋入厕，离开洗手间时，再脱掉它。

在日本，守时是很重要的。准时到达会议，并期待你的日本同事也会准时。由于这是一个群体社会，即使你与一人会面，但也要做好集体会议的准备。日本级别最高的人将坐在离门最远的位置上，剩下的人按级别递减分配座位，直到级别最低的人坐在最靠近门的位置为止。无论多么困难或毫无利润可言都不要拒绝别人的请求。日本人倾向于寻求长远的合作关系。

日本人喜欢积极的态度。他们几乎不说"不"，所以你必须提高警觉，观察他们的非语言沟通。最好是提出可以让他们回答"是"的问题。例如，你同意吗？在日本，集体决策和协商一致是很重要的。

书面合同是必需的。日本人在谈判中经常长时间保持沉默，当然他们喜欢协议内容涉足面广，谈判中希望相互理解，以便出现问题时，可以灵活地应对。

使用日本的律师，被看作是一个善意的姿态。要注意的是，日本律师是完全不同于西方律师的，因为他们更具有多面性。在谈判时，不要发脾气或提高嗓门。一些日本人在谈判中倾听时会闭上眼睛。

6.Africa 非洲

South Africa 南非

South Africa represents one of the most multicultural nations, earning it the nickname The Rainbow Nation. Those interested in doing business in South Africa must understand the way these cultures come together and affect business dealings. While certain rules seem to apply well in most South African business situations, you must also learn about the individual culture of the people with whom you plan to do business and try to adhere to those etiquette rules.

南非是多元文化特征最明显的国家之一，昵称为"彩虹国"。有意在南非做生意，必须清楚这些文化融合在一起，会影响到商务决策。在大多数商务情景下可以应用某些原则，但同时要了解与之做生意的对方的个人文化背景，以遵循相应的礼仪规范。

① Meeting & Greeting 会见和问候

There are as many ways of greeting one another as there are cultural groups in South Africa. However, when dealing with foreigners the default approach is to shake hands. Some women may not shake hands and merely nod their head. A simple nod back accompanied with a smile is all that is needed.

On the whole, people are fairly relaxed and informal in the business environment; when meeting people it is considered good form to engage in some personal dialogue based around one another's health, family, leisure time or sport. Getting straight down to business and rushing through these social niceties marks you as ill-mannered and may cause you to be perceived as uninterested.

Business cards are normal practice but little ceremony surrounds their exchange. The usual rules apply, i.e. treat the card with respect and store away properly rather than in a pocket. A short comment on the card is also polite.

South African business culture relies heavily on personal trust between parties. Whenever possible, schedule a face-to-face meeting to discuss business rather than communicating via email, letter or telephone. Maintain eye contact when you shake hands at your meeting to help build trust. If the individual or company you meet with has no knowledge of you or your business prior to your initial meeting, consider having a trusted third party send a letter of recommendation.

在南非，有多少种文化，就有多少种问候方式。但是，在和外宾做生意时，默认的问候方式是握手。有些女士可能不握手，只是点头致意。那么你只需要微笑点头回应即可。

总的来说，在生意场合，人们都相当放松和随意；见面时谈谈彼此的健康、家庭、休闲时光或运动是得体的。直奔生意主题，忽略这些社交细节会显得缺乏礼貌，而被认为淡漠无趣。

交换商务名片是常规的做法。通常要重视对方的名片，不要放进口袋，而要专门存放。简单评论几句是较礼貌的做法。

南非的商务文化注重人与人之间的信任。如果有可能，商谈业务应安排面谈，而不是只通过电子邮件、信件或电话联系。会面握手时应直视对方，以建立信任感。如果初次会见的人或公司对你的企业不了解，应请对方信任的第三方出具介绍信。

② Make and Keep Appointments 约见和赴约

Make appointments far in advance, at least a month prior to the meeting. The day before your appointment, call to confirm. Be on time for your appointment, whether it occurs in an office or at a restaurant over a meal.

在南非，至少提前一月预约见面。在见面的前一天，要电话确认。无论是在办公室还是在餐厅见面，都应准时。

③ Dress Appropriately 着装得体

If you are male, choose a dark, conservative business suit for business meetings. Women should wear dark business suits or conservative, modest dresses. South Africans may dress slightly more casual than this, but you should dress up when heading to an initial meeting.

如果是男士，选择适合商务会议的深色、传统的商务西服套装。女士应穿着深色或传统、低调的套装。南非人会比这个标准穿得稍微随意一些。但你在初次会面时应遵循这个标准。

④ Negotiate Properly 正确谈判

Negotiations move slowly in South Africa but do not hinge strongly on bartering for price. Set your price close to what you expect to get for your services. Approach the negotiations process with the attitude of working toward a mutually beneficial agreement. Add a deadline to your contract, but view it as flexible.

在南非若进行商务谈判则进程缓慢，并不是因为讨价还价。定价应接近于你的预期。谈判中应本着互利的态度去签订协议。合同上应标明终止日期，而南非人对此却很灵活。

⑤ Give Gifts to Hostesses 礼赠女主人

Even in business culture, you may receive an invitation to a South African home. If you do, you should bring a small gift for the hostess. A bottle of South African wine, flowers or chocolates work well as a hostess gift.

按南非的商务习俗，你也有可能受邀到南非人家中做客。如果前去拜访，应为女主人带上一份小礼物。一瓶南非产的酒、花或巧克力都是适合送给女主人的礼物。

⑥ Show Respect for Elders 尊重长辈

While South Africa has many different cultures within its country, most of these cultures have a strong sense of value for their elders. To avoid coming across as offensive, always behave respectfully around older individuals, even if they play a less important role in the business meeting than someone else.

南非国内有多种不同的文化，但大多数文化都极为看重对长辈的礼遇。为避免冒犯，在行为举止上要尊重年长的人，即使他们在商务会面中并不如其他人重要。

⑦ Communication 交流

Generally speaking, South Africans are direct (and often loud) communicators but they are also very aware of what, how and to whom something is being said. People will be conscious of what may or may not make someone uncomfortable. The communication style is very much dependent on the level of a relationship; the closer people are the more comfortable they will be with speaking openly and honestly. Relationships in their infancy require more tact and diplomacy.

South Africans follow the European approach to personal space, meaning people keep their distance when speaking. Unlike Latin or Arab cultures they do not appreciate touching and the like.

If you like to chat then South Africa is an ideal place for a good conversation. People will enjoy a good chin wag on a number of subjects. Being an outdoor nation they love sports and this is always a good place to start. The most popular sports are rugby, football and cricket. Other good topics of conversation include food, South African wines and international travel. Topics to avoid are comparing cities as people are very proud of their own cities. Do not raise controversial subjects such as race relations or local politics.

总的来说，南非人交流直接（经常高声地说），但他们也清楚该说什么、怎么说以及和谁说。人们会谈及让他们不自在的事。交流方式取决于关系疏密；关系近的人交流起来更为自由和坦诚。在关系建立初期，交流需要更多的技巧和策略。

南非人遵循欧洲人对个人空间的看法，即交谈时会保持身体距离。不像拉丁美洲或阿拉伯人，他们不喜欢触碰或类似举动。

如果你喜欢聊天，南非人是理想的交谈对象。人们会热衷各种话题的交流。作为一个户外的民族，他们热爱运动，而这也是一个不错的引发交谈的话题。在南非最流行的运动有橄榄球、足球和板球。其他不错的话题包括美食、南非产的酒和世界旅行。在谈话中避免拿城市进行比较，因为人们通常以自己的城市为傲。不要谈论有争议的话题，比如种族关系和当地政治。

⑧ Business Meetings 商务会见

Appointments should be made for meetings through the normal channels. It is often difficult to schedule meetings from mid December to mid January or the two weeks surrounding Easter, as these are prime vacation times.

Initial meetings are often but not always used to establish a rapport. Most meetings will start with some small talk but move swiftly to the business at hand. Come prepared and if possible send an agenda ahead of time to give your counterparts an idea of what you want to address. However, note that agendas are not seen as rigid in South Africa; people will digress and come back to issues in a circular fashion.

If making a presentation, keep it precise. Decisions are made on facts and figures rather than intuition or anything else intangible. Present your business case with statistics and case studies, including charts and graphs.

Although the majority of businesses work in English, there may be occasions where having materials translated into Afrikaans could make a good impression, especially if you are working with an Afrikaans company in areas like Bloemfontein or Pretoria.

会见应通过正式的渠道事先预约。一般很难在 12 月中旬到 1 月中旬或复活节左右两周安排会见，因为这段时间为南非主要的假期。

初次会面并不总是为了融洽关系。大多数会见会从闲聊开始，然后很快转入在谈的生意。应有备而来。如有可能，可提前给你的商业伙伴一份议事日程，使他了解你要表达的要点。但是，在南非，议事日程是可变的，因为人们议事时会兜圈子。

如果作展示，一定要简洁。决策基于事实和数字，而不是直觉或其他不可捉摸的事物。最好用包括图表在内的统计数字和案例分析来诠释。

尽管大多数商务交流都是用英语进行的，但有些情况下如将材料译成南非公用荷兰语会给人良好印象，尤其是在和布隆方丹或比勒陀利亚当地使用南非荷兰语的公司合作时，更要注意这一点。

(http://www.kwintessential.co.uk/etiquette/doing-business-south-africa.html)

Part II   The Cultural Taboos of Some Major Countries
主要国家的商务禁忌

1. The Taboos of Islam 伊斯兰教的禁忌

About 700 million people are adherent to Islam in the whole world currently. They are distributed mainly over the Arab countries in West Asia and North Africa, Pakistan of South Asia, and Malaysia, Indonesia, Brunei of Southeast Asia and other countries. According to the doctrine of "Koran", the residents which believe in Islamism have many taboos in their life.

It is Forbidden to consume pork or other oddly shaped animals, such as snapper, crab and so on. The animals which died by themselves and the blood, viscera of them are also not permitted to eat.

Meat from animals, except for pigs, is permitted under the Islamic dietary law as long as the animal was slaughtered according to the prescript of Islam (The animal must be slaughtered by a Muslim and its throat must be slit with a very sharp knife to ensure a quick death).

Alcohol is banned. Muslims generally not only forbid drinking alcohol or beverages contains alcohol, but also do not allow eating alcoholic foods, such as liqueur chocolate and so on. In particular, it has a more stringent ban of alcohols during Ramadan. For example, in Saudi Arabia, for those immigrants who bring alcohols without permission, the light punishment will be confiscating the alcohols; the serious punishment will be sentenced to detention or banished from the realm. The foreigners who have been overtaken in drink secretly also will be taken into custody.

No smoking during Ramadan. Annual Muharram is the Islamic holy month of Ramadan in

September. At this time, Muslims are required to abstain from food, drink and smoking during the day. Foreigners at this time can not smoke in front of the locals; otherwise it would cause great resentment.

目前全世界信奉伊斯兰教的居民约有七亿，主要分布在西亚和北非的阿拉伯各国、南亚的巴基斯坦，以及东南亚的马来西亚、印度尼西亚、文莱等国。根据《古兰经》的教义，信奉该教的居民在生活中有许多禁忌。

禁食猪肉及其他形状怪异的动物，如甲鱼、螃蟹等；自死的动物及动物的血、内脏等也禁食。除了猪肉以外的肉畜，只要是按照伊斯兰教规定进行宰杀（由伊斯兰教信徒宰杀，使用锋利的刀切断喉咙以确保快速死亡），伊斯兰教饮食法规定允许食用。

伊斯兰教徒一般不允许饮酒及喝含有酒精的饮料，也不允许食用含酒精的食品，如酒心巧克力等。尤其在斋月期间查禁更严。例如在沙特阿拉伯，对私自携酒入境者，轻者将酒没收，重者要处以拘留或驱逐出境。私自饮酒致醉的外国人也要受到监禁。

斋月期间禁止吸烟。每年回历 9 月是伊斯兰教的斋月，本地居民此时白天要禁食、禁水和禁止抽烟；外国人此时也不能在本地人面前吸烟，否则会引起极大的反感。

2.The Taboos of Colors 颜色的禁忌

Different countries and nations have different preferences of the color. In this regard, we should know ourselves as well as the enemies to avoid committing low-level errors when conducting international business.

不同的国家和民族对颜色也有不同的喜好。对此，在进行国际商务时，要做到知己知彼，才能避免犯下低级的错误。

United States: Most people like bright colors, such as red, pink, yellow, green and so on. The people in southwest like indigo. Local custom is: orange indicates orange, purple indicates grapes, and green indicates vegetables.

Japan: Black, dark gray, black and white, and green colors should be avoided. Red and white, gold and silver, is welcomed.

Italy: They regard the purple as a negative color.

Belgium: Blue is avoided. In case of an unlucky thing, people will wear blue clothes. Even when seeing blue things in the dream, they think bad things will happen the next day.

Turkey: Colorful color is an ill omen.

Brazil: Purple indicates sad; yellow indicates despair. With the two colors together, and it will cause bad omen. Brown is seen as unlucky.

Morocco: White is a symbol of poverty. People will wear color clothes, even though they are poor.

Mexico: Purple and black are disliked.

Ethiopia: People express deep condolences to the deceased by wearing.

Thailand: Bright colors are preferred. People are accustomed to use color to show the date within a week, dressed in different colors according to dates. Sunday is red; Monday is yellow; Tuesday is pink; Wednesday is green; Thursday is orange; Friday is light blue and Saturday is fuchsia. Black is for the funeral, and white is for the wedding celebration.

India: Consider the black, white and light color as an unpopular color.

美国：多数人喜欢鲜艳的颜色，如鲜红、粉红、黄色、绿色等色彩，西南部人喜欢靛蓝色。当地的习惯是：橙色表示橘子、紫色表示葡萄、绿色表示蔬菜。

日本：黑色、深灰色和黑白相间的颜色以及绿色应当避免使用。而红白相间和金银相间的颜色，是受人们欢迎的颜色。

意大利：认为紫色是消极的颜色。

比利时：忌蓝色。如遇不吉利的事，人们都穿蓝色的衣服。甚至认为梦中见到蓝色的东西，第二天会发生倒霉的事情。

土耳其：认为五彩缤纷的花色是凶兆。

巴西：认为紫色表示悲伤，黄色表示绝望，这两种颜色配在一起，会引起恶兆。棕黄色被看作是不吉利的。

摩洛哥：认为白色是贫穷的象征，人们生活再艰苦，也要穿花色衣服。

墨西哥：厌恶紫色和黑色。

埃塞俄比亚：穿黄色衣服意味着对已逝的人表示深深的吊唁。

泰国：喜爱使用鲜明的色彩。人们习惯用颜色表示一周内的日期，并按照日期穿着不同颜色的服装。如星期日为红色，星期一为黄色，星期二为粉红色，星期三为绿色，星期四为橙色，星期五为淡蓝色，星期六为紫红色。黑色用于办丧事，白色用于喜庆婚礼。

印度：黑色、白色及浅色为不受欢迎的颜色。

3.The Taboos of Being a Guest 做客的禁忌

If you are invited to an Arabs or Latin-American home, do not praise or admire the articles in the host's house excessively. Otherwise the host might really send this article to you as a present persistently, because they will think you like it very much.

If you are invited to Japanese, Malay or Canadian, do take your shoes off. The residents, adherent to Islam, consider that the right hand is more noble than the left hand. So we must use right hand when receiving or sending presents or accepting tea from the host. Otherwise it would be greatly disrespectful to the host.

到阿拉伯人家和拉丁美洲人家做客，不要过分地称赞主人家里的物品，否则主人极有可能坚持将此物品送给你作为礼品，因为他们会认为你十分喜欢它。

到日本人、马来西亚人和加拿大人家里做客时，一定要脱鞋。信奉伊斯兰教的居民，认为人的右手比左手高贵，所以当我们送收礼物或接受主人的茶点时，一定要用右手，否则就是对主人最大的不恭。

Situational Practice for etiquettes 礼仪口语实景

Make up or search for more situational conversations that may occur in the cross-cultural business communication and put them into practice.

Model 1

A: In my professional career, there are some cases in which cultural differences have led to misunderstandings in business.

B: Oh, go ahead please.

A: Koreans, you know, like to have time to think about their response and thus they gain time by nodding or simply saying "yes". So if someone says "yes" in Korea, it often means "I hear you" rather than agreement.

B: But this can often lead to confusion for Westerners.

A: Right. I remember a business meeting in Seoul with a sales representative from a French perfume company.

B: What did you work at then?

A: I was a buyer for a Korean department store. At the beginning of the meeting, the French salesman asked me if his company's perfume was selling well and whether it was competitive in the Korean market. I answered "yes" to indicate that I had understood his questions.

B: But he misunderstood you, right?

A: Yes. He thought I had answered "yes" to his questions and started to make proposals to increase the price and decrease consumer incentives.

B: Oh, it's so embarrassing.

A: Quite. As a matter of fact, his product was not at all competitive and I needed the time to decide how to present this negative information to him.

Model 2

A: Do you find that people in America often walk faster than people in China? Americans always seem to be in a hurry.

B: It's hard to come to a definite conclusion. Some Americans walk in a leisurely way, and some Chinese are hurry all the time. But on the whole, I think you're right.

A: What do you think are the reasons for that difference?

B: Americans treasure time. For them, time is tangible. It's a thing. "Time is money." You can "spend time", "waste time", "save time". You can even "kill time"!

A: Does this strong sense of time affect their lifestyle?

B: Sure. If you're 20 minutes late for a business appointment, the other person or persons will be annoyed. They may not trust you anymore.

A: But as far as I know, English-speaking people may be 15-30 minutes late for a dinner party.

B: That's true. For an informal occasion like that, punctuality is not so important. Also, a boss may keep his employees waiting for a long time.

A: But if his secretary is late, she's in trouble. She will probably receive a reprimand.

B: How true!

A: The American worship of time probably led them to create fast foods.

B: I agree. And globalization shrinks the differences between cultures. Now people everywhere are rushing, and anywhere you go, you find Kentucky Fried Chicken.

A: But plenty of Chinese are still making appointments saying, "If I am late, wait for me."

B: But with more intercultural communication, I think the gap will eventually be bridged, and Chinese will be hurrying everywhere.

 Terminology Related 相关礼仪术语

Cross Cultural Business Etiquette 跨文化商务礼仪

Cross cultural business etiquette is a tool to teach people to learn the ins and outs of global business. People often talk about how the world is getting "smaller," thanks to travel and technology. But the reality is that, even though we interact with different cultures more than ever, there are still major differences between countries. People often think differently, conduct business differently, and have different expectations. This makes living in a diverse world so interesting. However, it makes doing business a bit challenging—especially if you're not prepared. What's normal in your country might be a serious mistake elsewhere.

跨文化商务礼仪是一种帮助人们了解国际商务细节的手段。人们经常谈到由于旅行和技术进步，世界的距离在拉近。但是实际上，即使我们比起以往来，更为频繁地和不同文化进行交流。人们想法不同，做生意的方式不同，有着不同的预期。这使得生活在多元化世界中乐趣横生。然而，这也使得做生意变得更有挑战——尤其在你未做好准备时。在本国为正常的做法，换个地方，可能铸就的是严重的错误。

Useful Expressions for etiquettes 礼仪用语集锦

The followings are expressions you may use to introduce some core elements of culture:

❑ Culture is learned. It is not innate, so it is possible for a person to learn a new culture.
文化是可以学习的，不是天生的。所以，学习新的文化是可能的。

❑ Culture provides orientation. Generally, a particular group reacts in the same way to a given stimulus. Thus, understanding a culture can help to determine how group members might react in various situations.
文化指明群体取向。一般来说，对于外来文化刺激，特定的群体会以同样的方式做出反应。因此，了解文化有助于预见该群体成员在各种情景下会做出何种反应。

❑ In a cross-cultural partnership building, it is not that one culture dominates over the other, instead, parties from both cultures need to work together to create a third culture.
在跨文化合作中，不应该是一种文化控制另一种文化，而应该是来自不同文化的双方共同营造第三种文化。

❑ The third culture is not a simple compromise, but a new way of the original cultures and works effectively with the technology of the organization.
第三种文化不是简单的妥协，而是原文化的一种新的方式，可以和机构运行有效协作。

❑ Business partners are cultural adventurers. They are to develop an adventure's mentality towards cultures other than one's own.
商业合作者是文化探索者。他们会在本国文化之外，培养针对新文化的探索心态。

Exercises（课后练习）

I.Questions and answers: answer the following questions according to the information you have got in the previous reading.

1. What are the most obvious differences in manners between the north of Europe and the south?

2. What should be taken in consideration when setting up meetings in Northern and Eastern Europe?

3. Where is lightly kissing on the cheeks regarded as a way of greeting between friends?

4. What should be reminded when conducting business in the United States if you are from a culture that is more subtle in communication style?

5. What are the typical cultural taboos of Islamic countries?

II. Expressions: match the people in column A with their corresponding main characteristics in column B.

A	B
Northern Europeans	religious
Southern Europeans	logic and linear thinking
Englishmen	patience
Germans	non-confrontational
Frenchmen	indirectness
Mexicans	small talk
Americans	class distinction
Asians	fashion-conscious
Japanese	direct to the point of bluntness
Arabian	punctuality

III. Translation: translate the following statements into Chinese to ensure to stay away from Phone-call Faux Pas.

1. Always shake hands when meeting someone, as well as when leaving. French handshakes are not as firm as in the United States.

2. Germans do not like surprises. Sudden changes in business transactions, even if they may improve the outcome, are unwelcome.

3. The French have a great respect for privacy. Knock and wait before entering into a room. Additionally, do not "drop in" unannounced. Always give notice before your arrival.

4. Punctuality is necessity in Germany. Arrive on time for every appointment, whether for business or social. Being late, even if it is only by a few minutes, is very insulting to a

German executive.

5.Business can be conducted during any meal, but lunch is best.

6.Business is viewed as being very serious, and Germans do not appreciate humor in a business context.

7.Avoid drinking hard liquor before meals or smoking cigars between courses. The French believe this permeates the taste buds, compromising the taste of the meal.

8.Germans keep a larger personal space around them, approximately 6 inches more space than North Americans do. However, it is not unusual that when in line at a store cash register, Germans will crowd up very close to the person in front of them.

9.Good gifts to present include books or music, as they demonstrate interest in intellectual pursuits. Germans are strongly individualistic.

10.German men frequently greet each other with her or his "last name", even when they know each other very well.

IV.Cloze: choose the suitable statements from the box and complete the passage.

A.Long-term Orientation
B.Uncertainty Avoidance
C.Power Distance
D.Individualism
E.Masculinity

The Geert Hofstede analysis for the United States is very similar to other World Countries that have their heritage founded in Europe with strong ties to the British Isles (see Great Britain, Canada, Australia, and New Zealand). _____1_____ ranks highest and is a significant factor in the life of U.S. Americans. It indicates a society with a more individualistic attitude and relatively loose bonds with others. The populace is more self-reliant and looks out for themselves and their close family members.

The next highest Hofstede Dimension is _____2_____ with a ranking of 62, compared with a world average of 50. This indicates the country experiences a higher degree of gender differentiation of roles. The male dominates a significant portion of the society and power structure. This situation generates a female population that becomes more assertive and competitive, with women shifting toward the male role model and away from their female role. The United States was included in the group of countries that had the _____3_____ Dimension added. It is the lowest Dimension for the US at 29, compared to the world average of 45. Its low ranking reflects a freedom in the culture from long-term traditional commitments, which allows greater flexibility and the freedom to react quickly to new opportunities.

The next lowest ranking Dimension for the United States is _____4_____ at 40, compared to the world Average of 55. This is indicative of a greater equality between societal levels, including government, organizations, and even within families. This orientation reinforces a cooperative interaction across power levels and creates a more stable cultural environment.

The last Geert Hofstede Dimension for the US is _____5_____, with a ranking of 46, compared to the world average of 64. A low ranking in the Uncertainty Avoidance Dimension is indicative of a society that has fewer rules and does not attempt to control all outcomes and results. It also has a greater level of tolerance for a variety of ideas, thoughts, and beliefs.

V.Case study: in today's world, with global companies, it's important to develop good business relationships by taking the time to learn more about the gift guidelines for the country you'll be visiting. It will help make your meeting a success. Countries like Malaysia and Paraguay, concerned with corruption, frown upon any gift that could be construed as a bribe. In Malaysia you wouldn't give a gift until you had established a relationship with the person. In Singapore, government employees are not allowed to accept gifts, and the United States limits the acceptable dollar value to $25. However, in some countries like Japan, Indonesia and the Philippines, exchanging gifts is strongly rooted in tradition. Part of the tradition is the gracious style used to present and receive them.

Collect more corresponding materials and decide on the gift you will give to the business people from the following countries:

1. Germany
2. France
3. United States
4. Japan
5. Saudi Arabia

 Extension （拓展阅读）

Quick International Business Etiquette Tips

One of the most important aspects of being successful in international business ventures is learning and understanding the cultural context, traditions, customs and expectations of your counterparties. We will look in-depth at many intercultural business issues in the time ahead. But for a starter, here are a few quick international business etiquette tidbits to consider.

Japan

When planning to visit for business, bring some small token gifts—always wrapped—and present them with a little bit of personal ceremony. The nature or price of the gift is irrelevant. It is the pleasure of giving and receiving the gift which is important and is greeted with delight. Do not expect your gift to be opened in front of you. It will be saved and opened with relish in private.

Latin America

Especially for ladies, make sure your grooming is well-tended to, nails done, hair coiffed, makeup on, crisp clothing, polished shoes, etc. It is a sign of respect that you are presenting when you present yourself with polish.

Italy

If you are given an offer of employment, either accept it or reject it. It is considered "vulgar" to try to negotiate a better deal for yourself when provided with an offer.

Asia

Especially, but this is a good idea everywhere—treat business cards with respect. Accept them with both hands, study it for a moment and keep it visible to you if presented prior to your meeting. Do not stuff it into your pocket, fold it, write on it, or as we heard of one person doing, use the corner to clean your finger nails during a meeting.

Spain & Denmark

Adjust your private space zone when talking business with Spaniards, who like to stand very close. Do not step away to increase your private space or it may be seen as a sign of disrespect. This is the opposite of the Danish people, who prefer more space. Americans generally consider 18-inches between individuals a comfortable zone. Others feel differently.

Germany

Germans generally prefer more formality in their business dealings. Personal relationships are not required for successful business transactions. They opt for and appreciate direct communication, punctuality, written agendas for meetings (that are followed!) and conservative dress in business meetings.

France

Like Germans, French may also be direct in business communications, asking incisive and astute questions that may verge on blunt. However, trust and respect based on relationship

is important in creating business alliances. Meetings are often used to discuss issues, areas of concern, topical matters and so forth—not to make a decision on the spur of the moment.

India

Punctuality is not as highly prized in India business dealings as in many other countries. You could find yourself waiting some time even for a scheduled appointment. Be flexible and allow for margins of time with regard to your business meetings. Also, be prepared for a lot of interruptions, which allow for Indians to "multi-task" during the meeting. We were in one meeting where our Indian counterparty took no less than 5 phone calls on his mobile phone during a one-hour meeting. It is not a sign of disrespect; it is just a cultural difference.

Dubai

When shaking hands, use your right hand, as the left is considered unclean, and expect the handshake to be much gentler than in West. If you are a woman, you will need to extend your hand first, as it is considered inappropriate for a man to offer to shake your hand first. Refrain from multi-tasking and sit up straight in your meetings (e.g., checking your email or Smartphone). Meetings generally start with a little chitchat before getting to the business matters to be discussed.

Western Europe

Many people in these countries take vacation in late July and August, so it is best not to schedule meetings there during this time.

Also, for all your business dealings, it is a wonderful sign of respect, appreciation, and trust-building when you learn to speak the language of your counterparty. It may not be possible for you to become fluent in the languages of all the countries in which you plan to do business, but it is important, at a minimum, to provide some words of greeting and introduction to your counterparties. We will help you here in future issues with some of those phrases and greetings to get you started.

(http://poshports.com/node/44)

After-reading tasks（读后任务）

When you finish reading the text above, get into the groups and discuss with your group members about the following tasks and fulfill them.

Task 1

The text above provides more cultural etiquette in different countries which will surely benefit the readers a lot. In order to ensure the knowledge you have read will be kept in mind so as to put into practice in the later career life, it is recommended to take notes and make classification of the information contained in the text. First decide on the columns of the table below and fill the box with the corresponding information you can find in the text above.

Countries	Etiquettes
Japan	
Latin America	
Italy	
Asia	
France	
Spain & Denmark	
Germany	
Dubai	
West Europe	
India	

Task 2

Your group members may come from different countries or different areas in your own countries, so you can propose to talk about different customs and etiquettes that exist in respective hometowns. Sometimes it may be difficult to understand some of the customs or etiquettes, so the speaker may make great effort to clarify what it can be, for instance, the origin of the customs or the etiquette, the advantages of such customs and the etiquettes, or even the harm that may bring about if you do not pay enough attention to them.

Task 3

Usually we stay at home to spend holidays with our friends, relatives or family, but it may not be the case with the business people. So if you have to spend holidays with your business partners overseas, it can be essential to get acquainted with the local customs and the etiquettes there, which can tell you how to make the best use of the special days to facilitate the relationship between you and your business partner, and, at least, ensure that you can enjoy yourself in a foreign surrounding.

Self-study（自学反馈）

If possible, summarize what you have learned in this unit with the help of the following table.

Focus of this unit:

Guidelines for etiquette:

1.

2.

3.

...

Summary:

Application:

1.

2.

3.

...

Feedback:

参 考 答 案
Keys to Exercises

Chapter One

II.

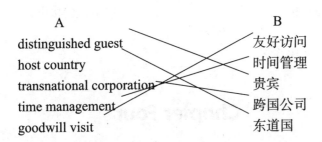

A

distinguished guest
host country
transnational corporation
time management
goodwill visit

B

友好访问
时间管理
贵宾
跨国公司
东道国

IV. 1. E 2. C 3. D 4. A 5. B

Chapter Two

II.

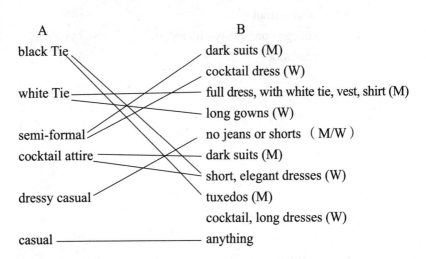

A

black Tie

white Tie

semi-formal
cocktail attire

dressy casual

casual

B

dark suits (M)
cocktail dress (W)
full dress, with white tie, vest, shirt (M)
long gowns (W)
no jeans or shorts （M/W）
dark suits (M)
short, elegant dresses (W)
tuxedos (M)
cocktail, long dresses (W)
anything

IV. 1. E 2. D 3. B 4. A 5. C

Chapter Three

II.

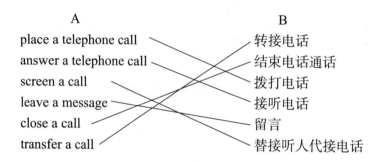

A	B
place a telephone call	转接电话
answer a telephone call	结束电话通话
screen a call	拨打电话
leave a message	接听电话
close a call	留言
transfer a call	替接听人代接电话

IV.　1. E　2. D　3. C　4. B　5. A

Chapter Four

II.

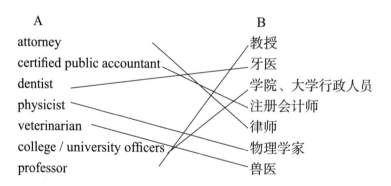

A	B
attorney	教授
certified public accountant	牙医
dentist	学院、大学行政人员
physicist	注册会计师
veterinarian	律师
college / university officers	物理学家
professor	兽医

IV.　1. E　2. A　3. C　4. B　5. D

Chapter Five

II.

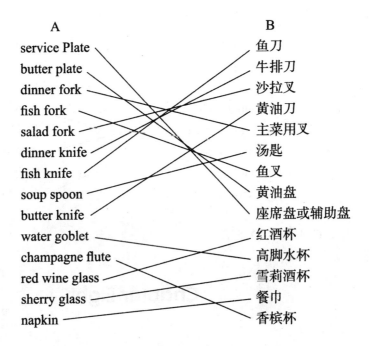

A	B
service Plate	鱼刀
butter plate	牛排刀
dinner fork	沙拉叉
fish fork	黄油刀
salad fork	主菜用叉
dinner knife	汤匙
fish knife	鱼叉
soup spoon	黄油盘
butter knife	座席盘或辅助盘
water goblet	红酒杯
champagne flute	高脚水杯
red wine glass	雪莉酒杯
sherry glass	餐巾
napkin	香槟杯

IV. 1. B 2. D 3. E 4. F 5. A 6. J 7. C 8. G 9. H 10. I

Chapter Six

II.

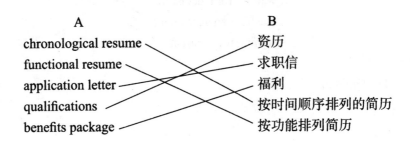

A	B
chronological resume	资历
functional resume	求职信
application letter	福利
qualifications	按时间顺序排列的简历
benefits package	按功能排列简历

IV.　Q1: D　Q2:B　Q3: A　Q4: C

Chapter Seven

II.

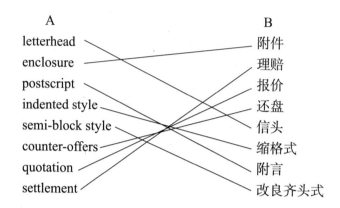

A
letterhead
enclosure
postscript
indented style
semi-block style
counter-offers
quotation
settlement

B
附件
理赔
报价
还盘
信头
缩格式
附言
改良齐头式

IV. 1. E 2. C 3. A 4. D 5. B

Chapter Eight

II.

A
greetings
small talk
presentation
deciding on strategy
waiting for a decision
reaching an agreement
signing the contract

B
决定（谈判）策略
问候
达成共识
签署合同
寒暄
等待（对方）决定
报告

IV. Omitted

Chapter Nine

II. Omitted

IV. 1. E 2. B 3. A 4. C 5. D

Chapter Ten

II.

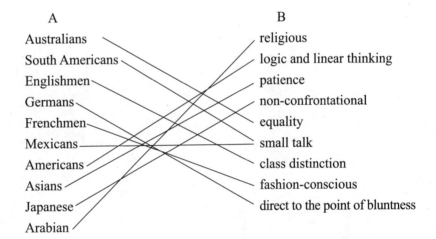

A	B
Australians	religious
South Americans	logic and linear thinking
Englishmen	patience
Germans	non-confrontational
Frenchmen	equality
Mexicans	small talk
Americans	class distinction
Asians	fashion-conscious
Japanese	direct to the point of bluntness
Arabian

IV. 1. D 2. E 3. A 4. C 5. B

参 考 文 献
Reference

1.Peggy Post, Peter Post. Emily Post's The etiquette advantage in business[M]. 2e. New York: Harper Collins Publishers, 2005.

2.Ann Marie Sabath. International Business Etiquette: Asia and The Pacific Rim[M]. Career Press, 1999.

3. 普拉斯（Plas, J.）. 实用英文秘书手册 [M]. 北京：商务印书馆国际有限公司，1998.

4. 约瑟芬·克林顿. 商务礼仪英语 [M]. 北京：北京大学出版社，1999.

5. 常骏跃. 礼仪英语会话 [M]. 大连：大连理工大学出版社，2000.

6. 张燕彬. 国际商务礼仪 [M]. 沈阳：辽宁教育出版社，2001.

7. 裴果芬. 国际商务英语洽谈 [M]. 上海：上海交通大学出版社，2000.

8. 吴云娣. 国际商务谈判英语 [M]. 上海：上海交通大学出版社，2002.

9. 全英. 国际商务谈判 [M]. 北京：北方交通大学出版社，2003.

10. 张翠萍. 商贸英语口语大全 [M]. 北京：对外经济贸易大学出版社，2005.

11. 钱清. 礼仪与风俗 [M]. 北京：外文出版社，2006.

12. 李敏，刘晓丽. 国外的礼仪与禁忌 [M]. 北京：中国社会出版社，2006.

13. 邱革加，杨国俊. 双赢现代商务英语谈判 [M]. 北京：中国国际广播出版社，2006.

14. 浩瀚. 商务英语情景会话模板 [M]. 北京：国防工业出版社，2007.

15. 欧玲. 西方礼仪文化 [M]. 重庆：重庆大学出版社，2008.

16. 浩瀚. 外企白领速成英语之礼仪高手 [M]. 北京：石油工业出版社，2008.

17. 李嘉珊. 国际商务礼仪 [M]. 北京：电子工业出版社，2008.

18. 窦然. 国际商务谈判 [M]. 上海：复旦大学出版社，2008.

19. 刘晖. 实用礼仪训练教程 [M]. 北京：电子工业出版社，2008.

20. 何传春. 新世纪实用英语培训系列·交际英语 [M]. 广州：广东旅游出版社，2008.

21. 戴卫平，蔡坤. 职场英语情景实战演练 [M]. 北京：中国宇航出版社，2009.

22. 杨文慧. 商务礼仪英语（第 2 版）[M]. 广州：中山大学出版社，2009.

23. 肖芬. 优雅与品位 [M]. 北京：外语教学与研究出版社，2009.

24. 联合国贸易网络上海中心. 如何与外国人打交道——海外商务文化礼仪习俗指南 [M]. 上海：世界图书出版公司，2009.

25. 钱放. 商务礼仪 [M]. 武汉：武汉理工大学出版社，2009.

26. 鸿升 . 8 天跨越求职面试英语 [M]. 北京：中国宇航出版社，2009.

27. 刘新法，刘浩 . 体味西方礼仪 [M]. 西安：西安交通大学出版社，2010.

28. 张宇，艾天姿 . 国际商务礼仪英文教程 [M]. 北京：北京大学出版社，2010.

29. 崔喜哲等 . 不可不知的 300 个西方文化经典 [M]. 北京：中国水利水电出版社，2010.

30. 赵嚚，蔡新芝 . 英语畅谈中国文化风俗 [M]. 北京：科学出版社，2011.

31. http://www.ehow.com/how_8200254_properly-set-table.html